Hans-Joachim Marseille

Hans-Joachim Marseille

An Illustrated Tribute to the *Luftwaffe's* "Star of Africa"

Robert Tate

Schiffer Military History
Atglen, PA

Dedication

First and foremost, to my Lord and savior Jesus Christ. Without You, none of this would have been possible.
To my wife, Minerva. Without her support and encouragement, this project would likely still be just a dream.

Book Design by Ian Robertson.

Library of Congress Control Number: 2008926100

Printed in China.
ISBN: 978-0-7643-2940-1

We are interested in hearing from authors with book ideas on related topics.

Published by Schiffer Publishing Ltd.
4880 Lower Valley Road
Atglen, PA 19310
Phone: (610) 593-1777
FAX: (610) 593-2002
E-mail: Info@schifferbooks.com.
Visit our web site at: www.schifferbooks.com
Please write for a free catalog.
This book may be purchased from the publisher.
Please include $3.95 postage.
Try your bookstore first.

In Europe, Schiffer books are distributed by:
Bushwood Books
6 Marksbury Avenue
Kew Gardens
Surrey TW9 4JF, England
Phone: 44 (0) 20 8392-8585
FAX: 44 (0) 20 8392-9876
E-mail: Info@bushwoodbooks.co.uk.
Visit our website at: www.bushwoodbooks.co.uk
Free postage in the UK. Europe: air mail at cost.
Try your bookstore first.

Contents

Acknowledgments

It would be impossible to complete a manuscript of this type without the help of numerous people. In my travels around the world and in writing columns and articles about Marseille over the years, I have had the pleasure of meeting some incredibly intelligent, gifted, and enthusiastic people who all share the same passion I have with the life and career of Hans Marseille. Some perhaps not to the same degree, but their knowledge and willingness to share their knowledge with me has been a blessing, not only in writing this tribute, but also helping me better understand the personality of the *Star of Africa*. I would like to thank those people here.

First I would like to thank my wife, Minerva, who after 22 years of marriage has watched me spend countless hours (and dollars) on my hobby. As usual, she has been totally supportive of yet another Marseille project. Thanks Mija.

Next I want to thank my dad, who way back in 1975 introduced me to Marseille. Who would have thought that such a small gesture to a high school freshman would have such far-reaching repercussions? I would also like to thank my brother Ed and sister Jacqui for their help in reading the drafts and showing me where I was being quite illiterate. Also thanks to Roger Siford, who has shown support through the years and allowed me to bore him with story after story of the real "Great One."

Roger Bender of Bender Publishing. Thanks for the use of your Marseille photographs, although they are quite sad.

Russell Brown: my good Aussie friend from down under and author of the book *Desert Warriors: Australian P-40 Pilots at War in the Middle East and North Africa 1941-1943*. I want to thank him for the generous use of his words, his photographs, interviews, and encouragement as I proceeded through this process.

Mr. Ron Cundy: although I have never met him face-to-face, his kind words and generous use of photographs and passages from his book *Gremlin On My Shoulder* have been an inspiration for me. It never ceases to amaze me how gentlemen of another generation so willingly want to help get their stories out. Mr. Cundy, a RAAF pilot in North Africa, is a wonderful man, and thanks again for the help.

Heide d'Alquen: I met Heide through a blind email one day after she had read one of my Marseille articles. It appears that when she was a little girl in Germany, Marseille's brother was her babysitter, and she has enjoyed a lifelong relationship with the Marseille family. Her insights and work between the scenes was greatly appreciated and incredibly helpful.

JP Hunerwadel: one of my coworkers from the College of Aerospace, Doctrine, Research, and Education (CADRE) at Maxwell AFB in Montgomery, AL. Of all the writers I have encountered in my days, I value his gifted tongue and amazing mastery of the English language. Undoubtedly, his review of my writing made it infinitely better than it otherwise would have been. JP, if "Killing my darlings" was a crime, I'd be in jail right now. Thanks again.

Friedrich Körner: My Friend Fritz. The late Herr Körner gave me wonderful insight into not only Marseille as a man and fighter pilot, but was instrumental in showing me how the *Luftwaffe* pilots in the desert lived. His friendship continues to be missed.

Michel Lavigne: like most of the professionals I contacted, Mr. Lavigne, author of *Kittyhawks Over the Sands: The Canadians and The RCAF Americans,* was more than generous, helpful, and kind in allowing the use of quotes from his book and several articles he wrote on Marseille for the Military Journal years ago.

Geoffrey Morley-Mower: I regret never having met him in person. Our discussions over the telephone and email correspondences were enlightening and informative. I wish I could thank you again for the use of your story about Marseille. Of all the stories and anecdotes presented in this book, it is perhaps this one story that best exemplifies what and who Hans Marseille really was.

Rafael Scheck: thanks for talking to me about life within the Reich and answering questions about Marseille and Matthias.

Frank Struppek: I met Frank when I was a pilot with the NATO AWACS program in Geilenkirchen, Germany. It was interesting to meet another guy with such a great passion for similar subjects. Through the years, Frank has been instrumental in translating many passages from German to English. Without his help, many of the areas of this book would have been impossible.

Christopher Shores: co-author of perhaps the greatest book chronicling the desert air war in North Africa, *Fighters Over the*

Desert (FOTD), Mr. Shores, like many other authors, was gracious enough to allow the use of quotes and other sections of his book. Truly the use of his book served as one of the backbones to this tribute to Hans Marseille.

Penn Templeman: another avid collector and Marseille aficionado, Mr. Templeman enthusiastically allowed the use of many of his private photos and items from his collection for inclusion in this book.

Nicolas Trudgian: undoubtedly one of the greatest aviation artists in the world today, I would like to thank him for his support and kind words as this project moved from concept to finalized version.

Paul Upton: my friend from the Jersey Islands. What can I say, Paul? Besides occasionally beating me out for Marseille items on Ebay (I still haven't forgiven you for the last one), he too was gracious enough to allow photographs and items from his private collection to be used in this project.

The Artists: I would like to thank the following artists for allowing their Marseille works to be used in this tribute: Jay Ashurst, Julius Cassani, Les Carter, Jerry Crandall, Tony Jackson, Konley Kelly, Heinz Krebs, Alexey Linkov, Lonnie Ortega, Mike Staley, Stan Stokes, Nicolas Trudgian, Tony Weddell, and Friedl Wülfing.

Ms. Martina Caspers at the Bundesarchiv in Germany. Without her help and support, many of the excellent photographs of Marseille would not have made it into this tribute. I want to thank her for her help. Lastly, I want to thank the other people who wished to remain anonymous.

Introduction

Wednesday, 30 September 1942 was forecast to be like most other late summer days in the North African desert; hot, dry, and unrelenting. For the men of German fighter *Gruppe* (*Jagdgeschwader*) I/JG 27, the anticipation of another full day of combat surely weighed heavily on everyone's mind, as well it should have. For the first time, Field Marshall Erwin Rommel's *Afrika Korps* was in a position to be thoroughly routed and forced out of Africa by the British 8th Army, who under the new and more aggressive leadership of Lt. General Bernard Montgomery, had gained their second wind and rekindled their highly touted fighting spirit. Not only were the men of JG 27 fully aware of Rommel's recent defeat at the Battle of Alam el Halfa in early September, but they seemed caught in a perpetual battle with the harsh desert climate, a severe lack of supplies, the constant strain of aerial combat, and the ever-present threat of British commando attacks against their airfields. As difficult as the situation appeared for the pilots of the *Luftwaffe*, and despite the recent loss of two of the more experienced pilots in the unit during the previous three weeks, individual morale remained surprisingly high. Under the watchful eye of their young "Jochen," problems affecting other *Luftwaffe* and Italian units in the Middle East seemed somewhat removed from the men at this lonely desert outpost in Quotaifiya, northern Egypt.[1]

Captain Hans-Joachim Marseille awoke that morning and was greeted as usual by Matthias, his personal batman from the Transvaal.[2] The strain of one and a half years of aerial combat showed heavily on his young 22 year-old face. Marseille, the youngest captain in the *Luftwaffe*, at this point in his life appeared to have everything going his way. He was a confident—even cocky—national hero, and by far the most successful fighter pilot in the North African desert. After a slow start on the Channel Front during the Battle of Britain, Marseille overcame his initial weaknesses as a fighter pilot and made his Messerschmitt Bf-109 fighter the scourge of the desert air war. During the previous 30 days he had been credited with shooting down 57 Allied fighter aircraft, 17 of those coming in one hectic day of combat on 1 September. On the third, he was notified of being the fourth man awarded Germany's highest military award: the Knight's Cross with Oak Leaves, Swords, and Diamonds. On the 19th he had been promoted to Captain, and with 158 total kills to his credit Marseille was well on his way to becoming among the first group of *Luftwaffe* pilots to shoot down 200 enemy aircraft.

Above: Marseille casually sporting his Knight's Cross. *Courtesy of E & C Collection* Oppposite: Poem, "The Ace" by Nelson Gilboe. *Courtesy of Mrs. Nelson Gilboe, Photograph courtesy of Seattle Museum of Flight*

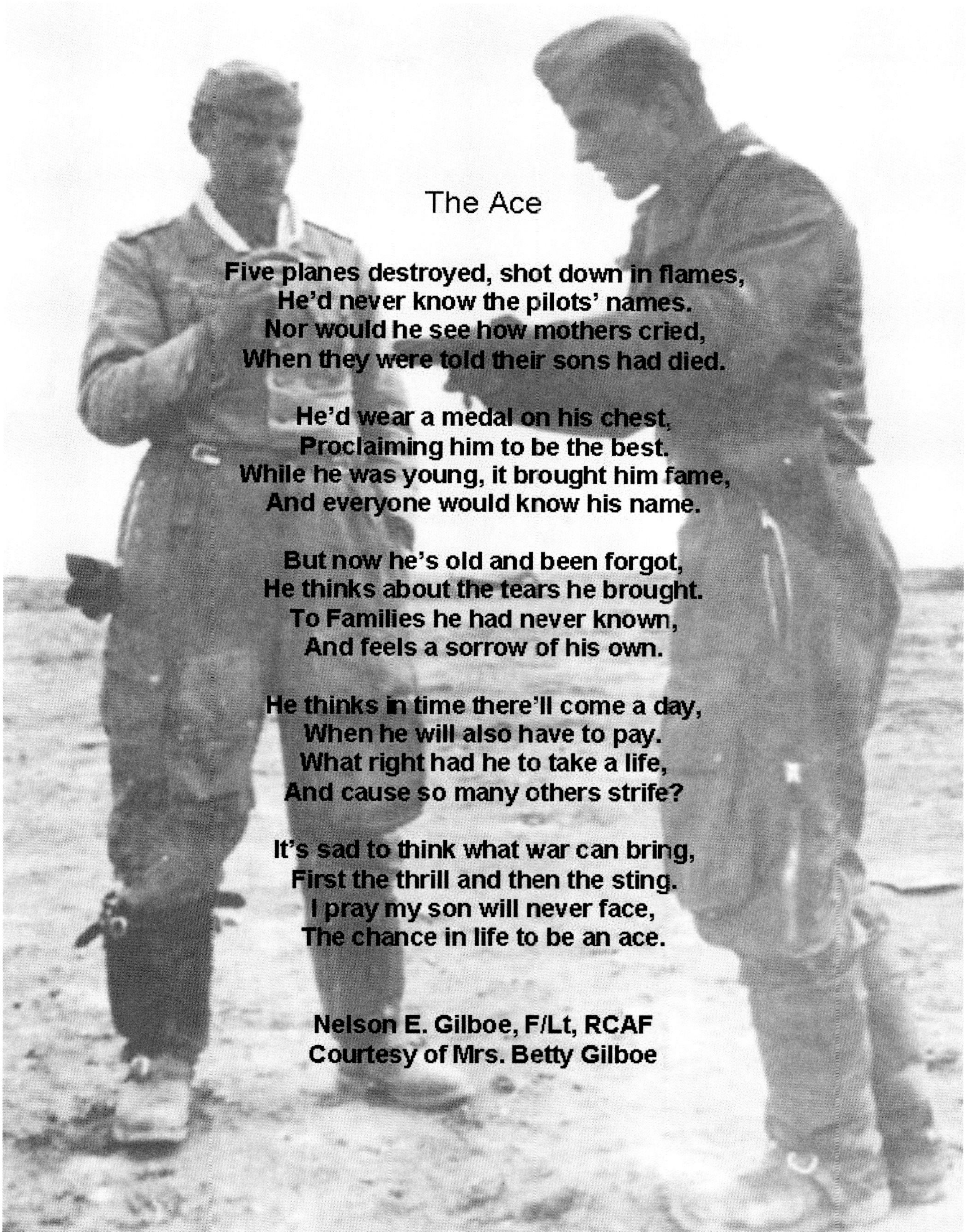

The Ace

Five planes destroyed, shot down in flames,
He'd never know the pilots' names.
Nor would he see how mothers cried,
When they were told their sons had died.

He'd wear a medal on his chest,
Proclaiming him to be the best.
While he was young, it brought him fame,
And everyone would know his name.

But now he's old and been forgot,
He thinks about the tears he brought.
To Families he had never known,
And feels a sorrow of his own.

He thinks in time there'll come a day,
When he will also have to pay.
What right had he to take a life,
And cause so many others strife?

It's sad to think what war can bring,
First the thrill and then the sting.
I pray my son will never face,
The chance in life to be an ace.

Nelson E. Gilboe, F/Lt, RCAF
Courtesy of Mrs. Betty Gilboe

Yes, 30 September brought the prospect of another day's hunt and success in the skies over Egypt. More victories and more glory bestowed upon the young man from Berlin. But this Wednesday morning, a freak accident would reduce perhaps the greatest fighter pilot of the war from the hero of the German nation to a lifeless historical footnote on the floor of the Egyptian desert.

I first "met" Hans-Joachim Marseille in September 1975 when I was a freshman at Manalapan High School in Englishtown, New Jersey. My German teacher, Herr Schmidt, had just given us our homework assignment, and we had to decide on a German name to use while we were in class. Conveniently killing two birds with one stone, I found myself reading about *Luftwaffe* aces while simultaneously searching through Martin Caiden's book *Me-109* and Constable and Toliver's *Horrido* for some "cool" German names. Certainly my new Teutonic name would of course have to be that of a successful *Luftwaffe* fighter pilot. Having already read Erich Hartmann's biography, *The Blond Knight of Germany*, I was familiar with Germany's top scoring ace, but for some odd reason, his name didn't seem quite German enough for me. So I settled on the very "manly" "Günther" for Günther Rall.

While I was searching for my new name, it seems my dad had been looking through Edward H. Sims' excellent book *The Greatest Aces*, and asked me about "this Marseille guy." I must admit that up to that point I had not really given him a second thought, except for the fact that I believed he had a rather odd name for a German. Being content in my ignorant 14 year-old high school mind, Marseille after all had "only" shot down 158 airplanes, was just 31st on the overall *Luftwaffe* victory list, and was therefore not even registering on my radarscope. My dad, in his quiet yet persistent way, insisted that Marseille seemed to be quite a lively character, and one heck of a fighter pilot. His interest piqued my curiosity, and I immediately read Raymond Toliver's and then Edward Sims' accounts of Marseille in their books. I was hooked. That began what has become an incredibly fulfilling 32-year journey of research, writing, public speaking, and collecting anything and everything having to do with one who I unashamedly believe was the greatest combat pilot of the Second World War, Hans-Joachim Marseille.

Within the last 32 years, a span of time 10 years greater than Marseille's own life, I can honestly state that not a single day has

Marseille climbs from the cockpit in either August or September 1942. *Courtesy of author*

gone by where I did not at least spend some time thinking about this young pilot who at the age of 22 died a hero of the German nation. Made famous by his exploits over Libya and Egypt, only *Feldmarschall* Erwin Rommel would achieve greater fame in the North African desert. Since 1975 all of my friends, college roommates, squadron mates—and many others would say my "poor wife" of 22 years—have heard, often in sickening detail, story after story about "The Great One." My business card claims "Marseilleologist ad infinitum," and like Egyptologists who study ancient Egypt, I enjoy studying all possible aspects of Marseille's life and career. My study of Marseille is truly a genuine labor of love and has in return opened many doors that would have otherwise certainly remained irrevocably closed. Whether it has been meeting some of his comrades from the desert air war, becoming close friends with the late 2/ JG 27 ace Friedrich Körner, speaking before large groups of military personnel, or simply bringing friends into my home for the "Marseille Experience," my "relationship" with Marseille seems to be more of a friendship than simply the study of a historical figure.

Sixty-five years after his stinging death, Marseille's legend continues to grow. Every country had its fighter pilot heroes from that war. America had men like Bong, Gabreski, Zemke, Boyington, and McCampbell, while the British Commonwealth had Johnson, Edwards, Pattle, Caldwell, Beurling, and Malan. Whether it was Sakai or Nishizawa of Japan, Kozhedub or Pokryshkin of Russia, Juutilainen or Wind of Finland, or one of the thousands of aces from numerous countries, no other fighter pilot, not even the higher scoring German aces, seemed to capture the imagination of their respective nations as did Marseille. Although often times at odds with military leadership and authority, Marseille's youthful exuberance, striking good looks, and unsurpassed success in aerial combat endeared him in the hearts of a grateful nation, as well as the men he flew with. As I write this tribute to Marseille, I have to ask what specifically was it that allowed him to stand out so clearly ahead of all his contemporaries in North Africa?

That is one of several questions this tribute will attempt to uncover. There has been so much written about Marseille that as historians, we are left to "separate the wheat from the chaff." As with any famous figure, so much fact and misinformation abounds that the legend of Marseille will likely never stop and, at some point, his myth will begin to outgrow reality. Although stories such as "his plane never being hit by enemy fire" or his plane "never

Marseille climbing into the cockpit of his Messerschmitt. In this photograph, the yellow under cowling is clearly evident. *Courtesy of E & C Collection*

Marseille with two unidentified men. Although Marseille is wearing his desert uniform, the background hints at Italy or Sicily. *Courtesy of Paul Upton*

skidding in turns" are fanciful delusions, I want to illustrate what has made Marseille one of the most popular and intriguing figures from any country to emerge from the annals of the Second World War.

Although clearly no superman, within the North African theater, Marseille was decidedly superior to his *Luftwaffe* peers in aerial combat. This statement is undeniable. Some historians and World War II veterans have argued, however, that Marseille was just lucky, or even worse, a lying, over claiming braggart who could not have possibly accomplished all that he claimed. Some have gone as far as to denigrate the skills and courage of his Commonwealth opponents in an attempt to justify or rationalize his alleged successes. Although Marseille was indeed lucky in the sense that he cheated death several times early in his career, I contend that no "lucky" man shoots down as many aircraft and in the manner in which Marseille did. At some point, "luck" must be acknowledged as consummate skill. Likewise, I am not willing to question the abilities of the pilots he flew against. Marseille was, however, able to exploit weaknesses in the tactics and methods employed by his enemies. There were too many eyewitnesses to Marseille's combat and aerobatic feats to simply dismiss them out of hand as some sort of Nazi propaganda.

What This Book Is/ Is Not

For all that I have tried to illustrate in this book, there are many things this "tribute" is not. First and foremost, this book is not intended to be an all-encompassing biography of Hans-Joachim Marseille. Authors like Franz Kurowski and Walter Wübbe have already written biographies detailing all aspects of Marseille's life. This is why I have intentionally chosen to ignore Marseille's early life and concentrate almost exclusively on his combat career in North Africa.

Likewise, each country that fought in the air war produced excellent fighter pilots, hundreds of men that represented their nations and air forces well. This tribute to Marseille is in no way meant to demean or marginalize their efforts and contributions, but

A group of I / JG 27 pilots before deployment to North Africa. Their "Emils" are still painted in European colors. Although difficult to tell, it looks like Marseille is the pilot standing at the far right. *Courtesy of E & C Collection*

rather is meant to focus on Marseille's successes and contributions. Certainly on any given day, one pilot could just have easily fallen prey to another.

Similarly, this book is in no way intended glorify or idolize the regime Marseille fought for. In my opinion, that would be an impossible task. At the same time, Marseille was clearly a young man who broke the stereotypical German officer mold. I believe Marseille was a pilot that can still be admired by people of all nations and generations, not only because of his technical expertise, but also what he stood for. Having flown the NATO AWACS in Geilenkirchen, Germany, for six years, I always found it interesting how the Germans in my squadron willingly ignored the accomplishments of their soldiers from World War II. Many of my German squadron mates would come into my office and look at my Marseille pictures on the walls and airplanes on the ceiling and shake their heads and laugh, because they could never do the same. Smiling, their response was normally along the lines of, "Only you could get away with this."

Although the Nazi regime will go down in history for the evil it was, I do not believe there is a need for people to be ashamed of men like Hans Marseille who fought honorably for their countries and not any particular political agenda. Whether we want to admit it to ourselves or not, in these politically correct and historically revisionist times, not all German soldiers were Nazis. Blanket stereotypes like this are not only counter-productive but demonstrate little critical analysis. This is much like saying, "All whites or all blacks are prejudiced." Certainly some are, but not all.

Hans-Joachim Marseille: An Illustrated Tribute to the Luftwaffe's "Star of Africa" is exactly that: a tribute. As a tribute, I have purposely given myself the latitude to present a more subjective view of the young man called the "Star of Africa." As with tributes to any historical figure, I realize that in many ways Marseille was a flawed character. As such, in no way am I in a position to extol virtues and characteristics where none is warranted. Nor will I ignore the realities of Marseille's humanness. On occasion he proved to be insecure and cocky; other times a conceited and boorish braggart. Likewise, he was a compassionate son and loving brother, a loyal comrade, and a damn fine fighter pilot. Is there a chance that he did not actually shoot down all 158 aircraft as claimed? Yes. Does any potential over claiming diminish his accomplishments in the desert? No. Did pilots from all nations make similar mistakes and over-claim? Yes. As a tribute, my goal is to look at Marseille's personality, character, and career primarily through the words of the men that flew with, lived alongside, and fought against him in North Africa. Similarly, the words and comments of historians have been used to paint a more rounded picture of Marseille's character and personality. After all, what better way to honor a man than to have the words of those closest to him, and even those of the men who fought against him, help tell the story of this fascinating historical figure?

In the late Winter of 1990 or 1991, my wife and I, along with some friends made a "pilgrimage" to Uetersen, Germany, to see the Marseille-Kaserne and museum. After a 6 hour trip through a blinding snow and ice storm, I am standing in front of the sign at the entrance. To the right is fellow NATO AWACS pilot Keith Stanley. When Germans in my squadron asked me the following week why we drove up to Uetersen in a snowstorm, the obvious answer was, "Because it was there." They expected as much from me. Unfortunately, Marseille's Knight's Cross with Oak Leaves, Swords, and Diamonds which was on display there for a while had by that time already been stolen, and we were obviously unable to see them. I did, however, get a good photograph of his 158 kill rudder which can be seen in the chapter *Victories. Courtesy of author*

Is this primarily a subjective look at Marseille? Absolutely. I unapologetically entered this project with the proposition that Marseille was indeed the finest fighter pilot in North Africa and arguably in history. That is my position, and I don't mind stating this in the beginning. If I didn't believe this, it is doubtful I would have written this "tribute." That being said, although there is much subjectivity to this book, comments and thoughts are supported, where possible, with historical facts. Keep in mind that I am not trying to *prove* anything, or necessarily convince anybody that Marseille was the best fighter pilot of the war or of all time. Whether I believe that to be true or not is inconsequential. Refer to the chapter *Victories* and the discussion of comparing pilots across time, theaters, and wars. Once again, this is simply my attempt to pay homage to the skinny kid from Berlin on the 65th anniversary of his death, a young pilot who by the time of his death at 22 years of age, had already won the heart of a nation while under difficult conditions maintained his dignity and values.

This tribute will show Hans-Joachim Marseille, like most historical figures, as a real, but flawed character, and not an iconic figurehead cloaked in unbelievable myth. But within this figure, what we will see is a young man whose career, not the regime he fought for, was worthy of admiration and study. I hope this is the true value of this book. As I relate different aspects of Marseille's personality, tactics, victories, and flying skills, I hope to showcase the depths of his abilities and the richness of his character. By now, most of us know of Marseille's unsurpassed tactical acumen; now sit back and enjoy the story of an incredibly charismatic "boy" caught up in a turbulent time in world history. This book hopes to round out the personality that became the "Star of Africa."

1

Marseille and the Historic Great Man[1]

"Just name a hero and I'll prove he's a bum."[2]
Greg "Pappy" Boyington

Anybody who has studied Hans-Joachim Marseille's career is well aware of his 151 aerial victories in North Africa (158 total), making him the highest scoring *Luftwaffe* "Experten"[3] against the Western Allies. Examining his score, we can determine that 138 of his 151 desert victories came during sorties where he scored multiple victories, and that all of these victories were achieved in only 59 sorties; a mere fraction of his 388 total sorties flown. In Mike Spick's book *Luftwaffe Fighter Aces: The Jagdflieger and their Combat Tactics and Techniques*, the author discusses the combat strike rates of the top *Luftwaffe Experten*. A strike rate is simply the number of victories obtained per sorties flown. Marseille's overall strike rate comes out to 2.42 sorties flown for each victory achieved. This is based on his 158 total kills achieved in 388 combat sorties flown. This places him as number 16 on the overall *Experten* efficiency list according to Spick. If we search further and look at his strike rate for the sorties only where he achieved his victories, we come out with a phenomenal .39 sorties per kill. This equates to almost 2.5 victories per sortie where he successfully engaged an enemy aircraft.

Many of us have read that according to Günther Rall, Marseille often averaged only 15 rounds of ammunition per kill as he decimated large segments of enemy squadrons while his awed squadron mates watched in stunned approval. Stories of his aerobatic acumen abound with him picking up handkerchiefs suspended from six-foot poles with the wingtip of his Messerschmitt and cutting ribbons with the tail of his airplane while flying inverted. He earned terms of endearment like "The Star of Africa," "African Eagle," "Eagle of Africa," "Southern Star," and "Star of the Desert." Likewise, he has been called a troublemaker, juvenile delinquent, "infant terrible," cocky, brash, and insecure.

Although universally recognized as an extremely gifted pilot, Marseille was booted out of 4/ JG 52 by his commander Johannes "Macky" Steinhoff (Knight's Cross with Oak Leaves and Swords, 176 kills) for his undisciplined, unreliable, and irresponsible way of conducting himself both in and out of the cockpit. Edu Neumann, Marseille's commander in North Africa, said, "With his bragging he desperately tried to compensate for his complex. He wanted to become a big man in our group right away, he needed that."[4] Like most historically significant figures, it is obvious that Marseille was neither a saint nor a perfect man. He was beset with flaws and

An excellent study of Marseille following the receipt of the Knight's Cross with Oak Leaves and Swords. For all of Marseille's documented successes in the desert, does his historical status rate that of the historical great man? *Courtesy of author*

many glaring contradictions. But there is much more to Marseille than those tangible facts, observations, and suppositions.

The study of human nature and of the individual's role in history is something to be approached with caution and objectivity. Through the years I have had to check myself with regards to Marseille's historical significance. Humans love to ascribe exaggerated characteristics and attributes to those people we want to revere or even despise. I have been among the most guilty of this regarding Marseille. It is easier for us to hate an enemy if we give him inhuman or morally reprehensible characteristics. Likewise, if we can portray our heroes as men overcoming severe adversity, fighting for righteous causes, or even giving them pleasing physical attributes, his status as a hero becomes more palatable. In a way, it was easy for the German nation to revere Marseille because of the combination of his good looks, his extreme youth, and the almost superhuman way—real or imagined—in which he manhandled his Royal Air Force foes in combat.

With the study of history, we often think of the past as places where our heroes have risen above all obstacles by the very nature of their superior moral, physical, and/ or spiritual qualities. We have a high regard for the hero, while we somehow ignore or forgive them for their faults and shortcomings; no matter how glaring. We put them on pedestals and think of them, or wish for them, attributes and characteristics that may not exist. In turn, it becomes increasingly easy to give them credit where no credit is due. This is human nature, and our study of history is replete with this idea of the "Great Man" doing things above and beyond the call of duty, somehow standing far above other men faced with similar situations and conditions. When history looks at Marseille within the context of his accomplishments in North Africa, can he possibly fit the bill of the historic "Great Man?"

In Sidney Hook's *The Hero in History*, the author examines two different historical personalities. One is described as the "Eventful Man" and the other as the "Event Making Man."[5] The

"Congratulations are in order." *Courtesy of Penn Templeman*

eventful man, also called *the determinist view*, can be described as the person who is simply in the right place at the right time. He is merely part of much larger events dominating his era and is born to forces far beyond his control. This man's conduct is influenced, determined, and controlled by outside pressures that he is reacting to. Although he may indeed be coping with outside stressors better than his counterpart and peers, in no way is he able to control them.

The event making man or the historical "Great Man," on the other hand, is the character to which we ascribe almost supernatural powers. Not a mere pawn of his surroundings, the Great Man finds the courage and intestinal fortitude to control his own destiny, and to successfully manipulate his surroundings to his advantage. Because of this ability to shape and control the events around him, the Great Man becomes a significant part of those larger events by driving them in one direction or the other. The Great Man, through his outstanding character, intelligence, will, and/or abilities has the capacity to accomplish his specific goals or purposes,[6] rather than allowing himself to be manipulated by his surroundings.

Signed formal portrait of Marseille. This photograph clearly shows the Knight's Cross with Oak Leaves and Swords. *Courtesy of Paul Upton*

The Great Man Theory states, "major developments of human history are accounted for by the great men who sometimes seem to exert an almost superhuman control over the fate of their generation."[7] It is important to realize that "Great Men" need not be "nice" men or those who fight on our side. History is full of evil men, who by the nature of their accomplishments can only be judged as evil, yet still maintain the status of historically great personalities.

Whomever this person may be, good or evil, the historical great man exists at some level beyond his own measure. These men (or women), by their very nature, are often so gifted, talented, or charismatic that the rules restricting the operation and movements of others seem not to hinder them at all. They appear to be in many ways, the master of their circumstances, and with that, their fate as well. They also tend to reshape and adjust their surroundings in order to fit their own ideas and concepts of the way they feel their environment should be. On the surface it seems possible to argue that Marseille's physical talents and keen understanding of the tactical complexities of aerial combat initially seems to place him within this category.

I believe a superior man, or rather a man of superior ability, can be decisive within situations where others' abilities wane. The Great Man's personality, stamina, education, physical prowess, values, integrity, character, charisma, oratory skills and/or judgment all play a part in setting himself apart from his contemporaries and rivals. All these attributes have an impact on the way he manipulates his environment. This is in essence what makes the great man "Great."

The eventful man, on the other hand, understands that outside forces are more prevalent and decisive, and in order to be successful, he only needs the proper tools in order to manipulate those forces.[8] This character needs a crises, social forces, social machinery and/ or certain ideas, not necessarily his own, in order to fulfill his "destiny." The determinists would argue, and I believe correctly so, that had Marseille not been sent to Africa in April 1941, the German propaganda machine under Josef Göbbels would have ensured somebody else like Homuth, Franzisket, Körner, Rödel, Schrör, or Stahlschmidt would likely have become the "Star of Africa." Basking in the aura of men like Rommel and the achievements of his *Afrika Korps*, the Germans were fortunate to have a young man of Marseille's caliber to make the creation of a hero that much easier.

The determinists further argue that the eventful man can only influence a situation when the time is right, and that his personality is in reality only the "voice of the group," only as good as the situation will allow him to become. There must be some catalyst or series of events that alone propels the eventful man forward. In effect, the eventful man is merely a prisoner of his environment, and will only become successful if he can navigate the myriad of situations presented to him.[9] The eventful man in reality doesn't cause his situation, he merely rides it. Marseille obviously didn't start the Second World War, but exploited that venue in order to achieve his successes. Much like being strapped in a roller coaster, the rider is unable to alter the coaster's course, change its speed, or more importantly, alter the outcome of the ride. It is on a preset destiny, and the rider, in this case the eventful man, is merely along for the ride. Whereas some riders may get sick or dizzy from the sudden and unpredictable changes of speed and direction, others may actually enjoy the ride. But nonetheless, they have no ability to change the inevitable outcome of the ride. The rider who bears the ride out the best is our eventful man. Without the roller coaster as a tool, he remains nothing more than a historically unobtrusive character.

Each country during the war needed their own hero. Richard Bong, for example, received the Congressional Medal of Honor for his actions during the war, and to a degree filled the same propaganda niche that Marseille filled for the Germans. There was no difference other than the quality of service of one man far exceeded that of the other.

The historical figures that we love to study, whether eventful or event making, must still deal with the situation given them. In order to achieve status as a historical great man, the hero must successfully deal with groups that back and oppose him, deal with conditions of the institution within which he must operate and with the people he must work with. Marseille arguably excelled in these areas where others of his class did not. *Luftwaffe* pilots of JG 27 all dealt with the same supply shortages, aircraft serviceability problems, and tactical concerns, yet only one pilot was able to adapt and succeed like Marseille. Fighting in the same desert environment, Marseille continued to excel far out of proportion to pilots of either the *Luftwaffe* or the Allied Desert Air Forces (DAF).[10] In an interview I conducted with my good friend, the late 2/ JG 27 pilot, Herr Friedrich Körner (Knight's Cross winner with 36 desert victories), he readily admitted and remained awed by Marseille's unique and superior tactical abilities. Of Marseille, Körner once said with an actual tear in his eye, "Yeah, everybody knew nobody could cope with him. Nobody could do the same. Some of the pilots tried it like Stahlschmidt, myself and Rödel. He, he was an artist. Marseille was an artist." Using his hands to illustrate. "He was up here and the rest of us were down here somewhere."[11] What more of a tribute to a fellow comrade could another pilot make?

Although it is true the pilots of Marseille's squadron did sometimes sit back and allow him to score victory after victory, certainly increasing his victory tally at the expense of their own,

Marseille the "artist." *Courtesy of E & C Collection*

it was still up to Marseille to maneuver his aircraft into a position to shoot down multiple aircraft day after day. This in itself was no small feat. Repeatedly entering enemy formations with the skill necessary to exploit his Messerschmitt's advantages without himself being killed, was something Marseille alone accomplished on a regular basis during his time in the desert.

In his book *Preface to History*, Carl Gustavson discusses four "maxims" concerning the historical great man. First, *long term trends are far less likely to be controlled or determined by an individual hero*.[12] There appears to be a limit to just how much an individual can do by himself in an attempt to change and shape the outcome of any historical event. In other words, no matter how successful Marseille was as an individual combat pilot, all of his tactical success and leadership could not turn the tide of the desert air war or prevent his own death in September 1942. The effect and impact of Marseille's success was limited to an eighteen-month period of time, confined to a limited area of operation, and restricted to tactical successes. Whatever "greatness" he may have achieved, it was done only within a local area and had no real long-range effects on the overall war effort. The fact remains that no matter how many fighter aircraft Marseille shot down, he and the *Luftwaffe's* inability to stop Allied bomber formations and the eventual defeat of the *Luftwaffe* in North Africa bear truth to this maxim.

Secondly, *most cases of great influence throughout history are indeed usually the right man at the right time*.[13] This is also true of Marseille. With his personality and apparent lack of respect for authority early in his career, had Marseille been in any other Air Force, he would likely have been thrown out before he ever completed training, no matter how good he was as a pilot candidate. Likewise, had a man like Edu Neumann, whose understanding and careful coaching of Marseille not been in place at the right period of time, Marseille likely would never have had the opportunity to compete as a combat pilot. Had the stern Prussian autocrat, Gerhard Homuth, been in Neumann's position, there is little doubt Marseille would once again have been sent packing like he was with Steinhoff in JG 52. Not only is this a case of the right man at the right time, Marseille needed the synergistic effects of factors, such as the war itself, the unique mix of leadership present in I/JG 27 at the time, the desert environment and other personalities to bring out, sharpen, and define his "greatness." Without the Second World War, Marseille would quite possibly have been just an average man living an average life, and obviously would never have become the "Star of Africa."

The third maxim is that *the occasional genius by extremely dexterous and willful actions, may achieve "historical mutation*."[14] In other words, can a person actually achieve world-changing greatness through his or her physical actions? Was Marseille such a historical anomaly? It may appear so. Behind Marseille's 151 desert victories, the highest scoring German aces were Werner Schrör, Hans-Arnold Stahlschmidt, Gustav Rödel, Gerhard Homuth, Otto Schulz, Günther Steinhausen, and Friedrich Körner with 61, 59, 52, 46, 42, 40, and 36 kills respectively. For the pilots of the Desert Air Forces, their top pilots were Caldwell, Marshall, Waddy, Mason, Wade, and Dodds with a total of 96.2 victories between them, and with Caldwell's 20.5 victories making him the leading Allied ace in the desert.[15] Even when considering the possibility, indeed unintentional likelihood of over claiming by Marseille, the fact that Allied pilots were rotated out of theater after a predetermined time, and thus had fewer opportunities to score, and that Marseille's victories were often against somewhat lesser skilled opponents flying marginally inferior aircraft, it remains obvious that Marseille's ability to bring down large numbers of enemy aircraft far exceeded that of any other pilot fighting in North Africa. Those pilots downed by Marseille were still Western trained pilots, and certainly not the quality of pilots the Germans faced in Russia in 1941-1942, nor the quality of *Luftwaffe* pilots the Allies faced over Germany from mid-1944 through the end of the war. These DAF pilots were the same quality and stock of men who handily defeated the *Luftwaffe* during the Battle of Britain in 1940. To dismiss them as "poor" pilots would be grossly unfair and incorrect. It would be far better to blame their archaic tactics and rigid dogmatic rules of aerial combat, haplessly pulled into the desert air war as the primary culprits of their ineffectiveness. Marseille's tactical genius in determining how to best exploit Allied tactical weaknesses alone, along with his unprecedented control as a pilot, accounted for his anomalous success in the desert. But his tactical successes had little or no far-reaching operational effects within his theater of operation, and although impressive, that alone cannot propel him into the category of the historical Great Man.

The fourth and perhaps most important maxim is that *every historical situation is unique and must therefore be judged on its own merit*.[16] No universal formula exists for the determination of the characters that will help shape and define a historical event. We must look at how the alleged "Great Man" affected or controlled his situation. It is impossible to determine exactly who is going to emerge as a significant historical figure. Marseille's accomplishments in the desert must be viewed from the context in which they were achieved. After his incredibly shaky beginnings as a fighter pilot during the Battle of Britain, and after being tossed out of his squadron by Steinhoff, few could have predicted any future greatness from Hans-Joachim Marseille.

In a period of time before the well-known atrocities committed within German concentration camps and the unimaginable slaughter on the Eastern Front, Marseille excelled in an era of reputed chivalry where relatively few civilian casualties were recorded, and soldiers fought one another without having to bomb and destroy cities. To this day, there remains a certain aura about the German *Afrika Korps* and Field Marshall Rommel's achievements in the desert. Throughout their lives, German soldiers that participated in that theater remained proud of their service there and in the knowledge they served with Rommel. A significant part of this legend of the *Afrika Korps* was certainly the *Luftwaffe's* participation in North Africa. And of course, there is no other person more highly associated with the *Luftwaffe's* success than Han-Joachim Marseille. The very nature of the conflict in North Africa during 1941 through September 1942 helped give birth to and nurture the Marseille legend. Marseille relentlessly shaped the aerial environment to his advantage like few other combat pilots ever have. An anomaly? Perhaps, but an incredible one nonetheless. Although he was only the 31st highest scoring German ace of the war, how did he achieve this historical anomaly? This will be looked at throughout this tribute.

In addition to several other aspects of Marseille's life and career, it is because of the factors mentioned above that I must squarely place Marseille in the category of the historical "event making man." Unquestionably the best fighter pilot in North Africa and arguably the greatest of all combat pilots in World War II, Marseille's tactical successes, and thus historical greatness, however, is overshadowed by his lack of any long-term operational or strategic effects. Likewise, he left no writings, as have other combat pilots that have helped to shape or change fighter tactics or theories. Had Marseille developed a tactic or strategy that enabled the *Luftwaffe* to be victorious in the desert, then perhaps he would more likely fit the Great Man theory. Marseille did successfully shape the tactical environment in which he operated, but in the end, the *Luftwaffe* failed strategically in the desert. Marseille "re-wrote" the book on advanced fighter maneuvers in engagements involving multiple aircraft, under similar circumstances succeeded where no other pilot from any nation did, and had the character and personality to greatly influence and impact those men around him. The fact that his unit was withdrawn from frontline combat duty for almost one month after his death is no small measure in determining the impact he had on his environment. The overwhelming amount of literature written about Marseille is yet another testament to his actual or perceived historical significance. Even though the argument can loosely be made that Marseille was a historical great man, in the context of what he accomplished in North Africa, he was really nothing more than an eventful man taking advantage of the situation placed before him. As the event making man, however, there was perhaps no other combat pilot that fit the bill better than Marseille.

Above and following: Series of photographs showing Marseille taxiing in and deplaning after a sortie. *Courtesy of E & C Collection*

Courtesy of E & C Collection

Courtesy of E & C Collection

2

Fighter Pilot Qualities

"He who can handle the quickest rate of change, survives."[1]
Major John Boyd

Regardless of any enduring attributes that defined Hans Marseille's character and personality, the one aspect that solidifies his status as a significant military figure was his mastery of those aspects considered essential to being a great fighter pilot. Historians, and more importantly, fighter pilots themselves have written and described these necessary attributes. Interestingly enough, when analyzing the careers of high scoring fighter pilots from any era or country, many of these characteristics seem universal and are shared, at least in part, by nearly all of these pilots. There is no doubt that Marseille was one of the few fighter pilots to ever embody most if not all of these seemingly constant characteristics.

In the book, *Aces in Command: Fighter Pilots as Combat Leaders*, author Walter J. Boyne describes two indispensable characteristics of the most successful fighter pilots. Boyne stresses that these pilots continually demonstrate the ability to adapt to both evolving tactics as well as rapid changes in technology. In relation to tactics, Marseille for example continually exhibited the ability to exploit both friendly tactics and expose the weaknesses inherent in the DAF formations. In terms of technology, these same pilots learned to cope with the technological advances thrust upon them. These technological advances range from the aircraft themselves, new and improved gunsights, and the range and accuracy of guns, and in the modern era, missile, early warning, and electronic systems to name just a few.

In addition to the characteristics listed by Boyne, successful fighter pilots have also had to demonstrate the ability to adapt to their physical environments. Whether it was climate, high or low altitude combat, or the intricacies of fighting in a specific theater of operations, the best pilots dealt with these adversities and managed

These two photographs, apparently taken at the same time, show Marseille preparing for another sortie. The first photograph clearly shows Marseille "fussing" with his ever-present shawl. *Both Courtesy of Penn Templeman*

There is little doubt that the Bf-109 Fs that Marseille flew in North Africa were superior to the fighter aircraft deployed by the Desert Air Forces. "How much superior?" is the question. If Bf-109s truly outclassed their opponents in every way, why didn't more German pilots score as did Marseille? *Courtesy of E & C Collection*

them better than their counterparts. For example, why did many high scoring *Luftwaffe* pilots on the Western Front not succeed in Russia while many successful pilots on the Russian Front failed in the West? Some pilots, however, were successful in both theaters of operation. Pilots of the past as well as those in the future will have to continually innovate, adapt, and devise tactics in any environment that keeps them in a position to exploit the enemy whenever and wherever possible.

In Mike Spick's book *The Ace Factor*, the author analyzes twelve factors essential to becoming an ace. Once again, aces of every era have demonstrated that they possessed many of these qualities or made the best use of the equipment they had. These factors can be used as a general template to uncover truths about the best of these pilots. Each of these factors is discussed in detail.

1: Better Airplane

Certainly the quality of airplanes engaged in the fight can have a decisive impact on the outcome of a dogfight, and there can be little doubt that the Messerschmitts used in North Africa were in most respects, with obvious exception of the Spitfire, superior to the fighter aircraft used by pilots of the Desert Air Forces. During Marseille's entire tour of duty in the desert, the majority of fighter aircraft he confronted were either Hawker Hurricanes or the American built Curtiss P-40 Kittyhawks and Tomahawks. Although most German pilots remained reluctant to get into a prolonged turning dogfight with these aircraft because of their extreme maneuverability, these Allied aircraft were still at a serious disadvantage to the Messerschmitt 109 *E* and *F* models, especially at higher altitudes.

The Germans smartly opted to maximize the advantages of their aircraft by generally avoiding protracted dogfights, instead choosing slashing attacks from higher altitude, diving past the enemy, extending and escaping. The Allied fighters had little chance of catching the diving 109s, and this in turn made the German tactics safer for their pilots. It was not until the Spitfire's arrival in the spring of 1942 that the Desert Air Forces finally had an aircraft equal in most respects—superior in others—to the Messerschmitt F-2/4 Trop. Unfortunately for the DAF, the numbers of Spitfires in the theater remained small compared to the other fighter aircraft deployed. Even though the Spitfire was certainly a considerable step up from the Hurricanes and American built P-40s, it is clear that Marseille still shot down his share of Spitfires over Libya and Egypt (15). Marseille often boasted that it is not necessarily the quality of the aircraft the man flies, but rather the quality of the pilot in the airplane that matters most.

There is no doubt, however, that much of Marseille's success came from victories over aircraft generally considered inferior to his Bf-109. Indeed, 132 of his 158 total victories (83.5%) came against these aircraft Does this mean Marseille's victories are somehow tainted or cheapened? Not at all. Keep in mind that every Bf-109 pilot in the desert flew against the same opponents and yet only one pilot, Marseille, was able to continually demonstrate such commanding superiority over his enemy. Although the technological advantages of opposing aircraft was clearly a factor in many of Marseille's successes, if the quality of the opposing aircraft was the only issue in North Africa, then the Desert Air Forces would have been destroyed in short order, but they weren't. Also remember that the majority of top scoring DAF pilots in North Africa, those who scored against these same Messerschmitt Bf-109s and gained air superiority over the desert, were successfully flying their "inferior" aircraft day in and day out against the *Luftwaffe*. There are certainly more factors at work than simply possessing a better airplane, although not many "super aces" are likely to emerge flying aircraft clearly inferior to those of his opponent.

2: Numerical Superiority

The question here is whether outnumbering your opponent is essential in ensuring one pilot's ability to continually score. Over time, it certainly has its advantages in wars of attrition, and it has been said that numerical superiority has a quality all its own. At some point, sheer numbers of opposing aircraft will certainly have a significant effect on overall tactical, operational, and strategic operations. Numerical superiority, however, can be a two-edged sword, especially when seen within the tactical realm of WWII, where the airspace was often clogged with hundreds of aircraft. In most fighter squadrons where intense competition for kills was evident, pilots often got in each other's way, obstructing other pilots' opportunities to score. In Saburo Sakai's book *Samurai*, the Japanese ace (64 kills) wrote about single handedly engaging 15 U.S. Navy Hellcats. Although Sakai's superb flying skills undoubtedly aided in his survival, he remarked that while each Hellcat pilot tried getting into the proper firing position, they continually got into each other's way. The result? The Americans, in a rush to each chalk up a kill, prevented one another from getting a clear shot at Sakai. In this way, numerical superiority may at times be detrimental and certainly no guarantee of success.

Likewise, in the air battles over Europe from early 1944 through VE-Day, although the American and British air forces held a substantial numerical superiority over the Germans, there were no Allied pilots with victories approaching those of the Germans. This in no way implies Allied pilots were not as skilled or competent as their German counterparts, but rather this shows that with so many pilots looking for kills, there were far fewer opportunities for each Allied pilot to score, especially in large quantities.

In the desert, rarely did Marseille or any German pilot have the opportunity to claim the advantage of numerical superiority over their enemy. In fact, the German tactic of the *Freie Jagd* (Free Hunt)

Marseille's Yellow 14 takes-off in the desert sand. *Courtesy of E & C Collection.*

ensured that two or four German pilots were almost guaranteed to encounter a superior number of Allied fighters. Regardless, while operating under these conditions Marseille was still able to consistently score against his DAF opponents, demonstrating that numerical superiority, although desirable for self-preservation, is not necessarily a prerequisite for tactical success.

3: Marksmanship

Marksmanship is one of the qualities considered most essential for success as a fighter pilot. Perhaps not seen as important today with less emphasis on using guns and more reliance on heat seeking and radar guided air-to-air missiles, during WWII the greatest aces had to master the many intricacies of aerial marksmanship if they wanted to succeed. Men like Marseille solved these problems, and in turn achieved incredible successes. He perfected his own technique that allowed him to shoot from any angle the situation created. As an extension of his airplane, Marseille would shoot and hit his opponents from some of the most extreme angles and distances. His mastery of aerial gunnery and deflection has been described as unearthly and eerie.[2]

"The Third Man." Günther Rall, 275 aerial victories. *Courtesy of author*

"The wartime combat reports of the *Luftwaffe* fighter pilot were highly detailed. Every evening you had this business to go through. Witness, air witness, ground witness, your account of the combat, the type of enemy aircraft, the kind of ammunition you fired, the armament of your aircraft, and how many rounds of ammunition. These reports were a nuisance to us, but when I was on the staff of Galland I saw how valuable they could sometimes be.

"We found that Marseille needed an average of only fifteen bullets per kill - which is tremendous. No other fighter remotely approached him in this respect. Marseille was the real type - an excellent pilot and a brilliant marksman. I think he was the best shot in the *Luftwaffe*."[3]

Günther Rall

Many aces who were not as talented with long range and/or deflection shooting often compensated by closing to almost point blank range with their enemy. "Squeeze the tit and fly through the shit,"[4] if you will. Even at close range, the pilot must still hit the target. Whether it was long range, close range, high deflection or no deflection, marksmanship is an attribute that any ace, to some degree, has to master. In order to shoot another aircraft down, the fighter pilot must solve several variables. Aerial marksmanship is much more than just firing your guns at an opponent. For the men of previous gun fighting eras, it was much more difficult than just aiming a rifle at a target on a range. Without the advantage of air-to-air missiles, air combat in WWII required the pilot to not only maneuver his aircraft into a favorable position to shoot, but also necessitated that he accurately judge the range to his fast moving, and often times maneuvering target. The pilot then had to accurately measure and judge the angle of deflection, speed, and finally the place where the enemy aircraft would be when his bullets arrived. Other factors such as G-force, bullet drop, environmental factors, etc. had to also be taken into account.

In effect, the WWII fighter pilot often had to maneuver his aircraft through turbulent air, judge the range, deflection, and speed of an enemy aircraft, and aim, fire, and hit his opponent all within a matter of seconds. Anyone who has flown over the desert in summer, for example, knows how extremely turbulent and bumpy the air is as it rises off the hot sand. Imagine trying to hit a moving target from more than a hundred yards away while inverted and simultaneously being pummeled by the unstable air. History tells us that very few pilots were very good at this. Marseille's record proves he was one of them.

"The best flyer, the best gunner, the best fighter pilot. He personified the boyishness, the nonchalance of a fighter pilot. And he had an unbelievably good eye and could shoot exceptionally well in a bank. He was, without doubt, a man who possessed a definite greatness."[5]

Hans-Joachim Jabs

"I think many will agree with me if I say that Marseille was the most talented of the fighter pilots - and also the most ambitious. He even trained between sorties in North Africa. And, according to the statistics, he had the most number of enemy downings using the least amount of ammunition."[6]

Günther Rall

"He (Marseille) can shoot like a young god, but above all he can fire accurately and spectacularly while in a turn, comparable only to such experts as Moelders and Galland. The rest of us shoot into empty sky."[7]

Hans "Fifi" Stahlschmidt

"Hans-Joachim Marseille was probably one of the very few fighter pilots who mastered one hundred percent the art of shooting in a curve. Most of the planes Hans-Joachim Marseille brought down, almost a hundred percent were shot in a curve. It's a special technique and a special tactic which you really have to master if you want to succeed."[8]

Friedrich Körner

"Shooting in a curve is the most difficult thing a fighter pilot can do. That means that the enemy flies a defense circle, it means they are already lying in a curve and the attacking fighter has to fly into this defence circle. By pulling his plane right round, his curve radius must be smaller but if he does that, his target disappears in most cases below his wings. So he cannot see it any more and has to proceed simply by instinct. He already has to shoot without being able to see the target. You have to calculate this interval between your own fire and the presumed hit of the bullets on the enemy plane. You have to guess, to sense it, and of course to score a hit."[9]

Friedrich Körner

"I had my work cut out counting his victories, noting the times and position, and simultaneously protecting his tail. His judgment of deflection was incredible. Each time he fired I saw his shells strike first the enemy's nose, then travel along to the cockpit. No ammunition was wasted."[10]

Rainer Pöttgen

Marseille's commander and mentor, Edu Neumann, climbs from his Bf-109. Neumann was a superb commander and ended the war with 13 victories. *Courtesy of E & C Collection*

"His instinct for aiming and shooting was such that he would open fire in a dogfight without actually having the enemy in his sights. He had the confidence in the air which enabled him to feel that in a battle of wits he could outmaneuver the Curtisses, the Hurricanes and the Spitfires even if the numbers were against him."[11]

Werner Schrör

"The key to Marseille's success was a shooting accuracy that bordered on absolute perfection. He scored his victories with a minimum expenditure of ammunition. His specialty was deflection shooting from a turn while either making a diving attack or pulling up from below. He was constantly practicing and, due to this, was so accurate in shooting from a turn that he worked out a system in which he would push the fire button at the moment when the enemy aircraft flying ahead of him disappeared under his nose.

"After his short burst he no longer bothered with his victim, but concentrated on the next aircraft in the circle in front of him."[12]

Edu Neumann

Author's Note: This likely accounts for the relatively high number of aircraft definitely damaged by Marseille that may have in fact been able to limp back home. A kill claimed by Marseille but in reality, only a damaged aircraft.

Victory	Date	Time	Place	Aircraft	Squadron	Air Force
19	24/09/41	1645	Buq Buq	Hurricane	1 SAAF	SAAF
20	24/09/41	1647	Buq Buq	Hurricane	1 SAAF	SAAF
21	24/09/41	1651	Buq Buq	Hurricane	1 SAAF	SAAF
22	24/09/41	1700	Buq Buq	Hurricane	1 SAAF	SAAF

"I Believe I've now got it."[13]

Hans Marseille to 'Fifi' Stahlschmidt

These victories were the first of nine times Marseille would down 4 aircraft on a single mission.

"His fast reaction is incredible. He knows automatically what are his opponents intentions, which he counters. He is absolutely sure that his burst of fire is lethal and attacks the next aircraft without waiting to observer results. Thus he is able to take every opportunity to shoot down one plane after the other."[14]

Unknown Squadron Member

"He was in effect a human computer. He was able in the twinkling of an eye, and while moving in three dimensions, to determine the exact moment at which to fire and the precise point in the heavens at which to aim, to make a lethal rendezvous between his bullets and the enemy plane, also moving in three dimensions. No one who saw him shoot in the air will ever forget his deadly precision."[15]

Raymond Toliver

4: High Quality Training

There is no doubt that Marseille benefited from the unrushed, unhindered pre-war *Luftwaffe* fighter pilot training. Although a natural pilot with the flair for aerobatics, Marseille's complete training is only partly the reason for his success. There is no evidence to support nor any reason to believe that the quality of the DAF pilots that graduated from Commonwealth training schools were in any way inferior to those of the Germans during this period. The quality of training between the two Air Forces was without a doubt on par with one another in relation to aircraft handling skills. Training with regards to tactics in the field and operational employment is one area where the Germans seem to have been significantly ahead of the DAF, at least in the early stages of the African campaigns.

In Ron Cundy's book *A Gremlin On My Shoulder*, he talks about the operational training he encountered prior to his time in the desert. He wrote:

"As I look back on it now, training methods were totally inadequate. Far too much time was spent in flying straight and level and doing rate one turns. In my opinion once we reached OTU [Operational Training Units], we should have been encouraged – in fact it should have been mandatory – to throw our aircraft around and really get confidence in their handling capabilities. More emphasis should have been placed on combat flying which could have been done by continually engaging in line astern chases, trying to follow competent instructors.

"The other aspect that was sadly lacking was practice deflection shooting. I recall that prior to joining a fighter squadron I had done practically no air-to-air gunnery. From memory I only fired at a drogue on about two occasions. Hence I was inadequately trained and it was some considerable time after I joined a squadron and having missed several 109's that I should have hit, that I became in any way competent.

"When one thinks of the total lack of combat training it is little wonder that we lost so many new pilots when they first came to the squadron. With no training in those skills they were sitting ducks for the experienced 109 pilots. Unless the new pilots were lucky enough to fly sufficient operations to gain the necessary confidence and experience, they were like lambs to the slaughter. Pilots like Eddie Edwards who had learned deflection shooting during boyhood while hunting on the prairies in Canada were exceptionally fortunate. . . . I can't understand why arrangements were not made for experienced fighter pilots to lecture us at OTU on fighter tactics – particularly how to react to attacks by enemy aircraft and how to maneuver to place ourselves in an advantageous position to attack them. Flying inferior aircraft did detract from our ability to attack but we were not taught how to take full advantage of those occasions when we were in a superior strategic position. Hence, too many valuable opportunities and pilots were lost."[16]

The DAF's insistence on holding onto and employing outdated tactics and formations with a glaring failure within certain operational training units to stress combat flying and gunnery training with its young pilots had the greater impact and attributed more to the successes of men like Marseille, rather than the unsupportable and contrived argument that the DAF pilots were simply inferior to the *Luftwaffe* pilots.

5: Leadership

"He can inspire a group only if he himself is filled with confidence and hope of success."[17]

Floyd V. Filson

The importance of having a leader that is neither intimidated nor jealous of a new "prodigy" cannot be overstated. In addition to firm and authoritative leadership, young pilots are often in need of mentorship from superiors. After his arrival to JG 27, Marseille had the fortune to have then Captain Eduard "Edu" Neumann as his group commander. Neumann's true value as a commander, and perhaps one of the most significant keys to Marseille's success, was recognizing the young Berliner's natural talents, giving his prodigy a long leash to try and perfect his tactics, build his skills, bolster his confidence, and finally shielding him from his squadron commander, Gerhard Homuth. This earned him Marseille's respect, and allowed his talents to grow and flourish in an unhampered environment. Instead of being threatened by what he saw in Marseille's flying ability and aggressive spirit, Neumann encouraged and nurtured this behavior.

Following several of Marseille's poorer performances early in his desert career, Neumann still had the foresight to admonish but not quell Marseille's drive. After being shot down and damaging some aircraft, Neumann could have grounded Marseille, but instead told him that he had the impression that Marseille was on track to become a good fighter pilot, but that the most recent occurrences were "not suitable to prove this expectation."[18] He went on to claim that Marseille was only alive because he had more "luck than brains," and that his maturation into a fine fighter pilot would only occur after Marseille replaced his misguided boldness with "clear and calm thoughts"[19] and well thought out tactical judgment. As a further indication of Neumann's insight, knowing that Gerhard Homuth did not like Marseille, Neumann stepped in to ensure they gave sufficient leeway into how they dealt with the young Berliner. Neumann told them to be "tough with Marseille, but take him seriously."[20]

Had Marseille had the misfortune to be commanded by a stern, no-nonsense disciplinarian, it is likely his development would have been arrested in North Africa. The results are obvious. More than one fighter pilot during his early career ran afoul of leadership within his chain of command. Marseille was no exception. It has been well documented that while flying with JG 52 in France under the command of Steinhoff, Marseille was unceremoniously tossed out of the squadron. Steinhoff wrote:

"Marseille was extremely handsome. He was a very gifted pilot and fighter-but he was unreliable. He had girl friends everywhere, and they kept him so busy that he was sometimes so worn out he had to be grounded. His sometimes irresponsible way of conducting his duties was the main reason I fired him. But he had irresistible charm."[21]

Without a doubt, the leadership of a commanding officer plays an integral part in either harnessing or stunting the growth of the overly aggressive fighter pilot. But in addition to the young pilot's acceptance or rejection of the leadership within his chain of command, the most successful fighter pilots likewise display characteristics of personal leadership. The desert war in North Africa allowed for a unique situation in that Marseille's squadron mates often sat back and allowed him to repeatedly score while they were relegated to covering and protecting his back. One interesting aspect of this phenomenon, however, is that Marseille, still hell bent on scoring victories himself, continued to unselfishly instruct and teach his pilots the finer points of his daring tactics. Unfortunately for his men, but luckily for the DAF, none possessed the flying skills necessary to take advantage of Marseille's tactics.

Leadership encompasses many things, and although by no means the greatest fighter leader of WWII, Marseille proved himself to be a capable commander once thrust into that position. When discussing leadership, generally there are two different types. There is one personality that once given a task or put

Courtesy of author

Once placed into a position of authority and command, Marseille proved to be a relatively competent combat commander. *Courtesy of author*

into a group responsible for determining a solution, this person immediately charges to the front, assumes command, and leads his group through a competent solution. This person, by the very nature of his headstrong personality, is often seen as a "natural" leader of men.

The other leader is the one who reluctantly assumes the mantle of "leader." Because of his superior talents and attributes, he naturally rises to the leadership position willingly or not. This is where Marseille fit in. Although he was quite unmilitary in his behavior and dress, initially a braggart who enjoyed relating embellished stories of sexual conquests and remained impertinent in his relationships with authority, once he found his rhythm in the desert, not only was he the most effective fighter pilot, but also a man that all of his comrades looked to for guidance and leadership. Although Hans Rings claims that he was "clearly no leader," I would have to disagree in part. He may have not been the personality to immediately jump to the forefront and insist on leading his men, but it was through his personality, physical talents, and burning desire to succeed, however, that he became a natural combat leader; one that men were willing to follow as he continually dove into and out of enemy formations. Yes, Marseille was an excellent combat leader in many respects. Unfortunately, in others he was not.

> "A true and safe leader is likely to be one who has no desire to lead, but is forced into a position of leadership by . . . the press of the external situation."[22]
>
> A.W. Tozer

As a combat leader, *Staffelkapitän* Marseille, by virtue of his 77 aerial victories at the time, was thrust into that position by recently promoted JG 27 *Kommodore* (Wing Commander) Edu Neumann. To his credit, Marseille readily accepted the role and successfully led his men into combat. As a fighter leader Marseille cared for his pilots, and devoted time and effort trying to teach and encourage them, and because of his talent, protected them as best he could while in combat. His boldness in attack gave little excuse for his men not to follow. Leadership by example and doing what he asked of his men endeared him to them. They literally loved him, and would do most anything for him. This, however, was not enough.

Perhaps the fundamental failure in Marseille's personal leadership was his inability to properly train and prepare a successor. Although he tried to teach his tactics and combat theories, he certainly realized most could never match his flying skills. For tactics that relied solely on unmatched aerial marksmanship and unparalleled aircraft handling, Marseille's theories became just that to the men around him: theories. Most of the men of 3/ JG 27 had little or no hope of enjoying the successes of their "Captain."

While the men of 3/ JG 27 basked in Marseille's glory and let him score time and time again, as a unit, it appears they were doing little in terms of preparing for the day when he would no longer be there to lead them into combat. Obviously, that day came on 30 September 1942, and with Marseille's death, the effectiveness

Squadron Commander Hans Joachim Marseille. *Courtesy of author*

of the entire I *Gruppe* diminished to the point where they were withdrawn from combat for a period of over a month. This type of combat ineffectiveness would be unusual and highly unlikely in most other fighter units. It would be hard to imagine, for example, America's 56th Fighter Group falling to pieces if either "Hub" Zemke, Dave Schilling, Francis "Gabby" Gabreski, Walker "Bud" Mahurin, or Robert Johnson had been shot down and killed. In fact, after Gabreski went down during a strafing run, the 56th successfully soldiered on without him. Although earlier in the month Marseille's best friend Hans-Arnold "Fifi" Stahlschmidt (59 victories) and Günther Steinhausen (40 victories) were killed, the devastating effect of one man's death on a fighter unit unfortunately illustrates the fundamental failure, albeit not entirely within his control, of Marseille's leadership. The more success he achieved, the more his men relied on him to carry the load, which he willingly did. His death—something seemingly not a concern of the men of I/ JG 27—had understandable and predictable consequences.

Regardless, Marseille, at 22 years of age, for the short time he was *Staffelkapitän* of 3/ JG 27, proved he was an excellent combat leader who boldly led his men into combat and attempted to prepare his men for it, but likely failed to both fully prepare a successor and to realize the effect his death would have on his unit.

> "After they [his squadron mates] realized his talent and skill, and saw the results he achieved, they became aware of his leadership and even magnetism, and looked up to him as to no other pilot."[23]
>
> Edu Neumann

> "Although a fine fighter pilot, Hans-Joachim Marseille was clearly no leader, being very much a 'lone wolf'. His promotion to Hauptmann was due to his incredible successes, rather than any other reason, and while commanding I Staffel, his pilots had little opportunity to shoot down any aircraft themselves, being left to ward off surprise attacks while the maestro showed them how it was done. In fairness, it must be said that his pilots aided in this. He looked after them in the air like a worried

From *Der Adler*, this photograph shows Marseille surrounded by personnel from his squadron. In the dirt he has drawn a circle and, as the other men look on, it is likely he is about to begin a lesson on the best way to attack the English Lufbery Circle. *Courtesy of author*

mother hen, but they were so bathed in the reflected glory of their brilliant leader that they sometimes voluntarily held back from attacking enemy aircraft to allow him to build his score still higher - an almost unique situation in a fighter unit!"[24]

Christopher Shores/ Hans Ring

"On the other hand Marseille, for example, was willing with pleasure to let his comrades share his tactics, and rejoiced greatly at each victory by his unit, but only a few pilots were able to gain from his experiences in combat because they lacked the natural talents." [25]

Edu Neumann

"More impressive than the arrival of the Americans, however, was the arrival of the first Spitfires in the skies over North Africa. In my opinion it was thanks to the merits of Marseille that we were able to reduce the unquestionable threat from this aircraft to a bearable degree."[26]

Edu Neumann

"Marseille was a legend for all of us, Germans and Italians alike. He was so successful! And we were grateful for somebody like Marseille who was able somehow to lift some of the pressure which the flying exercised on us. You see the material superiority of the enemy was so enormous at the time."[27]

Edu Neumann

"During the early days of the Desert war he would frequently walk alone in the Desert for long hours, working out tactical problems of air fighting."[28]

Christopher Shores/ Hans Ring

"I may thank you, Captain Marseille for your work. Without you, some things would have been impossible."[29]

Erwin Rommel

"This handicap [that relatively few pilots scored] was partially overcome by the morale effect on the whole Geschwader of the success of pilots like Marseille. In fact most of the pilots in Marseille's Staffel acted in a secondary role as escort to the 'master,' though this was of secondary importance when compared with the results achieved by this."[30]

Edu Neumann

"However, there is no doubt that my true schoolmaster was Marseille; I studied his tactics for attacking the British defensive circles for a long time, tried it myself often without success - and finally, learned the lesson."[31]

Werner Schrör

6: Superior Flying Skills

"Yeah, everybody knew nobody could cope with him. Nobody could do the same. Some of the pilots tried it like Stahlschmidt, myself, and Rödel. He, he was an artist. Marseille was an artist." Using his hands to illustrate. "He was up here and the rest of us were down here somewhere."[32]

Friedrich Körner

Superior flying skills, although desirable, are not necessarily a perquisite for a successful fighter pilot. For example, in North Africa both the Germans and the pilots of the DAF generally agree that the best aerobatic pilots in the desert were the Italians. Although universally recognized for their excellent flying skills, how did those skills translate into combat efficiency? Not very well it would seem. The highest scoring Italian pilot in the desert was Capitano Franco Lucchini, who reportedly shot down some

Formal Knight's Cross photograph of Friedrich Körner taken as a prisoner of war in Canada, September 1942. Körner spent exactly one year in the desert, arriving on 4 July 1941 and being shot down by South African Lt. Waugh on 4 July 1942. In that time Körner scored 36 aerial victories. *Courtesy of author*

20 aircraft between 14 June 1940 and July 1943 while flying over the Western Desert and Malta. Although a respectable score to be sure, the low victory tallies of the remaining Italian pilots shows that excellent flying skills do not necessarily translate into combat prowess. Similarly, several high scoring aces like von Richthofen in WWI were never credited with being outstanding "stick and rudder" pilots, but their combat efficiency cannot be denied.

Marseille unquestionably possessed superior flying skills and used them to both position himself for the kill and to escape from tenuous positions. As his physical skills seemed to improve almost daily, along with the physical increase came his awareness, almost a sixth-sense if you will, in the ability to anticipate and counter the movements and plans of his enemy. Fritz Dettmann wrote in *My Friend Marseille* that Marseille seemed to "play with the enemy" and to "beat them without the slightest effort."[33] Marseille accomplished this during times when the odds were even as well as when he was greatly outnumbered by his DAF opponents.

"You can't imagine a wilder daredevil."[34]

Walter Krupinski

"Marseille was one of the best. No one could follow him."[35]

Adolf Galland

"As a fighter pilot Marseille was absolutely supreme. . . Above all, he possessed lightning reflexes and could make a quicker judgment in a bigger orbit than anyone else. His senses and reflexes produced what, today, a modern computer would provide. Marseille was unique."[36]

Edu Neumann

"Landings and take-offs, however, fell well below usual squadron standards. Once he borrowed a new Macchi 205 from a neighboring Italian squadron and crashed it on landing. It left a poor impression of his general ability as a pilot."[37]

Werner Schrör

Author's Note: This incident allegedly occurred in September 1942 at Fuka, Egypt. It involved the personal mount of 4°Stormo, 96a Squadriglia's Flight Leader, Lt.Annoni (9 victories).

"I saw him using tricks in combat that others would never have contemplated. He would close the throttle, lower his landing flaps and drop the undercarriage to reduce speed and fox an attacker. By using his flaps and working the throttle he could increase the maneuverability of his aircraft and tighten his turns."[38]

Werner Schrör

"There was no one else like him. I could always pick him out by the way he flew."[39]

Edu Neumann

"But none of us could emulate his skills and few could achieve victories in the way that they came to him."[40]

Werner Schrör

Marseille climbs out of the cockpit of W. Nr. 8673. Note the black outline around the visible portion of the "1." This is the only aircraft known to have carried the distinctive I/ JG 27 emblem on the nose. *Courtesy of E & C Collection*

"Though it sounds more legendary than factual, several surviving comrades insist that his Messerschmitt-109 pulled vapor trails in quick turns (from the wing-tips) when no other fighter in the formation did so."[41]

Edward Sims

"He and his plane were one unit and he was in command of that plane like nobody else."[42]

Emil Clade

"He always flew at a very, very high speed, you could see the white eddies at the end of the wings. You recognized him immediately in fight. That is Marseille!! He understood and reacted at the speed of lightning."[43]

Edu Neumann

"I forgot to fire as I watched Marseille wading into the enemy formations."[44]

Ludwig Franzisket

"His eyesight was exceptional; he seemed to have a third eye in his head. His flying reflected his flamboyance and his dash. He was never one for sticking to the usual disciplines of the air – even when he was a junior officer in the squadron. But there was a genius, a flair about his flying which enabled him to exploit a situation, to shoot from almost any position. When he found himself at a tactical disadvantage he had the opportunism and the speed of mind to extricate himself from it and turn the tables on his opponents."[45]

Werner Schrör

"Marseille flew slowly over the airfield. The aircraft dropped lower, drawing ever closer to the ground. A bamboo stick had been stuck into the ground and a handkerchief tied to it about a meter above the earth. Marseille was going to pick it up with his wingtip. Astonished, the Generals stopped laughing. There was an outburst of applause when the young pilot took the handkerchief with the wing of his aircraft. The Messerschmitt pulled up and roared over the heads of the visitors at high speed."[46]

Unknown

"I've fully integrated all the motions in air combat and with difficult maneuvers. It begins as I close with the enemy. I've now come so far that I can keep control of the Bf 109 in any situation, even in the tightest turns and at the lowest possible speeds. In combat I make all my motions unconsciously. This lets me concentrate fully on the attack and fly my plane as though I had wings."[47]

Hans-Joachim Marseille

"His movements were faster than average."[48]

Edward Sims

"At the time, the English used to form the well-known defensive circle, where each man protects the aircraft in front and is himself protected from behind, but I flew several missions with Marseille and saw how he managed to penetrate this circle and destroy his victim so quickly that the next English pilot in the circle had no time to fire at him. Of course, only a pilot possessing extraordinary abilities could achieve this."[49]

Friedrich Keller

"Marseille was much more, however, than just a superlative marksman. Since his shaky beginnings as a cadet pilot, he had developed an aerobatic ability so pronounced that he could thrill even veteran German aces with his flying."[50]

Raymond Toliver

7: Judgment

Judgment in air combat often relates to knowing when to fight and when to fly away. It is the ability to avoid situations where superior flying skills may be required to save one's neck, or more likely, one's lack of skill will result in getting shot down. Several famous fighter pilots throughout history have used their keen insight to codify air combat principles based upon common sense and their experiences in air combat (See Appendix 2). In World War I, German ace Oswald Bölcke (40 kills) wrote his 8 rules for air combat, his so-called "Dicta Bölcke." During WWII, the great RAF fighter leader from South Africa, Adolph "Sailor" Malan (27 kills plus 7 shared), wrote his Ten Rules for air fighting, while German ace Erich Hartmann (352 kills) wrote his "See-Decide-Attack-Reverse or 'Coffee Break'" rule. American fighter leader John "40 Second" Boyd[51] wrote extensively on his OODA-Loop. Each of these men used their personal experiences to write a method for other pilots to use when engaged in combat. Unfortunately, there is no evidence that Marseille wrote any such document.

As for Marseille's time in North Africa, there appear to be three distinct periods in his level of maturity and sophistication in relation to judgment. The first period appears to be from his arrival in North Africa until December 1941 when he returned to the desert armed with the new Bf-109F. The second period is from December 1941 through 17 June 1942 where Marseille seemed to fully perfect his tactics, and the third period came after his summer leave. It is during this hectic period of a little over one month that Marseille achieved his greatest successes.

Period 1: Although there was never any question of his abilities as a gifted pilot, in his quest to become the best fighter pilot in North Africa, it was his rash and often ill planned decisions to repeatedly attack overwhelming elements of DAF aircraft that resulted in his being shot down and damaged on several occasions. Although it laid the foundation for his future successes, it is only by luck and the grace of God that he was not killed in his early days in the desert. Even members of his squadron agreed during this period that Marseille's last days could be "counted by the fingers of a hand" if he continued on as he did.

Period 2: After having finally fully analyzed the faulty DAF Vic and Lufbery formations, Marseille appeared to take a much more scientific approach to his attacks, allowing for his experience and tactical expertise to replace unbridled bloodlust. Although he definitely showed a lack of maturity and judgment early in his African career, that was somewhat replaced by his technical abilities through June 1942, although he still showed a propensity to push himself too hard and attack formations when he probably should not have. It is apparent that his excellent flying skills kept him alive even against overwhelming odds. Early during this time period, it was said that Marseille seemed "cheerful and untroubled," although he was not scoring as quickly as he would have liked. They did remark, however, that Marseille had become more calm and cool-headed while finally being able to control his ambition.

Period 3: Finally, upon his return to the desert in August 1942, although still armed with his superior flying abilities and the knowledge of how to defeat the English formations, Marseille, according to several pilots that flew with him, seemed like a man possessed, appearing ever more reckless and impetuous in his battles against the DAF. Of all the characteristics of the successful fighter pilot listed by Mike Spick, this is the one area where Marseille demonstrated his greatest weakness and immaturity. In his quest to succeed and be the best pilot in North Africa, Marseille deliberately entered combat at times where he may have been better served disengaging. If judgment can be summed up as not allowing oneself to act recklessly, regardless of Marseille's success, it is within this area that he repeatedly failed.

> "I think Jochen felt that things couldn't go on as they were and that sooner or later his luck would run out. He may, in the end, have begun to question his success and his genius."[52]
>
> Werner Schrör

8: Luck

Luck is an intangible that cannot be planned for, yet remains instrumental to the success or failure of many pilots. Why does one pilot survive a shoot down while another one dies? On one occasion when Marseille was shot down by French pilot Sous-Lt Denis, bullets nicked the back of his flight helmet while two others went just inches in front of his face. Any slight deviation fore or aft would have left Marseille's head a bloody shambles, yet instead, he walked away to fight another day. Now that's luck!

Luck also plays a part in the number of aircraft a pilot can actually engage. Some pilots flew entire tours of duty rarely ever seeing an enemy aircraft, while others were able to engage the enemy on an almost daily basis. In Marseille's situation, the *Freie Jagd* and a supportive commander both led to excellent scoring opportunities.

An excellent photograph with Marseille pointing to battle damage he received in his Emil before arriving in the desert. At this point, I/ JG 27 was flying in the Balkans in early April 1941. *Courtesy of E & C Collection*

In the end, however, the successful pilot must be lucky enough to find and shoot down enemy aircraft, and of course be lucky enough to survive enough encounters to become more proficient.

> "The luck is on my side."[53]
>
> Hans Marseille talking to Stahlschmidt

9: Determination

The most successful of fighter pilots are usually those driven to be the best. There is something in their makeup that makes them want to be the best; they seem to live it, breathe it. There is no doubt Marseille wanted to become the best fighter pilot in the desert. He would spend hours walking alone in the desert, carefully working out the details of defeating the British formations. He could be seen turning in small circles with his arms flailing as if in a deadly duel with enemy fighters. In the air, following missions he would pass the lead onto others in the flight so that he could practice his tactics and simulate attacks against the men in his squadron, while late into the night he would talk with his comrades at length on how to best defeat the Allied pilots. Although it took almost one year for him to develop the maturity and skills necessary to be considered among the *Luftwaffe's* elite, it was Marseille's determination to become the best pilot in North Africa that paid dividends through practice, training, and hard work.

> "He practiced incessantly, and slowly he worked out the split-second timing and sighting for accurate deflection shooting."[54]
>
> Edward Sims

10: Fearlessness

This idea is too often misunderstood. No pilot that I have ever interviewed said they entered combat completely devoid of fear. Successfully managing their fear, however, was their goal. Regardless of the risks involved, the best combat pilots must still to some degree willingly embrace the danger inherent in aerial combat.[55] This is not to say the best pilots must continually seek combat, but neither do these pilots shy away from it, especially when the chances for a successful engagement are on their side. This pilot, when seeing the enemy, must have the stamina and guts to position his aircraft to a point where he risks combat and places himself in an environment that greatly increases the risk of his own demise. Next, he must maneuver and engage the enemy. If it is true that 65% of pilots able to enter combat somehow figure out a way to avoid it, this shows that these aces are indeed a cut above most fighter pilots. For the top scoring among them combat is not only unavoidable, it is desirable. But for many, the continued stress of air combat proved to be too much.

In the book *Messerschmitts Over Sicily* by Johannes "Macky" Steinhoff, he describes the three types of men that turn away from combat:

A serious Marseille mission plans for an upcoming sortie. *Courtesy of author*

> "Usually the report that someone was turning back came shortly after take-off and before there was any real danger. It was invariably accompanied by an expression of regret; for instance: 'Oh sod it, my engine keeps cutting. I'll have to turn back.' In some cases the regret was perfectly genuine, in others less so, and it needed long experience of command to distinguish between them.
>
> "Those who turned back could be divided into three categories. First of all there were the genuine cases which were by no means rare since technology is a law unto itself and cares little for the reputation of a fighter pilot. The reliable veterans of numerous campaigns, the old hands, knew their aeroplanes and made little of it when they had to turn back. Instead of profuse explanations, they simply gave the leader a factual report of the trouble. They knew that what they said would be accepted without question.
>
> "The second category consisted of experienced pilots who, having suddenly reached the end of their tether, either could not or would not acknowledge the fact. Having survived hundreds of patrols and battles, each time learning more about how to master themselves, how to circumvent the perfectly natural instinct of self-preservation, they had all at once found themselves unable to cope any more, unable to resist the temptation

of making a timely excuse. Thereafter they would turn back more and more frequently. In such cases it was better to take them off operations before they were killed.

"The third group was composed of young pilots posted to the front from fighter replacement wings. Among them there were always a few who would yield to the temptation of a minor deception so as to avoid battle. They were horrified and utterly overwhelmed by the pitilessness of the air war in the Mediterranean. Many had been misled by communiqués which, though full of heroic deeds, said nothing about the superiority the enemy had gradually achieved. None of the fighter training schools was in a position to prepare the young pilots for what really awaited them.

"When someone in this category turned back, the older, experienced pilots would test his machine after their return from the operation. As often as not they found no sign of the alleged trouble, thus instantly demolishing the boy's fragile edifice of petty lies. Some never repeated the attempt; others reappeared, much later, in category two, while the majority were either killed or posted home 'for other employment.'"[56]

It is apparent that Marseille, at least in the company of his comrades, dealt well with the potentially crippling affliction of fear. In combat he was certainly relentless, but I believe it would be a bit optimistic to claim he flew without fear. Indeed, his long walks into the desert night when he couldn't sleep, his nightmares, persistent thoughts of death, and his sometimes morose attitude demonstrated the effects stress had on him. But like all great fighters, he was able to channel those fears in a positive direction and continue to fly and fight.

11: Great Distance Vision

All great combat pilots are attributed to having this one characteristic: the ability to see small objects at substantial distances. This gift is essential in locating enemy aircraft before they can see you. In air combat, the ability to find the enemy first is often the difference between life and death. Allegedly, 80 percent of the pilots that survive being shot down in combat report either never seeing the enemy airplane that shot them down, or they saw it too late to effect the outcome of the combat. Marseille's 41st and 42nd victories both reported never seeing Marseille's attack. His vision was legendary among pilots that flew with him, and he would often pick out enemy formations a full minute or more before anyone else in the formation saw anything other than empty sky. This allowed him to gain the element of surprise and thus seize the initiative even during times when he and his element were outnumbered by the enemy. This factor alone contributed highly to his success as a fighter pilot.

"He possessed outstanding eyesight, so that he was able to spot his enemy long before he was spotted and take the appropriate actions."[57]

Edu Neuman

"His eyesight was extremely good (it is said he adapted his eyes to the desert by staring into the sun for long periods)."[58]

Edward Sims

"Marseille had fantastic eyesight; he was able to see the enemy long before anyone else and he had devised a special attack method which only he could use."[59]

Friedrich Keller

"His eyesight was exceptional; he seemed to have a third eye in his head."[60]

Werner Schrör

"Marseille combined many qualities which are important in a fighter pilot. Firstly he had very good sight and in the air three-dimensional vision is very important. You need to be able to look into the depths of space in order to recognize the enemy as soon as possible. Then you have a decisive advantage. You can position yourself in the most favorable place for an attack and maybe you can even carry out a surprise attack which puts you at a great advantage."[61]

Emil Clade

12: Skill of Opposing Pilots

"The Tommies will soon be sending you a medal for damaging our planes."[62]

Edu Neumann

"Oh I have been shot down because I'm still an ignorant person. I have been lucky."[63]

Hans-Joachim Marseille

The skill of opposing pilots cannot be ignored when looking at the records of fighter pilots from any nation. The historian must look carefully at the competition any ace had to confront in combat. In the 1982 Lebanon war for example, Israeli fighter pilots downed close to 100 Syrian fighter aircraft to a loss of zero. This complete domination of an opponent is impressive by any standard. The question one must ask, however, is "what about the quality of the Syrian pilots and their aircraft?" Although not belittling the Israeli accomplishments, there can be little doubt that their Syrian opponents were clearly not up to the challenge of facing Israeli pilots flying American-made F-15 and F-16 fighters.

If the opposing pilots as a whole are truly unworthy opponents, wouldn't one expect consistently large scores on one side versus another? In North Africa, Marseille faced pilots from England, Canada, Australia, New Zealand, South Africa, and perhaps several pilots from the U.S. in September 1942. Some historians, I believe in an attempt to challenge the successes of Marseille, have in turn marginalized or questioned the quality of pilots he faced in the desert. I am unwilling to dismiss out of hand the qualities of the DAF pilots. If these pilots were in fact of such lesser caliber, why were there not more high scoring German aces? Granted, the top German aces scored well above those of the DAF, but this is accounted for in part by the DAF's shorter tour rotations. If the Allied pilots were truly inferior, how could they have been so clearly victorious over the *Luftwaffe* in the desert? Although clearly outnumbered by the DAF, had the Germans so completely outclassed the DAF pilots, large scores by *Luftwaffe* fighter pilots would have negated any Allied numerical superiority. That, however, was not the case.

So many other factors like extended *Luftwaffe* tours in the desert helped give an illusion of alleged German superiority. There can really be little doubt that had men like "Stocky" Edwards and "Killer" Caldwell remained in the desert for one and a half to two years, their scores would have likely rivaled those of many *Luftwaffe* pilots (provided they survived). Of the ten top scoring *Luftwaffe* pilots in the desert, also keep in mind that half survived that conflict while four were killed in action, and one, Friedrich Körner, was shot down and made a prisoner of war. In other words, the top ten *Luftwaffe* pilots suffered 50% casualties in the desert.

Obviously, the quality of opposing pilots plays an essential role in either the success or failure of a fighter pilot. Remember, Marseille was shot down and damaged several times by these same pilots. Thus it is illogical to argue that Marseille's successes hinged solely upon poorly trained DAF pilots while at the same time acknowledging the overall German unwillingness to engage the DAF in prolonged dogfights because of their skill and the superior maneuverability of their aircraft. If the German pilots fighting for their lives maintained a healthy respect for their DAF opponents, why would we, 65 years later, dismiss this reality? Unlike the highly "under-trained" German pilots sent up to be slaughtered over Europe in the "defense of the Reich" in 1944-45, the pilots Marseille faced in North Africa were highly qualified and skilled. Rather than insisting the pilots themselves were substandard, I believe it was more a case of good pilots employing outdated tactics and flying marginally inferior aircraft, along with Marseille's unique talents that contributed to his success.

Marseille: the Consummate Fighter Pilot

When we take into account all of the characteristics discussed by Mike Spick and Walter Boyne, we can ascertain that Marseille was a pilot with exceptional eyesight and the ability to see enemy aircraft long before he himself was seen. He possessed superior flying skills, and while continually training, he adapted and modified his tactics to successfully exploit the archaic and tactically restrictive DAF formations. Although often displaying a certain lack of judgment brought on by an intense desire to be the best fighter pilot in the desert, he trained relentlessly and used his superior Messerschmitt to exploit his flying ability and marksmanship to down pilots of the DAF at rates unlike any other German pilot regardless of the numbers of opposing enemy aircraft.

While all successful fighter pilots display most or some of these essential characteristics, Marseille and probably only a handful of other pilots in the history of aerial combat have clearly possessed them all. Perhaps most telling is an overarching characteristic that is a synergistic result of the other attributes listed by Mike Spick. This attribute is called Situational Awareness (SA).

Situational Awareness seems to be another characteristic most successful fighter pilots have in common. SA is the ability to be cognizant of all aspects of the airspace surrounding the fight. The pilots with superior SA seem to know where every aircraft in the fight, both friendly and enemy, is at all times. Even though there may be upwards of 20 to 30 aircraft involved, pilots with superior SA somehow seem to keep track of them all. Not only do they appear to know where these aircraft are, but they also seem to know where they are in relation to themselves. Werner Schröer stated that Marseille seemingly had a third eye in his head, being able to keep track of the movements of every aircraft in the area.

> "He had an incredible eye. I want to say, he seemed able to divide the air into slices. We others sometimes looked through the enemy and looked at the other side and didn't see what was in front of us. He was a talented pilot. Extraordinarily talented, a unique talent."[64]
>
> Edu Neumann

In Mike Spick's *The Ace Factor*, the author discusses one study that attempted to objectively quantify SA. In air combat exercises, it concluded that pilots with the best kill ratios also had the best SA scores in multiple aircraft engagements. Not surprisingly, those same pilots with the highest SA ratings consistently scored better than pilots with lower SA scores. In other words, pilots that have the best awareness of their surroundings continually have the best chances for surviving and scoring victories.[65]

In the end, in terms of those qualities necessary for high scoring fighter pilots, one can objectively ascertain that Marseille was a superior pilot in possession of outstanding physical, mental, and emotional qualities. These together made him a fighter pilot who will always stand out among all his peers.

> "Certain attributes were essential; airmanship, motivation, guts, aggressiveness, good eyesight and the ability to shoot straight. When you are with him you find that the "hero" is a myth. He is armed with no callous disregard for life and death. He is not fortified with some peculiar toughness of the body or spirit. Behind the glamour of their daring and devotion lie their personalities, which to my thinking are more fascinating still. Nor do their great deeds lose in stature if we regard them as performed, not by heroes, but by ordinary men. The fighter pilot then is an ordinary man – as scared as the next."[65]
>
> Derek Gilpin-Barnes
> Intelligence Officer

3

Tactics

"Secondly, Marseille developed his own special tactics for shooting down a plane which differed significantly from the methods of most of the other fighter pilots. When we attacked we always attached great importance to flying at high speed so that we could escape from a precarious situation if necessary. Of course Marseille too flew at a high speed. But besides that he did something extraordinary: In Africa it frequently happened that the enemy formed a defence circle that means when 5, 6 or 7 planes fly in a circle, the one behind could cover the one in front. So there was practically no one without cover. Marseille flew into this defensive circle. And in fact nobody else ever copied this tactic because when he entered from on top, he only had a very short time to shoot. But many times he dived through and attacked the defensive circle from below and by using this tactic he had to fly very slowly. He even took it to the point where he had to operate his landing flaps so as not to fall down [stall] – because of course, he had to fly his curve more tightly than the upper defence circle."[1]

Emil Clade

The air war in the desert presented unique opportunities for the fighter pilots on both sides of the conflict. For the pilots of the DAF, in addition to their marginally inferior aircraft, it was the unfortunate adherence to dogmatic ideas of fighter combat and archaic fighter formations—those poorly adapted to the aircraft they were flying—which continued to plague them against their *Luftwaffe* adversaries. For the German pilots, possession of the premier fighter in North Africa meant more opportunities to score and led to varied uses of their aircraft in the tactical role. It is interesting to see how the different air forces applied tactical air power and dealt with the effects of that application of power. In discussing Marseille's tactics, historians would be remiss in ignoring the impact of overall fighter tactics, formations, and fighter doctrine in use during Marseille's time in North Africa. These factors contributed most significantly to his success in the desert.

Marseille with the Knight's Cross, Oak Leaves, and Swords. *Courtesy of Bender Publishing*

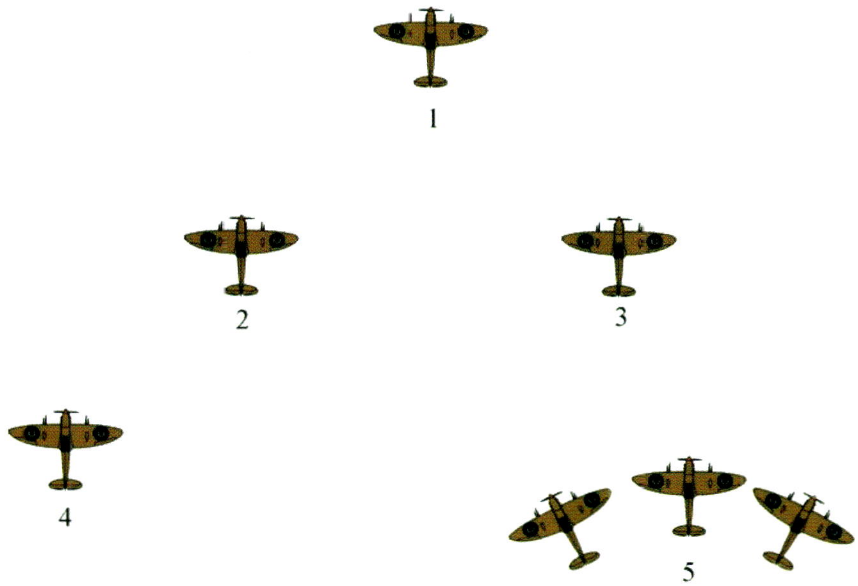

Figure 3-1: The Vic. *Image by author*

British Tactics

Tactics employed by the pilots of the Desert Air Forces were initially a mix of old, unimaginative formations like the three- or five-ship "Vic" and the desperate Lufbery Circle. Although both of these formations, especially the "Vic," were outdated by spring of 1941, they enjoyed wide use in the desert campaign.

Vic

The Vic, or "V" formation, was a tightly flown formation that usually consisted of three or five aircraft arranged in a pattern resembling the letter "V," with these aircraft normally spaced 50 to 60 yards apart. Tactically, this formation was difficult to wield in a combat environment. The Vic was standardized by the Air Fighting Development Establishment (AFDE) during the 1930s,[2] and was developed as a way to bring the most guns to bear on what was then seen as the primary aerial threat at that time: unescorted enemy bombers. Conventional wisdom of the time envisioned less fighter-to-fighter engagements and more bomber interceptions. Three Hawker Hurricanes arranged in the Vic, for example, could bring to bear some 24 .303 machine guns onto an enemy bomber. Since the Vic was envisioned as a single large gun platform, this formation had the ability to cut a swath through any enemy bomber formation: in theory. Dogmatic, tactical doctrine at the time also demanded tight formation integrity unless otherwise specified by the flight lead. Pilots were expected to maintain formation integrity at all times, and this uncompromising insistence on tight formation flying, as will be shown later, severely hampered DAF pilots in North Africa.

The Vic's weaknesses were many. The first figure in this chapter illustrates that with an odd number of aircraft in the formation, there was always an "odd man out." That is to say, one aircraft remained without cover by another aircraft. In this example, aircraft number 5's primary responsibility was that of the "weaver," also known as the "Tail-End Charlie." This pilot was responsible for covering the six O'clock position of the entire formation. This aircraft would weave back and forth, clearing the area of potential enemy aircraft and warning the rest of the formation of an imminent attack. This left the weaver vulnerable to attack in that he was left alone without mutual support and generally out of sight of the rest of the formation. Here, alone and in the rear, the Germans could, and often did make quick work of this tail-end Charlie, sometimes without other squadron mates even realizing he was missing until they returned to base. Likewise, it was usually the less experienced pilots that flew this position. Inexperience coupled with the tactically vulnerable weaving position made this exceptionally dangerous.

Although this formation looked good flying over public gatherings, airshows, and parades, there was another inherent weakness of the Vic. In the combat environment where the pilots were so absorbed with trying to maintain a tight formation, they were unable to properly clear the area for enemy aircraft. Instead of looking for German or Italian fighters, pilots in the Vic spent an inordinate amount of their time looking at the lead aircraft and trying to maintain proper alignment. The inflexibility and rigidity of this formation often doomed the pilots, since they relied upon the lead aircraft and the weaver to spot attacking fighters. The Germans, having long foregone this inflexible formation, immediately recognized the inherent vulnerabilities and exploited their aircrafts' superior performance. There was very little useful combat effectiveness in the Vic. It is no surprise that RAF Fighter Command officially discarded this formation in early 1941. During the Battle of Britain the *Luftwaffe* had already shown the Vic to be obsolete, and many RAF fighter units had already taken it upon themselves to stop using that formation altogether. What is surprising is that pilots of the DAF continued to use this archaic formation long after its flaws and weaknesses had been utterly exploited by the *Luftwaffe*.

> "We learned tactics pretty quickly, but there wasn't much time during the Battle [of Britain]. We learned to

> spread the Vies. One chap was put in as 'weaver' – arse-end Charlie – weaving about behind our formation, keeping a look out. They were often shot down, weaving behind and never seen again."[3]
>
> Alan Deere

The Lufbery Circle

The Lufbery Circle, generally attributed as being developed by WWI American fighter pilot Raoul Lufbery, can best be described as a three dimensional version of "Circling the Wagons." When wagon trains of the old west were attacked, for mutual protection the settlers would form their wagons in a circle, thus preventing the attackers from gaining an advantage through any exposed weaknesses. At any given time, an attack by the enemy would be met by fire since no area was exposed or vulnerable. The Lufbery Circle was used for this same reason. It was designed as a method for pilots in slower but equally maneuverable aircraft to set up a defensive barrier against pilots in faster and generally more capable aircraft. As a defensive formation, the Lufbery proved effective against most *Luftwaffe* pilots that encountered it.

In theory, once defending aircraft formed up in the Lufbery, any attack by enemy fighters would have dire consequences, since entering or attacking the Lufbery, any German or Italian fighter would immediately have an Allied aircraft in position to fire upon the intruder. This formation gave excellent covering fire for each of the defending aircraft and provided the DAF pilots with an opportunity to negate many of the advantages of the German Messerschmitts, and was also sufficient in most cases to dissuade all but the most aggressive of German pilots.

Although the Lufbery may seem to be the perfect 2-dimensional defensive formation, it too had its serious drawbacks. First and foremost, air combat takes place in all three dimensions, and the Lufbery often failed to account for the vertical aspect of potential

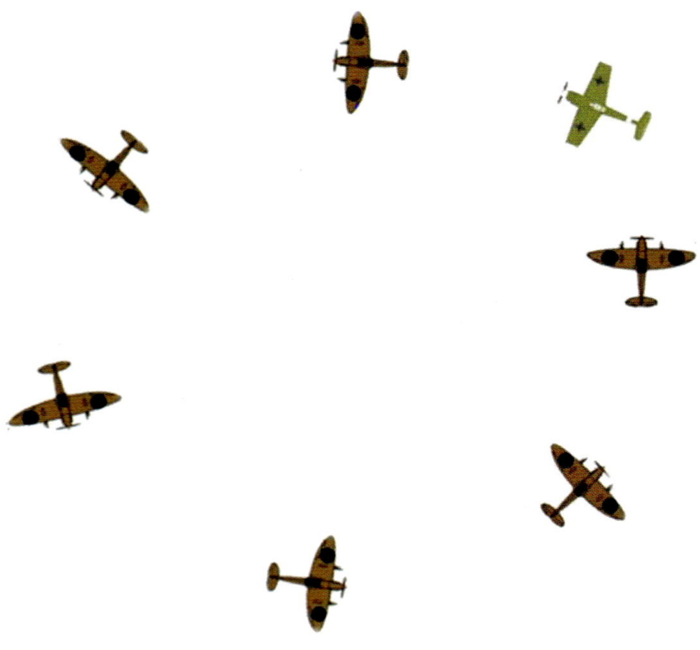

Figure 3-2: The Lufbery Circle. *Image by author*

Luftwaffe attacks. Next, by going into a defensive posture, DAF pilots willingly ceded initiative to the Germans. The *Luftwaffe* pilots could, and did, choose when and if to attack, thus dictating the course of battle.

Perhaps the most significant flaw of the Lufbery was that it was usually flown at higher altitudes as opposed to lower to the ground. Pilots like Marseille could maximize the performance of their aircraft and exploit the vertical dimension by attacking the circle from either above or below. Figure 3-2 illustrates that an intruding Messerschmitt would immediately come under fire by other aircraft in the formation. What the diagram fails to indicate is that attacks from either above or below often achieved success since the Lufbery failed to account for, or rather was ill-prepared to counter such vertical exploitation. For the Lufbery to have been fully successful, the pilots of the DAF would have been better served either forming up or quickly working down toward lower altitudes, thereby preventing vertical attacks such as those eventually devised and employed by Marseille. With the formation only several hundred feet above the ground, such aggressive attacks would have been impossible for likelihood of striking the ground. Even with this significant flaw, the Lufbery remained an effective defense during the early to mid stages of the North African campaign.

During the research for this book I had the opportunity to interview Colonel George Daniels at Maxwell Air Force Base. As an F-15 pilot, he gave interesting first hand insights to the Lufbery Circle. He mentioned how A-10 Thunderbolt II pilots will sometimes employ a similar defensive formation called "Circling the Hogs." When confronting a superior fighter aircraft, the A-10 pilots will form the Lufbery as did the pilots of the DAF. The theory remains as it did 65 years ago, but the main difference is that the A-10 pilots typically fly this formation lower to the ground in order to deny the enemy the ability to attack from above or below using guns.

Likewise, by flying this formation lower to the ground, the A-10 pilots have less of the sky to search for enemy aircraft, greatly reducing their workload of flying and clearing for enemy aircraft. The DAF pilots flying the Lufbery at higher altitudes against an aggressive pilot like Marseille were at a disadvantage in that they not only had to fly their formation and keep the tail of the preceding aircraft clear, but their visual scan had to encompass the entire sky, looking for attacks from above, below, and from the same altitude. This was not an easy feat, and the overall success of this formation speaks volumes for the skill of the many DAF pilots who flew it.

When confronting A-10s in this formation during exercises, I asked Colonel Daniels the best way to attack and, not surprisingly, he mentioned from above with a missile attack and then to extend and escape. I then asked him if he only had guns how he would then attack the A-10 formation. His response was, "I would not go into a formation of A-10s. You have to give them proper respect." I also interviewed Lt.Col. Donald Cornwall, a pilot with experience in the F-15E, F-117, and with 646 hours of A-10 time. I asked him about "circling the hogs" and how it worked for him during Red Flag type exercises. He said that in 10-15 times of encountering

112 Squadron pilots posing in front of one of their shark-mouthed Kittyhawks. S/Ldr Neville Duke is standing second from the left. *Courtesy of Michel Lavigne*

fighter aircraft while flying this formation, not once did any of his squadron mates get "shot down" by guns.

What I found interesting about Colonel Daniels' and LTC. Cornwall's comments were how similar they were to some *Luftwaffe* pilots about the DAF use of the Lufbery. As the Messerschmitt was faster than the Hurricanes and P-40s but not quite as maneuverable, the same is true of the faster F-15 versus the quicker turning A-10. Putting this in proper perspective, it is even more impressive what Marseille was able to accomplish.

> "We flew in 'fluid sixes' or fours, all weaving. As the Germans nearly always had the advantage of height, when attacked we sometimes went into a defensive circle tactic which was derived from experiences during shipping patrols and the inferior performance of our aircraft. The standard German attacks were either to dive and climb, or to dive, fire, and continue down through the formation, but on rare occasions a 109 pilot would turn with you, and this was a fair sign that you were in for trouble as they generally turned out to be tough customers."[4]
>
> N.F. Duke

German Tactics

The German *Finger Four*, the primary *Luftwaffe* combat fighter formation, was the most effective employed during the desert air war. By allowing the *Luftwaffe* pilots to seize the initiative, it proved to be far superior to both the Lufbery Circle and the Vic. First employed by the German Legion Condor during the Spanish Civil War, it was named because when looking from above, the formation resembles the fingers of an outstretched hand.

The Finger Four offered the German pilots increased flexibility and mutual support. No longer did a single pilot fly on the outskirts of the formation acting as the weaver trying to clear the six o'clock position for the rest of the formation. Rather, each aircraft was paired with another for mutual support. When flown as either a *Rotte* (2 aircraft team) or a *Schwarm* (4 aircraft team), each pilot could expect covering support from his wingman. In Figures 3-3 and 3-4 aircraft 1 and 3 are the element leaders, while aircraft 2 and 4 are the wingmen responsible for covering the tail of the lead aircraft.

In addition to covering one another, the Finger Four was "looser" and far more spread out than the Vic. This allowed each of the German pilots to scan the sky for enemy fighters, rather than having to concentrate on maintaining a rigid formation. Instead of two sets of eyes trying to keep constant vigil for enemy fighters, in both the *Rotte* and *Schwarm*, every pilot had the opportunity to search freely for enemy aircraft. Since we have already discussed how the man who generally sees the enemy first has the better chance of success, this formation presented the *Luftwaffe* pilots

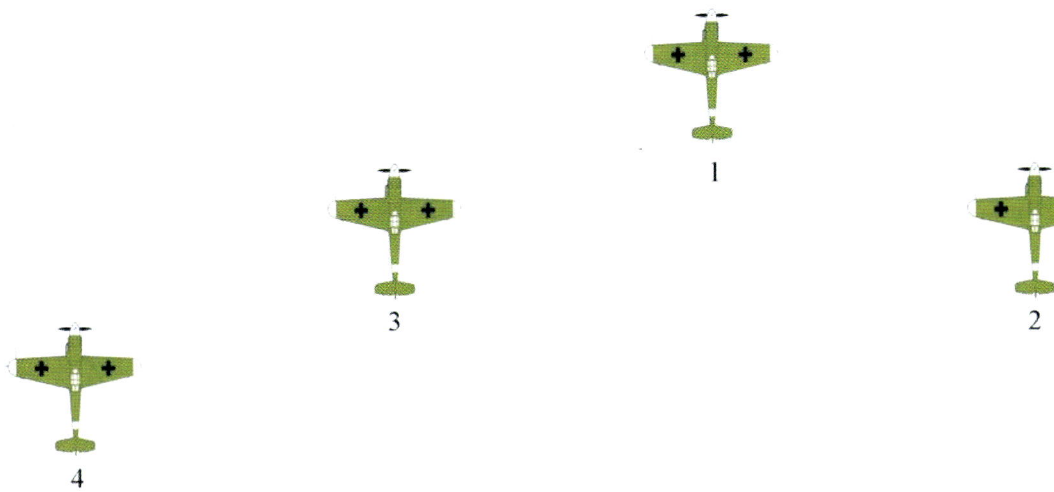

Figure 3-3: *Luftwaffe Schwarm*. *Image by author*

with a significant tactical and psychological advantage over the pilots of the DAF.

Other advantages of the Finger Four were both its offensive and defensive adaptability. Not only did the *Freie Jagd* (see next section) allow the Germans to seize the initiative in most fighter-to-fighter combats, since the Finger Four was more extended and spread out, it was more difficult to see all the Germans in the formation as they closed in or moved away from the fight. Colonel Daniels further explained that the more dispersed the formation, naturally the more difficult it becomes to see all the players. Employment of the two or four ship teams meant these formations were spaced far enough apart that it was possible for DAF pilots to miscount the two or four ship elements. A DAF pilot might spot a German *Rotte* but not see the second element of two 109s. If this mistake was made, the results could be obvious.

Another advantage of the Finger Four, in contrast to the Vic in particular, was its superior flexibility in maneuvering. By employing crossover turns, no aircraft was left out of position on the outside of a turn. Unlike the slow turning Vic, pilots in the *Rotte* or *Schwarm* were able to make precise and rapid turns while maintaining an effective combat formation. There was no longer any need for the pilot on the inside of a turn to pull his power way off and slow down just to remain in position. Pilots could now

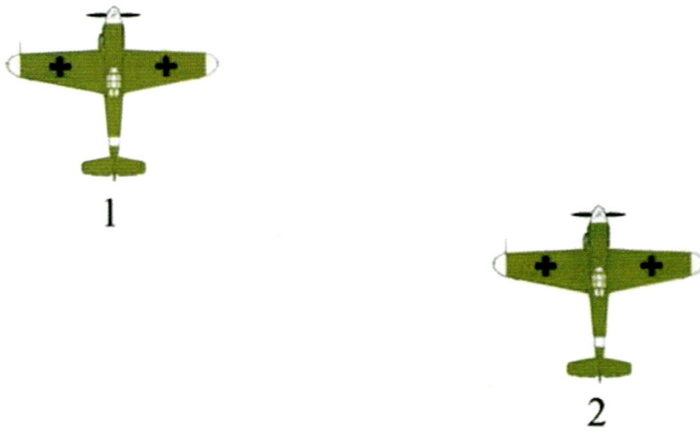

Figure 3-5: *Luftwaffe Rotte. Image by author*

complete all maneuvering turns at full speed and under normal power.

Perhaps the most important aspect of the Finger Four, whether employed in two or four man elements, was that each pilot was afforded some protection by at least one other aircraft in a formation. As long as the element leader and his wingman were still flying, mutual support existed. A single aircraft's time is numbered in a combat environment, and German tactics minimized this possibility as much as possible.

In addition to the *Rotte* and *Schwarm*, German tactics in the desert were developed to maximize the capabilities of their Messerschmitts while, not surprisingly, minimize their weaknesses. It had already been established during the Battle of Britain that the English Hurricanes were aircraft to be reckoned with in a turning dogfight. These aircraft, although slower than the Messerschmitt, were more maneuverable, and *Luftwaffe* pilots recognized this. Even the American built P-40s were maneuverable aircraft, and were to be respected if a *Luftwaffe* pilot was going to try and turn with them in combat. Of course, the legendary performance of the Spitfire was well known, but unfortunately for the DAF, it was the Hurricane and P-40 Kittyhawk and Tomahawk aircraft that made up the lion's share of fighters during the period when Marseille operated in North Africa.

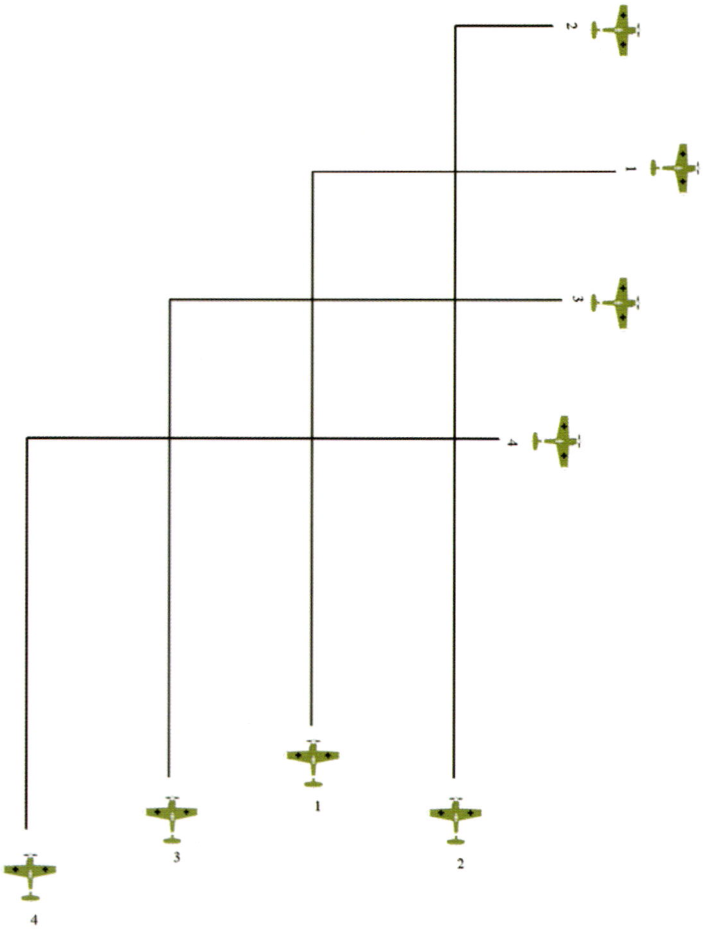

Figure 3-4: Crossover Turn. *Image by author*

> "However it was a deadly mistake for a Bf 109 pilot to try and enter a dogfight with the Curtiss's. I have seen the death of two or three of my comrades in dogfights with Curtiss's, among them Leutnant Heinz Schmidt in June 1941."[5]
>
> Ludwig Franzisket

> "Dogfights in the style of Richthofen or Marseille I did not fight to a conclusion. The superiority of the British types in dogfights was notorious, and the Spitfires added their higher speed to this. . . . This fear was in many cases unfounded – because the excellent Spitfire needed an excellent pilot."[6]
>
> Werner Schrör

Series of photos: Completion of another sortie. *Courtesy of E & C Collection*

Although the Allied aircraft could generally out-turn the Messerschmitt, it was in the area of overall speed, altitude, and vertical maneuverability where the Germans held a distinct advantage. German tactics thus evolved where they attempted to enter their engagements from a higher altitude and then complete diving, slashing attacks with the option to dive away freely or climb back into the vertical for another attack. Interestingly, this was the same tactic employed by Claire Chennault and his Flying Tigers against more nimble Japanese fighters over China. This tactic nullified the real or perceived turning superiority of the Allied fighters while maximizing the climbing, diving, and speed advantages of the Messerschmitt. It also had the benefit of limiting exposure of German pilots to enemy fire. It was only the extremely confident pilots that would routinely turn and "mix it up" with the Allied fighters. Although the classic view of the "heroic" turning dogfight is the stuff of legends and Hollywood pictures, the reality of air combat in the desert was far different. These hit and run tactics were sometimes viewed as "unfair" by pilots of the DAF, but if the object is to kill and not be killed, these tactics definitely benefited the German pilots. Although you could engage in a turning dogfight, why would you?

> "However, it is self-evident that we preferred to gain our victories with the least danger. I understand very well the bitter feeling the British pilots often had about the 'bad' Messerschmitts – but why should we have exposed ourselves unnecessarily?"[7]
>
> Rudolf Sinner

Freie Jagd

> "There is nothing better than the *Freie Jagd*. But we don't know how long this freedom in combat will remain to us. The development of communications and the reporting offices keeps us more tightly on the leash day by day. I'm afraid that the hour will soon come when Manfred von Richthofen's theory will no longer be applicable; 'Fighter pilots should be allowed to operate in their assigned areas as they see fit. When they spot an enemy, then they attack and shoot him down. Everything else is nonsense.'
>
> "But Richthofen will always be right in one thing; the only person who is an effective pilot is the man who attacks the enemy whenever he sees him, who is willing and able at all times to jump into combat without wondering whether it might not be himself this time who will be lying on the ground with shattered limbs at the end of the fight."[8]
>
> Hans-Joachim Marseille

The *Freie Jagd*, or *Free Hunt* was the basic tactic that formed the backbone of *Luftwaffe* fighter operations in North Africa. The *Freie Jagd* consisted primarily of *Rotte* (two man) or *Schwarm* (four man) hunter/killer teams that operated independently of overall *Luftwaffe* operations. Like many military formations and operations, the *Freie Jagd* was born out of tactical and operational necessity. Due to the overwhelming naval superiority of the British Royal Navy in the Mediterranean, supplies such as fuel and aircraft parts were a continual problem for the *Luftwaffe* in the desert. Often times, the Germans could not field entire squadrons of aircraft for lack of fuel and serviceable aircraft. This led to a special dilemma for *Luftwaffe* squadrons. During the times when squadrons could not operate at full strength, which for the *Luftwaffe* was almost daily, the question became how many aircraft could they actually fly and who would man those aircraft?

The logical decision dictated placing the most capable pilots and their wingmen in those aircraft whenever possible. This increased the operational and tactical flexibility within the *Jagdwaffe*. Tactically, the *Rotte* or *Schwarm* was, as previously discussed, much more fluid, maneuverable, and allowed the German pilots the ability to move much more unhindered than their DAF counterparts. Operationally, these hunter/killer teams could easily be directed to an area of interest faster than an entire squadron of aircraft. They could then find the enemy, attack quickly, and escape. Often employing in only *Rotte* strength, the Germans had the added advantage of being more difficult to spot than a larger formation of aircraft.

As with any combat formation, the *Freie Jagd* too had its own serious drawbacks. Since these hunter/killer teams were employed in two or four man units, if the German pilots engaged a formation of enemy fighters they were inevitably outnumbered, and if that formation happened to consist of a pilot of the caliber of James "Stocky" Edwards, Clive "Killer" Caldwell, or any number of excellent DAF pilots, the results were often devastating to the Germans.

On 7 September 1942, for example, a I/ JG 27 *Schwarm* was attacked by seven Spitfires of 601 Squadron RAF. During this attack, Marseille's best friend Lt. Hans-Arnold "Fifi" Stahlschmidt, third highest ranking ace in the desert with 59 victories, and Lt. Karl von Lieres zu Wilkau (24 desert victories) were shot down. Both men, obviously very skilled fighter pilots, still succumbed to the quality and number of DAF fighters they encountered that day.

Another negative aspect of the *Freie Jagd* was the poor operational and strategic return in investment. Although the German pilots more than held their own in combat with fighter pilots of the DAF, these small hunter/killer teams, and indeed *Luftwaffe* fighter operations in general, did very little to turn back the increasing number of Allied bombers attacking German airfields and *Afrika Korps* forces on the ground. Many of the *Jagdwaffe* pilots seemed to treat Middle East and North African operations almost as a game or a joust, trying to prove who was the best fighter pilot in the desert. In doing so, these men unfortunately ignored more critical operational and strategic issues, eventually losing the air war in North Africa.

Likewise, even if these simpler German formations were able to shoot down a handful of Allied aircraft on a daily basis, the question that begs to be asked is, so what? If the DAF lost four or five fighters and their pilots in a day, they were more readily replaced by the Allies. Where the Germans could ill-afford to lose a significant number of aircraft or men, the DAF could more readily absorb those losses. If the *Jagdwaffe* could have employed a hundred four-ship hunter/killer teams daily to sweep the sky clear of enemy opposition, this tactic may have seen significant operational or even strategic success. But the Germans could not generate those numbers and as a result, the *Freie Jagd* had very little, if any, overall strategic or operational effect on the outcome of the air war in North Africa. Nonetheless, the *Jagdwaffe* did what it could with the materials, pilots, and supplies it had. The *Jagdwaffe's* failure in North Africa was certainly not for a lack of will within the ranks of *Luftwaffe* fighter pilots.

> "The natural rivalry among pilots meant that, with some *Experten*, high scoring appears to have become an object in itself, while the hit-and-run tactics adopted to compensate for numerical inferiority meant that it was enemy fighter squadrons which tended to suffer. The bomber squadrons were rarely mauled, pounding both airfields and Axis communications almost unopposed, while the *Jagdflieger* pursued their private war, leaving the *Landsers* of all ranks cowering under enemy bombs."[9]
>
> *Desert Warriors*

Perhaps the most insidious failure of the *Freie Jagd* in the desert was the attitude born inside certain *Luftwaffe* squadrons. Since it was usually the most capable of pilots that flew the majority of the *Freie Jagd* sorties, it was also these pilots that tended to run up the most impressive scores against the DAF. This created a two-edged sword that eventually became too unwieldy to handle. On the one side, there were men like Marseille, Schrör, Stahlschmidt, Körner, and Rödel whose natural talents lent them perfectly to this hunter/killer method of fighting. Marseille in particular would enter a fight, shoot down an aircraft or two, and hope that his wingman was keeping his tail clear of enemy aircraft. The problem here is obvious. Certain pilots became very proficient while others served only to protect the flight lead. Only a select few ever became *Rotte* or *Schwarm* leaders, while the rest remained wingmen with little chance to score. Indeed, Marseille's primary wingman, Lt. Rainer Pöttgen, flew over one hundred missions with Marseille before claiming his first victory.

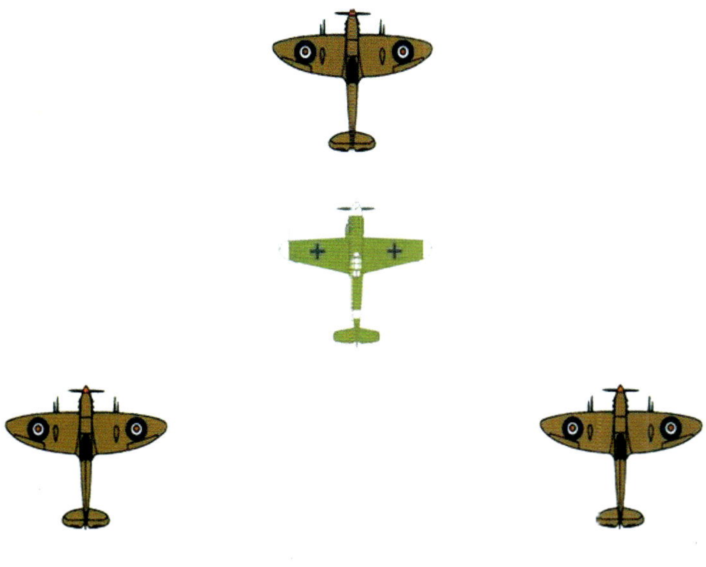

Figure 3-6: Marseille Against the Vic. *Image by author*

This bred a unique dynamic not seen in Allied squadrons, where intense competition to score was the name of the game. Whereas German wingmen in North Africa, often given little chance to score themselves, sat back and watched other pilots score time and again, the distribution of victories among pilots in German squadrons was skewed toward just a few men. The result? If and when these high scoring aces failed to return from an operation, their loss was much more acutely felt within their squadron. After Marseille's death in September for example, the entire I/ JG 27 was removed from combat for over a month in an attempt to regroup from his loss.

Marseille's Tactical Genius

> "Tactics should diminish the possibility of resistance and it seeks to fulfill this purpose by exploiting the elements of movement and surprise."[10]
>
> Liddell Hart

Marseille was certainly on the leading edge of tactical thought. His aggressive tactics were augmented by his superior control over his aircraft. Together these proved deadly and, for a time, seemingly unbeatable. Marseille was comfortable fighting and shooting from any angle, from a left or right hand turn, while in a roll or inverted, and believed attacks from straight behind were not necessarily the best for successful air combat. It took complete mastery of his aircraft to consistently succeed under conditions where most pilots struggled or failed to score. Perhaps equally important as his flying skills and marksmanship was his tactical genius and the intuitive analysis he used in defeating enemy formations. For example, against the enemy Vic, Marseille would often avoid attacking the Tail End Charlie, rather flying through the middle of the formation in order to hit the most experienced pilot in the formation, thereby dislocating the rest of the formation. Some would argue that his tactics were sheer genius, others: madness!

Dislocation and Exploitation

Unfortunately for the historian, Hans Marseille left no writings describing his own tactics or thoughts on air combat. Unlike Oswald Bölcke or Sailor Malan, there is no record on the rules of air combat according to Marseille. If there were such writings, they have long since been lost to history. What we do have, however, are the eyewitness accounts of the men who fought alongside and against Marseille. It is through their words and recollections that we can accurately piece together Marseille's actions over North Africa.

Between the wars, British Army captain Liddell Hart became one of the most prolific military historians and strategists of the last century. Among his many writings, his magnificent book *Strategy* discusses the concept of dislocation and exploitation. This concept focuses on two areas: rapidity of movement, and the psychological effect an attack produces within an enemy system. A boxer, for example, quickly positions himself to strike his opponent in an attempt to upset his balance. This is dislocation. Then, before his opponent can recover, the boxer strikes his opponent again and again, hopefully defeating him. This is exploitation. The key to this theory is that your opponent is never given an opportunity to respond or recover.

In combat this theory still holds true. Sun Tzu wrote, "The condition of a military force is that its essential factor is speed, taking advantage of others' failure to catch up, going by routes they do not expect, attacking where they are not on guard."[11] Hart made the most of this concept in his theory. Napoleon further wrote that the key to success in combat was "rapid and audacious attack,"[12] once again without giving the opponent a chance to respond. Not only were the attacks to be bold and decisive, success likewise relied upon attacks conducted along a line of least expectation. Hart wrote, "A direct approach to one's mental object, or physical objective, along the line of natural expectation for the opponent, tends to produce negative results."[13] In other words, if you attack where expected, you increase your chance of failure. This is because the enemy, knowing an attack is coming, will prepare himself and guard against it. In order to increase your chances of success, one must hit the enemy where he least expects it.

This leads to perhaps the most important piece of the dislocation/exploitation theory; the psychological impact such attacks have tend to pay the biggest dividend. Napoleon wrote, "The moral is to the physical as three is to one."[14] Exploitation by its very nature surprises, shocks, and disrupts the enemy. If conducted properly, it can generate confusion within the enemy's ranks, and it can shatter the cohesion of an enemy formation with paralyzing effects. Since exploitation rests largely within the psychological sphere, it is often more difficult to determine its effects yet remains something to strive for. Hart wrote, "Psychological dislocation fundamentally springs from a sense of being trapped."[15] He further states, "In most campaigns the dislocation of the enemy's psychological and physical balance has been the vital prelude to a successful attempt at his overthrow."[16]

It is relatively certain that Marseille left behind no writings on his theories of air combat. What is certain, however, is that there were keenly intuitive processes that Marseille used to develop his tactics against the British formations. Marseille, through careful analysis of the enemy formations, their tactics, and his own trial and error, intentionally chose to attack via lines of least expectation. By deftly maneuvering his aircraft from either below or above the Lufbery or through the middle of the Vic, Marseille made his attacks in such a way that his rapid movements were both nearly impossible to follow and had the added effect of seeming to create confusion among the enemy pilots. His movements generated surprise that in turn gave him freedom to maneuver and thwart his opponent's abilities to counter his attacks. Marseille endeavored to string together a series of lightning fast attacks, neither of which came from the same direction or method, being dictated by the tactical situation of the moment.[17]

Analysis of Marseille's tactics, however, encapsulates the true genius of his flying. Undeniably an outstanding pilot and superb marksman, it was his intuitive knowledge of the art of dislocation and exploitation that made his other attributes so successful. By wading into enemy formations when they were clearly not expecting an attack, Marseille was able to gain the advantage and then exploit it before the enemy pilots could analyze and counter his attacks. Whether against the Vic, Lufbery Circle, or simply fighter vs. fighter combat, from April 1941 until his death in September 1942, Marseille alone was able to continually succeed against the DAF at a level approaching his own. He scored when others did not, and while outnumbered, Marseille repeatedly out-flew the more maneuverable Allied fighters and their highly trained pilots. If Marseille's accomplishments could have been easily copied, if the general level of DAF pilots had somehow been consistently below that of the *Jagdwaffe*, or if the archaic formations flown by the DAF could completely explain Marseille's successes, there would have been many rivals to his dominance in the air. There were none.

> "But the tactics are all wrong. We are too inflexible. Fighters in front, fighters above, fighters on each side of the bombers. We are so closely tied to the bombers that we get in each other's way. The fighters must be free of the bombers. We must disrupt the British formations, not they ours. Why must we always fight as units, never as individuals? We must disperse them by planned attack and pick them off one by one!"[18]
>
> Hans-Joachim Marseille

Author's Note: This quote from early in Marseille's Battle of Britain career alludes to his thoughts of Dislocation and Exploitation, as well as his lone wolf tendencies which suited the *Freie Jagd* in North Africa so well.

> "Marseille exploited the confusion into which the enemy formations were thrown by his sudden attack, making certain that one of them broke out of the safety chain and then shooting him down in a tight turn back."[19]
>
> Rainer Pöttgen

> "During the early days of the Desert war he would frequently walk alone in the Desert for long hours, working out tactical problems of air fighting."[20]
>
> Hans Ring

> "Against the enemy's wedge formations [Vic] he would attack from behind, not firing at the aircraft formed up on either side in order to flush out the lead aircraft in the center. He made a fast enough approach to escape the avenging fire of the two planes flying on the flanks and scored his kills with lightning-like accurate bursts."[21]
>
> Edu Neumann

"As long as I look right into the muzzles, nothing can happen to me. Only if he pulls lead am I in danger."[22]

Hans-Joachim Marseille

"Marseille knew that it is not the number of aircraft that decides the outcome, but the better man."[23]

Fritz Dettman

On Marseille's tactics for the Lufbery Circle

So much has been written and discussed over the years about Marseille's tactics that a rehash here might seem redundant. Still, a short discussion is in order. Later we will let the words of those pilots who witnessed Marseille in action give a clearer insight to his tactics.

Marseille's method for attacking and displacing the Lufbery was as unique as it was bold. When reading combat reports and comments by both DAF and *Luftwaffe* pilots who witnessed his attacks, apparently no two were necessarily the same. Marseille refused to let his tactics become dogmatic and predictable; rather, he allowed them to evolve based on the situation he was in at the moment, and of course depended upon the actions of the DAF pilots confronting him.

Starting at a point laterally displaced and above the circle, Marseille would dive down below the formation, zoom up, and attack from underneath. There, under the crushing G-Forces of his pull-up, he would select one aircraft, line him up in his sights, and hammer one very short and deadly burst of cannon and machine gun fire. After his firing run, Marseille would use his speed to climb through the top of the formation, and then he would set himself up for another repeat attack. Sometimes, however, instead of immediately positioning himself up for another climbing attack, he would continue his climb until stalling his Messerschmitt. There he would spin safely down below the enemy formation, thus preventing enemy fighters from following him through his maneuver. Once complete, Marseille would position himself for another attack.

Other times he would assault the circle while diving from above, shoot his victim with a well-placed burst of fire, and slice through the turning formation, not allowing DAF fighters the chance to engage his high speed attack. Unbelievably, it has been reported that at other times Marseille would actually do the unthinkable and enter the circle of highly maneuverable Hurricane or Curtiss fighters, out-turn them, and use his excellent marksmanship to hit his target while in a steep turn and from incredible angles and distances. By manipulating his throttle and landing flaps, he was able to slow his Messerschmitt enough to decrease his turn radius inside that of his opponents, thereby nullifying the designed purpose of the Lufbery.

By repeating this and other variations of this deadly sequence, Marseille often shot down two, three, and four aircraft in a single sortie. His movements were so audacious that during his time in North Africa, according to other very successful pilots like Friedrich Körner, Marseille was the only *Luftwaffe* pilot with the skills necessary to consistently pull off these complicated maneuvers, hit his enemy, and generally escape unscathed.

An Enemy Perspective

The following is an excerpt that illustrates Marseille's tactics as observed from an enemy pilot. This combat took place on 13 May 1942. During this mission, Marseille and Rainer Pöttgen attacked

An informal shot of Marseille with journalist and author of *My Friend Marseille*, Fritz Dettmann. *Courtesy of Penn Templeman*

12 Kittyhawks of 3 RAAF squadron over Gazala, Libya. On this sortie, Marseille destroyed Kittyhawks flown by FO H.G. Pace (KIA) and Sgt. MacDiarmid (bailed out). FO Geoff Chinchen fired at and hit Marseille's 109 in the oil cooler and propeller.[24] Notice Chinchen's account mentions how on all but one attack, it was only Marseille that appeared to fire while Pöttgen covered his tail:

> "Enemy attack – dive and zoom and occasionally endeavouring to follow their target in a turn. On one occasion a head on attack.
>
> "My first attack was astern to rear quarter on Me 109F attacking one of our a/c. The distance was too great to be a good attack.
>
> "A Me 109F attacked an a/c lower than my a/c and I came down and climbed with him. I was apparently unobserved as he did a stall turn while I was approx. 400 yds away. I closed to approx 200 yds. Firing all the way and he seemed to be hovering in my tracer. He fell away and as I was [at] the stall I had to correct and lost sight of him.
>
> "E/A started an attack on one of our a/c and observed [me] about to make a front quarter [attack] on him, so he came in and made it a head on [attack] on me.
>
> "He flew right up my fire and at the last moment broke away. I could not observe him firing during this attack.
>
> "Beam to rear quarter attacks were made on e/a attacking our a/c. In each case the enemy broke off his attack but no result of my firing was observed.

Note: The pair of e/a circled line astern approx 1,000 – 1,500 ft. above me and 2,000 – 2,500 ft. above the main body of our a/c. As I kept my a/c pointing in their direction I was not attacked on [any] occasion. Each attack was made on an a/c whose tail was towards the e/a, in some cases during a turn. The leading a/c always attacked and did so by starting with a wingover which gave one a little time to anticipate his target and get position. Only on one occasion were the two e/a attacking together."[25]

Another Enemy Encounter

The following combat report is from 19 May 1942 when Marseille and Pöttgen attacked three aircraft of 450 Squadron while on a *Freie Jagd*. Marseille claimed two victories, his 61st and 62nd, including Sergeant Ivan Young who, although wounded, was able to make it back to Allied territory:

> "Section of three sighted two Me 109F approaching on same level when at 16,000 ft. nine miles South of Gazala. These immediately climbed 2,000 ft. above and delivered two abortive attacks out of the sun, pulling out 500 ft. above. In third attack Black 2 received several shells in wing and rudder and fired ineffective bursts at attacker, avoided further action, returned and force landed at Gambut Main. Result of action disclosed several hits in wing with explosive bullets, these exploding inside wing. Rudder hit and rudder cable severed, wheel burst, A/C airframe Cat. II engine serviceable. Black 1 saw attack, turned left to attack E/A No. 2 from under, went into spin, coming out in cloud, lost sight of section and returned home. (Unfortunately the ORB does not record who Black 1 and 2 were, but it is likely that they were Sgts. Law and Oakley, as they landed at 0846 and 0840 respectively, earlier than the other group of four. This left Sgt. Young, who was Blue 1, alone.) Blue 1 witnessed E/A attack Black 2 then climbed to 3-4,000 ft. above, circling about. He attempted to climb to them, got to within 1,000 ft. when they also climbed with him to 20,000 ft. Blue 1 spiral dived to cloud at 4,000 ft. followed by one ME 109. He pulled up in steep turn to go into cloud when second ME 109 came through hole in cloud and fired burst of cannon into Blue 1's engine, putting it out of action. Blue 1 attempted forced landing, doing violent weaves, leveled out approx. 10 ft. The first 109 attacked from astern, registering several hits. Blue 1 made steep left turn and stalled onto ground. Pilot got out and ran. First 109 strafed and set A/C on fire. A/C totally destroyed. Blue 1 during engagement fired an ineffective burst. Pilot unhurt. Picked up by 6th South African Armoured Cars. Cloud 6/10 1 to 5,000 ft."[26]

Author's Note: There are several interesting elements of this combat report. First, when discussing the outstanding flying skill and marksmanship of Marseille, during this combat, as well as the fight mentioned on 13 May where Marseille downed two aircraft, his extreme tactics still resulted in several abortive attacks. Although he did down a total of four aircraft in these two combats, he did so only after several complex and ineffective attacks, one of which resulted in his aircraft also being damaged.

Another interesting aspect of this second combat report is that the pilot mentions the "second ME 109 came through hole in cloud and fired burst of cannon into Blue 1's engine, putting it out of action. . ." He then goes on to mention, "The first 109 attacked from astern, registering several hits. . . ." Assuming that his eye witness account is accurate, and there is no reason to believe it is not, it is apparent that Marseille's wingman, Rainer Pöttgen, should have been given at least partial credit for this victory since he either fired the shots that put Sgt. Young's engine "out of action," or delivered the *coup de grace* that forced him into the ground. According to this combat report, clearly both 109s fired at and hit Sgt. Young's aircraft.

> "I'll pass one or two times through the circle from above, then move in behind the aircraft I've chosen. On the third pass, however, when the enemy expects something totally different, I dive from my higher altitude past the defensive circle, build up more and more speed and pull up again into a half loop, then do a half roll and shoot down the closest one while on my back."[27]
>
> Hans-Joachim Marseille

"Against all this there were the serious talks we had in the long evenings when we would all discuss tactics with him [Marseille] - how to break up a defensive circle of Curtiss fighters protecting British ships, how to attack elements supporting the surrounded fortress of Tobruk. He would work out the tactics he thought best and fly them according to his instinct, leaving the rest to try to do the same."[28]

Werner Schrör

"During the fights over the convoys to Tobruk, the British introduced the defensive circle. It was very efficient, but then Marseille disenchanted it; he would dive down near the circle, pull out and zoom into it from below. He reached the level of the circle just before stalling, just in time to level off, shoot down a Tommy and start to spin to sea level, where he pulled out at the last second (it was impossible to follow him). He then climbed back to his own formation and repeated the performance until the circle broke up. No other German pilot was able to copy Marseille's tricks, although all made attempts to do so, and sometimes succeeded in breaking up the circle."[29]

Werner Schrör

"Marseille, he was very, very forthright here. He had good resolve in shooting out of the turn, but he never did a turning battle, round n' round, because the Messerschmitt 109 wasn't able to fly such a narrow turn like the other type aircraft. So it was stupid to go into it. Only go into it, shoot, and get away from it. So, this is what he did. This was his thinking. And I, for my . . . I must say personally, I never had the idea to mix or to mingle with an aircraft in a squadron or unit which were better constructed for narrow flight or narrow turns. . . . Why, why should I? My tactics were completely different."[30]

Friedrich Körner

Körner went on to state:

"I think the only one who could do it was, this was Marseille. Because he was an expert in shooting out of, in a circle. He had the additional sense for not seeing the aircraft but seeing the target shooting at that direction and the aircraft reach the point immediately or in this, and the bullets reach it."[31]

On 19 March 1942, Friedrich Körner shot down JG 27's 1000th airplane for his tenth victory. These two photographs show Körner following this mission.
Both Courtesy of Author

"You asked if me if I had seen him. Yes I have seen him. So one day we flew an escort, very important over the Leer [Sea] and Tobruk. And it was a very short sortie. We had to bring a reconnaissance aircraft back and the time left, the time you have you go back over enemy territory and fly the *Freie Jagd*. So we brought the 109 reconnaissance, we brought the 109 aircraft back, said bye bye, and we turned back in direction of Tobruk, El Adem area. So Marseille flew right of my position, I flew left close to the coast [Author's note: aircraft were heading east], and suddenly I saw a big number of aircraft. And I said to him, 'Aircraft on your right side.' Closer to him, but he hadn't seen them. Fortunately, he had excellent eyes. He said, 'Where are they so I can get into position.' And finally he found them and I had turned into them. So he attacked from the right side, I attacked from the left side. I came out I think with one or two aircraft shot down and he did this one, two, three, four, five, aircraft. Yes, an artist. An artist."[32]

Friedrich Körner

Author's Note: Analyzing these comments from Friedrich Körner and comparing them to both Marseille's and Körner's victory logs, it is possible to determine that this particular combat likely took place on 16 June 1942, one day before Marseille scored his 101st victory and departed the desert for an extended vacation in Germany and Italy.

When comparing the victories of both men, this is the only day where both men scored within the same area and close to the same time. Although on several occassions their victories did overlap, if Körner's recollections were correct, this is the only day where both men scored over the El Adem area. According to Christopher Shores and Hans Ring in *Fighters over the Desert* (FOTD), 4 Bf 109s of I/ JG 27 took off at 1750 and another 5 took off at 1820 on *Freie Jagd* sorties. According to their research, both flights of 109s engaged enemy fighters over the El Adem area. Although Körner recounts the escort of a reconnaissance 109, Shore and Ring do not mention this. Since most *Freie Jagd* sorties consisted of either 2 or 4 aircraft, the fifth aircraft mentioned in FOTD may actually account for this odd numbered airplane that the *Schwarm* was assigned to escort.

According to FOTD as well as other sources, Marseille claimed 4 victories over Hurricanes of 73 Squadron RAF and Kittyhawks from 2, 4, or 5 SAAF that afternoon at 1902, 1910, 1911, and 1913. Körner claimed a single victory in a fifteen minute dogfight over the Kittyhawk flown by Pilot Officer Cable of 250 Squadron at 1950 (1850 according to his personal log). By comparing the similar times of these air combats and the general location of this action, it is more than likely that this is the combat described by Körner.

The only other sortie that closely matches Körner's description took place on the afternoon of 8 February 1942. On this day, Marseille shot down his 47th through 50th aircraft in two sorties to become the highest scoring pilot in North Africa. This was a title he never relinquished. On the second sortie of the day Marseille shot down 2 Hurricanes of 73 Sqdn. RAF at 1420 and 1430, while Körner shot down a Kittyhawk of 112 Sqdn. RAF at 1430. The only problem with these victories is that the location was over the Bay of Bombay, some 25 miles west of El Adem.

Final Thoughts

Without a doubt, much of Marseille's success can be attributed to possession of a superior aircraft, the poor operational training and preparation of some DAF pilots, and the restrictive DAF tactics coming up against the more fluid German formations. In addition to this, it was clearly Marseille's superior flying skills and a seemingly intuitive knowledge of dislocation and exploitation that increased his effectiveness against the DAF. Although the *Luftwaffe* tactics at the fighter vs. fighter level were more efficient, it still took a pilot of Marseille's caliber to fully exploit those efficiencies.

4

Victories

"The first thing I saw was a Spitfire just below me. I knew I must fire at once. . .but I could not press the gun button. Why couldn't I shoot? In an instant I would lose my right and someone else would get him. I wished he were not there. . . Suddenly a great wave of anger swept over me and I said if you do not shoot now you will never be a fighter pilot. I pressed the button at once.

"I could see the tracer bullets ripping into his wing. He began to smoke and went down. That's all there was to shooting a plane down. . . I do not suppose that everything I thought took more than a second but it seemed a terrible eternity to me, comforted by the fact that I knew that now I would never be afraid to shoot again. . We reformed . . . The voice of the *Staffelkapitan* said in my ears: 'Congratulations on your first!'"[1]

Hans-Joachim Marseille

"For the seven victories I got over the Channel in 1940, I was shot down three times. Each time I succeeded with the greatest of difficulty to crash-land my plane. And always at the same place, near Cap Gris-Nez. Funny enough that each time there was the same Army surgeon. The third time I think he hesitated to examine me. And each time my plane was full of holes from bullets and shrapnel, in 15 to 20 places. Somebody would certainly think that I was doing it maliciously on purpose."[2]

Hans-Joachim Marseille

Historically, the most tangible measure of a fighter pilot's prowess remains his number of aerial victories. According to author Walter Boyne in his book *Aces in Command*, only 5% of fighter pilots who have ever entered combat have earned the status of ace (five or more aerial victories). He further states that only a scant .0005% of all airmen trained as fighter pilots have achieved those same lofty heights.[3] There definitely seems to be something special about the pilots who can claim this level of competence. And if this is the case, what does that say about the qualities of the men from any nation who have risen to the status of super ace, or "Experten," as the *Luftwaffe* termed them?

Regardless of outstanding leadership qualities, aerobatic skills, marksmanship, or tactical comprehension, for most historians it remains that tally sheet, first and foremost, that defines the true

Marseille with Knight's Cross, Oak Leaves, and Swords: Summer 1942. *Courtesy of author*

A rare photograph taken of Marseille during the Battle of Britain. *Courtesy of E & C Collection*

Marseille shakes hands with a "black man" following another sortie. *Courtesy of Seattle Museum of Flight*

measure of the successful fighter pilot. Since the First World War fighter pilots have competed for the right to claim they were the best. Comparing pilots between theaters or spanning different eras, however, is by no means an exact science, and likely not objectively possible. With so many factors involved in the making of a great fighter pilot, subjective comparisons cloaked in alleged "objective criteria" can become unimaginative and counterproductive.

In the chapter dealing with the essential qualities of successful fighter pilots, while we showed that some objective standards might possibly be used to measure a pilot in relation to his environment and his peers, I believe there are some comparisons that cannot be accurately made.

Comparisons Across Time

In making the claim that one fighter pilot was the greatest of all time, the historian must realize that making such objective comparisons across time is difficult at best, but in reality, nearly impossible to do. I must admit my guilt ascribing this title to Marseille from time to time. At best, unfortunately, the historian is left with a subjective opinion: great for discussion but bad for definitive analysis. How can the historian legitimately argue that Albert Ball flying in Europe during WWI was somehow better than Saburo Sakai flying in the Pacific in WWII? In other words, more numbers of airplanes shot down is not necessarily an adequate indicator of pilot prowess. Trying to compare different pilots over the vastness of time is a nearly impossible endeavor, much like trying to compare heavyweight boxers from different eras. Once again, what we are left with is conjecture and speculation usually based upon a mix of subjective and objective criteria. How does one measure the qualities of a fighter pilot from either World War to Korea, Vietnam, or the Gulf War? What about pilots from the era of open cockpits and metal gun sights to electronic gun sights and radar guided missiles? To say von Richthofen's 80 WWI victories are somehow more significant than Kozhedub's 62 WWII Russian front victories makes an interesting argument, but to what end?

For example, the *Luftwaffe* claimed 34 "Experten" with more than 150 kills and another 60 with kills between 100 and 150. Together these 94 aces are credited with an astonishing 13,997 aerial victories. Does this prove German pilots were *naturally* superior to others? I don't believe so. How can the historian objectively compare a pilot's scorecard who flew 100 missions as opposed to a pilot who may have flown more than 1,000 combat missions? Provided both of these pilots survive, the man with more than 1,000 missions and perhaps 500 or more engagements obviously should have had many more opportunities to score. And provided he did just that, does this necessarily make him the better fighter pilot, or is he perhaps just the more opportunistic? Certainly no combat pilots of any era flew the number of sorties and engaged their enemies as often as the Germans in WWII, and their records reflect that reality.

Once again, with so many variables coming into play, a legitimate argument for the natural superiority of one group of pilots or a single pilot over another, albeit fun to argue and discuss, in the end is likely to be largely subjective in nature. Does success in the past equate to superiority over pilots of today? Not necessarily.

Comparisons Across Theaters

For some reason, many historians continually denigrate the successes of the German fighter pilots who fought on the Russian front during WWII. Because of the massive successes of the *Luftwaffe* during the opening shots of Operation Barbarossa, many incorrectly extrapolate that the large German claims were either figments of German imagination, German propaganda, or that Russian pilots and equipment were simply far inferior to the Germans. Although this may have been true in 1941, it bore no semblance to the realities of late 1943 through 1945. To openly ignore the loss of 88,000[4] known Russian combat aircraft during the war is interesting to me. In the West, some believe if the German claims were in fact correct, their victories must have come easily, since Russian pilots were not as good as other Allied pilots. Once again this ill-conceived logic ignores that the top Allied aces of WWII were Russian, and that the highest scoring German pilots didn't start building up their scores until well after Barbarossa first launched in 1941. Erich Hartmann, Germany's top ace, didn't get his first kill until 5 November 1942, and didn't achieve his 100th victory until 20 September 1943, just in time for the resurgence of the Red Air Force.

Victories in the West are still regarded as more difficult to have achieved, and are therefore considered more a testimony to a pilot's skill. But once again, how does one come to the conclusion that Erich Hartmann's 352 Russian Front victories are not as significant as Marseille's 158 victories against Western pilots? What of the Pacific? Are Hiroyoshi Nishizawa's 100+ victories against U.S. pilots more significant than Eino Ilmari Juutilainen's 94 victories against the Russians? When attempting to compare pilots across theaters in a particular conflict, it appears this is done primarily to emotionally build up one theater (thus the men of one side as opposed to another) while minimizing the importance or difficulty of another. This unfortunately continues the process of injecting ethnocentric or nationalistic beliefs that one group of pilots is somehow naturally superior to another.

We have witnessed this type of discussion regarding Marseille in North Africa. Many historians and critics still claim Marseille's successes were in large part because the quality of pilots he encountered in North Africa was substandard. This in addition to the alleged "inferior" aircraft flown by the DAF in the desert all certainly contributed to his success. For the elitist historians arguing that the war in the desert was somehow substandard, I would dare them to convince me that the quality of German pilot the Allies faced from mid-1944 until the end of the war were in any way equal to the quality of DAF pilots the German faced in North Africa. Consider that when extolling the virtues of Allied pilots over Europe in the closing stages of WWII. Comparing across theaters can indeed be a very sticky and subjective proposition.

Comparisons Across Air Forces

Again, not only is it difficult to compare pilots from the same conflict, but what about pilots from different air forces? Painting broad-brush comments like "Germans were the best, just look at their scores" adds little objectivity to this debate. Different air forces in the various theaters dealt with diverse objectives, opportunities to score, tactics, strategies, and climatic conditions. When the historian interprets the impressive victory tallies of the Germans, for example, he must also consider the many complex factors that led to those victories, and not simply claim that one air force's pilots were better than another's solely based upon victory totals. Keep in mind it was many of these high scoring German aces that died by the hundreds in the skies over Germany during the defense of the Reich.

Yes, the Germans may have scored many victories in all theaters in which they fought, but what of their strategic and operational successes? In North Africa, for example, it has been argued that while the German fighter pilot fought a war of fighter-to-fighter combat, in their eagerness to increase their victory totals, the more important tasks of defeating Allied bomber formations went unnoticed. Therefore the "game" of scoring victories ultimately led to their defeat in the desert. Indeed, of Marseille's 151 desert victories, only four were enemy bombers. Although a large victory tally is impressive to look at on one's rudder or underneath a pilot's cockpit, if these same pilots failed to achieve their operational objectives, how important do these aerial victories actually become?

The Only True Comparison

If we make suppositions as to the greatness of one fighter pilot over another, there can only be one legitimate, objective comparison. In order to say one pilot was better than another, I believe we can only look at that pilot in the context of 1) his theater of operations, 2) the time frame in which he fought, and 3) how he fared in relation to both his peers and the opponents he fought against. That is it. Only here with pilots flying similar aircraft, using similar weapons, and working within the same operational environment with the same logistical and doctrinal restraints and constraints can we get an accurate and relatively objective view of how one pilot may have been superior to any other. This is the context in which we will look at Hans-Joachim Marseille's achievements.

Marseille's Victories

Simply looking at Marseille's 151 desert victories, one is faced with a sense of awe. But there is of course much more to Marseille's success than sheer numbers. If we claim that Marseille was the greatest fighter pilot in North Africa, we must look at his victories in the context of that particular air war itself.

Confronted with one of the harshest climates during the war, pilots of both the DAF and *Luftwaffe* were faced with unique and challenging environmental conditions. Although faced with the desert environment, pilots on both sides went up almost every day to fight each other, and out of these air battles several interesting

Series of photos following the completion of what appears to be another successful sortie. Rainer Pöttgen, Marseille's wingman, shakes Marseille's hand as he climbs down from his 109 and stands at the far left in the third photograph. *All Courtesy of E & C Collection*

Compairson of Top *Luftwaffe* and Commonwealth Pilots in the Western Desert with Five or More Kills

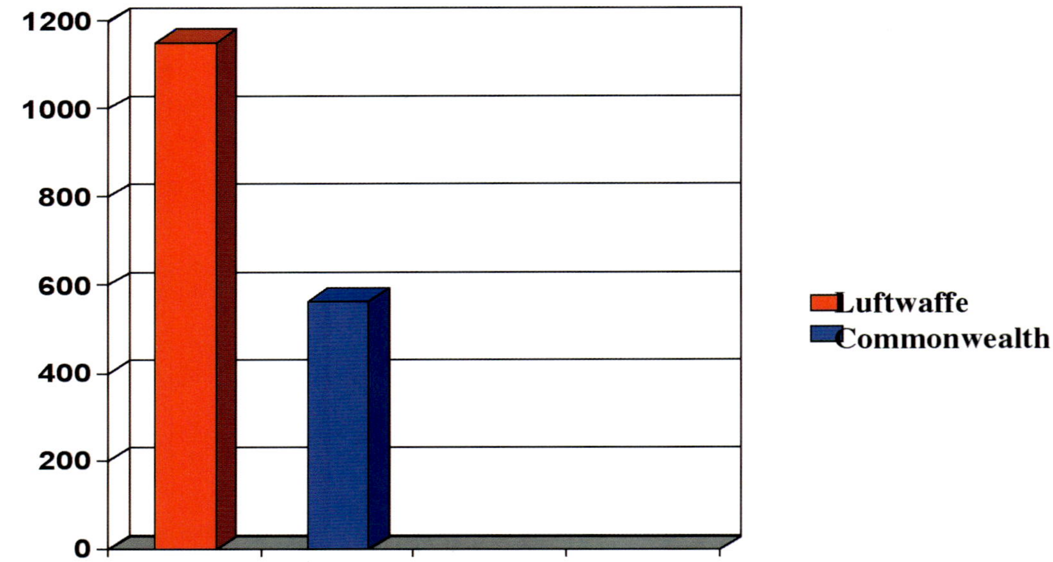

Figure 4-1

Top 71 *Luftwaffe* Pilots (1152 Victories)
Top 75 Commonwealth Pilots (565 Victories)

things emerged. As previously discussed in the chapter on Tactics, with the birth of the *Freie Jagd*, German pilots had a tendency to allow the most gifted pilots to increase their personal scores while the less talented scored less often, or in most cases, not at all. This is not the case, however, within the ranks of the DAF.

Figure 4-1 shows that the top 71 *Luftwaffe* pilots scored almost exactly twice as many kills as did the top 75 Commonwealth pilots, while the total numbers of aerial victories between both sides in this campaign were nearly even. Certainly there are reasons for this, including the better performance of the Messerschmitt over the Hurricane and P-40s, longer tours for the German pilots in the desert, the tactically ineffective Lufbery and Vic formations, and once again the interesting dynamic of the *Freie Jagd*. Figure 4-2, on the other hand, paints a significantly different picture of *Luftwaffe* vs. Commonwealth victories. Although the Commonwealth had only one pilot credited with more than 20 victories through 1942 (Clive Caldwell, with 20.5 desert victories), looking at the number of minor DAF aces, these are more than comparable to the *Luftwaffe*, and the DAF actually had more than twice the number of pilots with kills in the 6-10 range. This clearly shows that within the DAF, more pilots scored on a regular basis and more pilots contributed to the success of the DAF in North Africa.

Compairson of Top *Luftwaffe* and Commonwealth Pilots in the Western Desert with Five or More Kills through December 1942

Number of Pilots

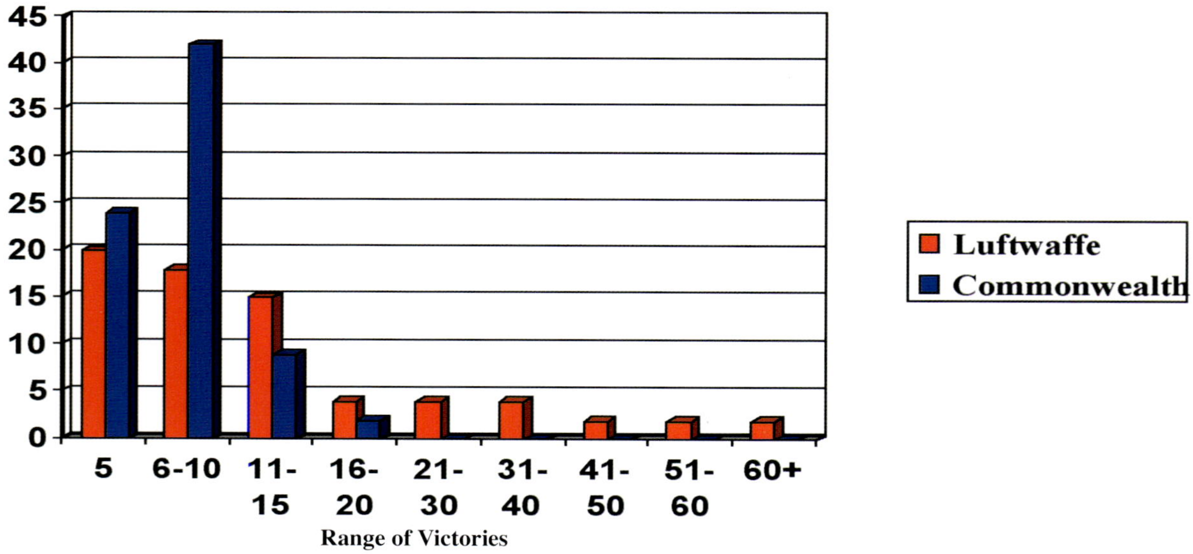

Figure 4-2

Canadian James "Stocky" Edwards. Highest scoring Canadian pilot in the Western desert with 19 1/2 aerial victories through April 1943. *Courtesy of Ron Cundy*

It is not until the range of victories increases to 11-15 that the *Luftwaffe* surpasses the DAF. Indeed, according to Hans Ring and Christopher Shores in *FOTD*, of the 674 German aerial victories where the pilot is known, just 15 pilots account for these. Out of close to 1400 total *Luftwaffe* victories in North Africa, these same 15 pilots account for approximately 48 percent of all victories. Taking into account the number of *Luftwaffe* pilots that fought in the desert, this represents a fairly significant reality.

By analyzing this data, it becomes apparent that the two air forces in the desert had far different operational methods Although there were definite "Top Guns" within their ranks, the Desert Air Forces fostered an atmosphere that more evenly distributed the number of victories throughout their squadrons. The *Luftwaffe's* top pilots once again tended to increase their personal scores at the expense of the less experienced. Be that as it may, this still does not fully account for Hans Marseille's phenomenal rise. Even when considering the *Freie Jagd*, the superiority of his Messerschmitt to most Allied fighters in North Africa and the failed tactics and formations of the DAF, why did Marseille succeed so overwhelmingly as compared to any other pilot operating with or against him in his theater of operations? If Marseille was not significantly superior to all other fighter pilots in the desert, would we not expect to see similar results from other pilots? When faced with the same climatic conditions, supply shortages, and the same enemy opposition, Marseille's successes outshined those of any other pilot, friendly or enemy, in the Western Desert.

Let's consider that in 388 combat sorties, Marseille is generally credited with shooting down 158 Allied aircraft. What is even more remarkable is that 138 of his 151 desert victories were multiple kills. In other words, on sorties where Marseille shot down at least one airplane, approximately 91% of the time he shot down at least two aircraft. In fact, no less than 45 times Marseille shot down 2 or more aircraft during a single sortie. Seven times he downed 3 aircraft, 10 times he downed 4, twice he downed 5 aircraft, and once each he downed 6, 7, and 8 aircraft on a single sortie. On the sorties where he engaged the enemy and downed an aircraft he averaged 2.6 kills per sortie. During the last month of his life Marseille downed 57 aircraft, 17 of those on 1 September 1942. Perhaps equally impressive is that during Marseille's first 6 months in the desert, from 18 April to 15 October 1941 when 3/ JG 27 left North Africa to train on the Bf 109F aircraft, Marseille had gained a very modest 15 victories. Upon returning to the desert on 3 December through 26 September 1942 when he gained his final victory, in just over 10 months (for 3 of those months he was home on leave, so in effect, within seven months of combat) Marseille downed 136 aircraft.

If Marseille's numbers appear staggering, they are. No other pilot in the desert remotely approached this level of destruction, and although it is difficult to compare the achievements of one pilot over another across time, theater, or air forces, historians and aviation enthusiasts will be hard pressed to dispute the significance of Marseille's achievements. Certainly, other *Luftwaffe* pilots shot down more aircraft than did Marseille on other fronts. He was only 31 on the list of top pilots, and yet Marseille's superiority over enemy pilots in the North African desert remains unquestioned. He shot down almost 2 1/2 times the number of aircraft of his nearest German competitor, Werner Schrör, and more than seven times the highest scoring Allied ace, Clive Caldwell. With this in mind, what do others have to say about Marseille's victories?

Comparative Analysis of Top Ten *Luftwaffe* and Commonwealth Pilots in the Western Desert

Top Ten Luftwaffe Pilots in Western Desert April 1941-December 1942

Pilot	Victories
Hans-Joachim Marseille	151
Werner Schrör	61
Hans-Arnold "Fifi" Stahlschmidt	59
Gustav Rödel	52
Gerhard Homuth	46
Otto Schulz	42
Gunther Steinhausen	40
Friedrich Körner	36
Karl-Heinz Bendert	36
Rudolf Sinner	32
Total	555

Top Ten Commonwealth Pilots in Western Desert June 1940-December 1942

Pilot	Victories
C.R. "Killer Caldwell	20.5
A.E. Marshall	16
J.L. Waddy	15.5
E.M. Mason	15.4

Marseille describes a mission to squadron members. *Courtesy of E & C Collection*

L.C. Wade	15
J. Dodds	14
B. Drake	14
P.G. Wykeham-Barnes	13
A.W. Barr	12.5
V.C. Woodward	12.5
Total	148

> "Above everything, it was in pilot experience that the Germans gained their greatest advantage. Nearly all the pilots who came to Africa initially, in all the four main Gruppen were already combat-tested veterans, and the majority remained in the area from their arrival until the final retreat, except for the occasional leave. That their expertise increased by leaps and bounds during this time is unquestionable, and it is noticeable that none of the very large claims made by Marseille, Schulz and other 'experts' were made until they had been in the area many months, and built up formidable scores in ones and twos. It is also noticeable that when they did claim four, five or six aircraft in one sortie, their opponents were almost always formations of inexperienced pilots, or squadrons new to the Desert."[5]
>
> Hans Ring

Author's Note: Hans Ring makes an excellent point, but keep in mind that the words "inexperienced pilots" do not necessarily equate to "poorly trained" pilots. It simply means many of these pilots were new to the Middle East, and may have been in the process of becoming familiarized with the theater. This process could be disastrous for a new pilot if encountering veteran *Luftwaffe* pilots more familiar with the theater. This also held true for new *Luftwaffe* pilots coming into contact with DAF pilots who had been in the theater for a long time.

> "If Marseille was often able to shoot down one aircraft after another out of a defensive circle, this was an isolated success. So far as I know his outstanding successes could not be repeated by other German pilots. The defensive circle was, however, of necessity; such a defensive maneuver could not produce victories and was only profitable when outnumbered by aircraft of equal speed."[6]
>
> Ernst Düllberg

> "Marseille was the unrivalled virtuoso among the fighter pilots of World War II. His achievements had previously been regarded as impossible and they were never excelled by anyone after his death. In the short span

General of the Fighters, the dapper Adolf Galland. *Courtesy of author*

of little more than a year his life as a pilot completed itself. During this period he flew in 388 actions, shot down 158 enemy planes, 151 of them in Africa."[7]

Adolf Galland

". . .a Blenheim came roaring down over our heads at about 50 feet. There was a terrific rattle of machine gun fire and at first I thought the Blenheim had made a mistake and was firing at us, or choosing an awkward spot to clear his guns. Bullets whistled around, so we dived into the slit trench. A Messerschmitt, hot on the tail of the Blenheim, was responsible for the bullets. The Blenheim roared down the Wadi, out to sea, trying to escape from the Messerschmitt, but the Messerschmitt was too close. The Blenheim fell out of the sky and crashed into the sea. The plane disappeared completely not leaving a trace."[8]

BUP correspondent, Jan Yindrich

Author's Note: This is one of the more interesting and well-documented victories attributed to Marseille. In the book *Hurricanes over Tobruk*, author Brian Cull mentions that this Blenheim was dispatched on 28 April 1941 to evacuate staff officers of 258 Wing Headquarters. Among the five passengers was the commanding officer, Wing Commander David Victor Johnson, and Chaplain to the RAF in the Western Desert, Squadron Leader Reverend J.E. Cox. Also on board were passengers Squadron Leader D.P. Barclay, Pilot Officer S.E. Beloe, and an army officer, Captain R.S. Oughwright. The plane was crewed by the pilot B.C. de Gardanne Allan and the gunner Sergeant L.W. Morling. This Blenheim was Marseille's second victory in the desert. There were no survivors.[9]

What makes this victory so interesting is that several authors have identified this particular Blenheim as Marseille's second victory, while another author's eyewitness account begs to challenge the accuracy of the claim. There is little doubt that Marseille scored his second North African victory over a Blenheim in the Tobruk area on Monday morning, 28 April 1941. This rather detailed and personally witnessed aerial victory, as described by Jan Yindrich in his book *Fortress Tobruk*, however, allegedly took place on Sunday, 11 May 1941.

The problem here, at first glance, is obvious. As a war correspondent keeping a detailed chronological journal of his time in Tobruk, you might assume Jan Yindrich's date for the combat he described is correct. This particular ill-fated Blenheim that plunged into the ocean off the coast of Tobruk, in view of Yindrich, crashed two weeks after Marseille's only Blenheim claim in the desert. If we are to accept Yindrich's journal, this victory cannot possibly be credited to Marseille. However, in our modern day vernacular, "Not so fast!"

In *Fighters Over the Desert*, no Blenheims are reported being shot down on 11 May. One is recorded shot down on the tenth by a CR 42 that crash-landed east of Sollum, Libya. Likewise, in Tony Woods' outstanding compilation *O.K.L. Fighter Claims: Mediterranean and Southern Front 1941-1942*, no *Luftwaffe* fighter claims for a Blenheim are registered for 11 May 1941.

In an attempt to locate and confirm the correct dates, a search of the Commonwealth War Graves Commission (CWGC) led to information confirming the previous research of Christopher Shores, Hans Ring, and Brian Cull. The CWGC lists the deaths of each crewmember and passenger on this aircraft, with the exception of Captain R.S. Oughwright, as being 28 April 1941. The CWGC contains no listing at all for a Captain R.S. Oughwright, although there is a listing for a Captain Ronald Plowright. By looking at this information, it is possible to conclude that Jan Yindrich, in his own daily journal, somehow got his dates mixed up. It then appears that Marseille did in fact shoot down 45 Squadron Blenheim on 28 April 1941.

Despite confusing the dates in his journal, as an interesting read Yindrich further wrote:

> "One moment there was a Blenheim fleeing out to sea, the next, there was nothing, except the Messerschmitt, which banked and flew inland again.

"Fitchett looked at me, I looked at Reg and we all felt a funny feeling at the bottom of our stomachs. At least, I felt a strange feeling and asked the others if they felt the same. They said they did.

"'That's good-bye to Bob,' I murmured.

"'Nobody will have got out of that lot alive,' remarked Reg.

"We went back to the tent and sat down. Ian poured out a drink. We saw Bob Low yesterday and he said he was leaving this morning by plane for Cairo. The plane we had seen dive into the sea. An enthusiast for R.A.F. and crazy about flying that is the way he would have wanted it. The last of the corps of war correspondents to arrive in the Middle East, he had only got to Cairo a couple of weeks before the beginning of the siege of Tobruk.

"Several dispatches of mine were on the plane. Now they are at the bottom of the Mediterranean. It must be the first time a war correspondent has seen his dispatches shot down into the sea before his eyes. Fortunately, I have copies, although when there will be another plane, I don't know.

"Suddenly a cheery voice sang out: 'Hello folks, what are you all looking so glum about?' It was Low.

"'Why, Bob, we thought you were dead, over there, in the sea,' Reg said.

"Bob looked puzzled, so we told him what had happened. He said that he was on the plane right until the last minute, just before it took off.

"'My kit was put on board and I was to go. There were eight people on board and the pilot said that if it was urgent for me to go, he would take me, although that would make nine and a bit too much of a load. I said that I would wait until there was another plane. So they took my kit off and I did not go.

"'There was a wing-commander and the padre aboard her. The plane should have taken off at dawn, but they were waiting for someone, so when you saw her flying over here, she had just taken off. By that time, three Messerschmitts were over the aerodrome, hiding in the sun. As soon as the Blenheim took off, one of them dived on her tail and chased her out to sea, before she had time to get any altitude, or get back on the ground.

"'The station commander wanted to wait until tomorrow, as it was so late and he was afraid enemy fighters would be around, but somebody had urgent business and insisted on taking off, in spite of the late hour.'

"By now Low was beginning to realize the narrowness of his escape, so he had a drink. The padre was a particular pal of his. We went for a bathe in the sea."[10]

Author's Note: According to the CWGC, the men onboard this flight are listed at the Alamein Memorial in Egypt:

1) Pilot: Pilot Officer Bruce Cartwright De Gardanne Allan, RAF Volunteer Service, 45 SQDN, no age
2) Air Gunner: Flight Sergeant Leonard Woolford Morling, 45 SQDN, age 31.
Passengers:
3) Wing Commander David Victor Johnson, 45 SQDN, RAF, no age.
4) Squadron Leader Reverend James Ernest Cox, Chaplain, RAF Volunteer Reserve, age 32.

The Alamein Memorial, which forms the entrance to the El Alamein War Cemetery, El Alamein, Egypt. *Courtesy of the Commonwealth War Graves Commission*

5) Squadron Leader David Pringle Barclay, 45 SQDN., RAF, age 28.
6) Pilot Officer Stephen Edward Beloe, 45 SQDN. RAF Volunteer Service, age 36.
7) Captain Ronald William Plowright, Royal Armoured Corps, Queen's Own Yorkshire Dragoons, age 28.

Next are some accounts of several combats against Marseille. The following excerpt covers Marseille's 32nd victory. Sergeant Malcolm Canty of Yarmouth, Nova Scotia:

"After two more successful sorties on the 9th, the boys of No 250 Squadron moved to Tobruk on the 11th [December 1941]. Early the same day, they flew a patrol with their comrades of the Fleet Air Arm. They were scheduled to patrol the Gazala area. Flying further west, they caught Me 109s from I/JG-27 just after they had taken off from Tmimi for an escort to 24 Ju 88s of I/KLG-1 and 3 Me 110s of III/ZG-26. A whirling dogfight followed with P 40s and Me 109s milling all over the sky. The famous virtuoso of the Luftwaffe in the desert, Leutnant Hans-Joachim Marseille of 3/JG-27, was part of the show. In the course of the battle he was attacked by two Tomahawks, that he avoided in a steep climbing turn. Marseille was one of the rare Me 109 pilots who could turn with the maneuverable Allied fighters. He was turning at low speed when another Tomahawk appeared in front of him – only 50 yards away.

"This P 40 Tomahawk was AN344 flown by Sergeant Malcolm Canty from Yarmouth, Nova Scotia. Marseille watched as Canty went into a turn – the only thing to do to save his life. But it was not enough for Marseille who turned inside the P 40's maneuver, always at low speed, and fired in the Canuck's line of flight. The P 40 flew right through the cannon shells, which hit the fuselage. Marseille then broke upward and looked for his victim over his shoulder. The Tomahawk flew straight and level for a few seconds, then weaved from side to side, black smoke trailing. The undercarriage went down, then the Tommy turned on its back and went down to crash about 30 miles SE of Tmimi. For Marseille, it was victory No 32, claimed at 09.30 Axis time. Malcolm Canty had survived his first combats with the 109s but he did not survive the famous Marseille – one of the best shots in the whole Luftwaffe. . .

"At First, Malcolm Canty was reported as missing in action. Later, the burnt-out wreck of his Tomahawk was found and his parents were advised on the 29th of December that he had been killed in action. The Allied report stated that he was shot down about 30 miles SW of Tobruk and it links perfectly with Marseille's combat report. Sergeant Canty was probably buried beside his aircraft by enemy troops who found him. A further report that he could have been buried at Sollum is not confirmed. In Nova Scotia, a memorial service was held in Faith United Church of Canada, Hebron, on Sunday evening, 16 August 1942, when a table was unveiled in loving memory of Sergeant Malcolm Allen Canty, RCAF."[11]

Michel Lavigne

Author's Note: On the afternoon of 13 December 1941, Marseille's 22nd and final birthday, he engaged Tomahawk IIs of 3 SAAF. Marseille claimed FO Trimble (the account below) at 1600 near Martuba, Libya, and another Tomahawk ten minutes later near Tmimi. These two victories were Marseille's 33rd and 34th.[12]

"Tommy was being attacked by two Messerschmitt 109s and I (Bobby Gibbs) saw what turned out to be Marseille send him down in flames. I thought I hit his Number Two, who went spinning down. The bastard [Marseille] had a crack at me too that day, but missed."

"As Trimble recalls: "One day we were told to do a fighter sweep. . . . We were short pilots and I had to help make up some numbers. Anyway, I was about to shoot at a 109 which was on the tail of one of our blokes and there was another 109 coming around behind me and I kept looking at him and thinking he couldn't turn to get a shot at me. But it happened that he did.

"As I started to fire, he started to fire. We had different targets. It was a dull day, very filmy cloud. We were fairly low, maybe 5,000 ft, it was raining and his cannon shells came out of the boss of the airscrew, they looked really beautiful.

"I thought: Oh, he's going to miss me. But at the last moment I received two shots on my wing root which fractured lines to a fuel tank. Another shot belted my tail. A fourth one hit me just on the top of the cockpit canopy, which was half-open, and dented it several inches in front of my head.

"Well, this shell that did the damage also blew out the Perspex canopy and the flames curled up into the cockpit. The airplane was burning and I was knocked out; I was unconscious and the flames came right up. Of course, when I came to I was in a bit of a panic. I could see out of one eye just fractionally because the other one had seized up where my face was burnt.

"Luckily, I was wearing leather gloves which shriveled up but saved my hands from being burnt.

"I got out of the spin and headed south. Then both eyes closed up and I could sense that I wasn't spinning. I gradually descended until I felt the airscrew touch the ground and then I just belly landed."[13]

PO Tom Trimble, 3 RAAF

Much like the discussion surrounding Marseille's Blenheim victory on 28 April 1941, history shows that there can be a lot of confusion and questions raised about specific victories. This is evident with Marseille's 53rd victory over 260 Squadron pilot Squadron Leader "Pedro" Hanbury on 25 April 1942. In the preparation for this book, I was lucky enough to receive some correspondence from former RAAF pilot Ron Cundy (5 victories with 2 shared). In a letter, he wrote:

"... Since receiving you welcome letter I have done some research through my records. In writing my book (*A Gremlin on My Shoulder*) I obtained from the Public Record Office in England a copy of the Intelligence Officer's records for the period I was with 260 Squadron. The enclosed is a copy of the I.Os. record for 25 April 1942.

I have a very clear recollection of one of the pilots reporting that he saw Hanbury attacking a JU87 and taking return fire from that aircraft's rear gunner. Shortly after his engine seized and he was seen to force land. I think it is significant that at no time did Hanbury deny that he had been shot down by the rear gunner of the JU87.

Unfortunately the I.Os. record does not show either the number or the code letters of the aircraft flown by the various pilots on that (or any other) day. . . ."

The record of the 260 Squadron Intelligence Officer reads:

"2 A/C returned early. 6 Kittyhawks were ordered to intercept enemy formation that had just bombed Tobruk about 2/3 miles off Gazala. 11 JU87s were sighted. The squadron attacked & was subsequently split up during the individual combats which ensued. S/Ldr Hanbury destroyed 1 JU87 and 1 Mc202; he force landed near Gazala. P/O Miller destroyed 1 JU87 & also force landed near Gazala. Both pilots were unhurt. P/O Hindle destroyed 1 Me109 which crashed on the shore near Ras-el-Tin. Sgt Carlile shot down an Me109 over the sea off Gazala. P/O Black attacked JU87 & got in good burst without definite observed results. Sgt Wareham is missing from this operation. Casualties to aircraft were as follows: 1 Cat(III), 3 Cat(II) 1 Cat(I)."

The recollections of Mr. Cundy are very interesting indeed. In *Fighters Over the Desert*, the authors make it clear that Squadron Leader Hanbury was one of two victims downed by Marseille that day. The other aircraft was the P-40 flown by the South African Sgt. Wareham, who was killed in this encounter.

There can be little doubt about the confusion inherent in the air combat environment. Is it possible Hanbury was brought down by the gunner of the Stuka instead of Marseille? Yes. Is it possible that it was the other P-40 flown by P/O Miller that was also forced to crash land after his encounter with a Stuka? Yes. Likewise, is it possible that Hanbury was initially hit by the Stuka gunner and Marseille put the finishing touches on his aircraft before he slid to a stop on the desert floor? Of course it is.

I find this description by Mr. Cundy to be very interesting. Because of his vivid description and recollection of this particular event, it is likely that a Stuka gunner did, at least in part, participate in the downing of Pedro Hanubry on 25 April 1942. Perhaps most telling is that Hanbury never denied being hit by the Stuka gunner. I find this humorous because having participated in Red Flag exercises, there is very little more interesting than watching the reaction of a fighter pilot, in this case an F-15 pilot, being "shot down" by a B-52 tail gunner.

Courtesy of Michel Lavigne

Two photographs of Squadron Leader Osgood V. "Pedro" Hanbury. *Courtesy of Ron Cundy*

Either way, thanks to Mr. Cundy, and yet another interesting insight to a Marseille victory claim.

"And how many of these twelve did you get?" asked the Field Marshal (Kesselring).

"Twelve, sir!"[14]

Upon Marseille's return from his second sortie
1 September, 1942

"Today I have experienced my hardest combat. But at the same time it has been my most wonderful experience of comradeship in the air. We had a combat in the morning, at first with forty Hurricanes and Curtiss, later some twenty Spitfires appearing from above. We were eight Messerschmitts in the midst of an incredible whirling mass of enemy fighters. I flew my 109 for my life, but although the superior strength of the enemy was overwhelming, not one of us shirked our duty, all turning like madmen. I worked with every gramme of my energy, and by the time we finished I was foaming at the mouth and utterly exhausted. Again and again we had enemy fighters on our tails. I was forced to dive three or four times, but I pulled up again and rushed into the turmoil. Once I seemed to have no escape; I had flown my 109 to the limit of its performance, but a Spitfire still sat behind me. At the last moment Marseille shot it down, fifty metres from my 109. I dived and pulled up. Seconds later I saw a Spitfire behind Marseille. I took aim at the Spitfire, I have never aimed so carefully, and the enemy dived down burning. At the end of the combat only Marseille and I were left in the dogfight. Each of us had three victories. At home we climbed out of our planes and were thoroughly exhausted. Marseille had bullet holes in his 109, and I had eleven machine gun hits in mine. We embraced each other, but were unable to speak. It was an unforgettable event."[15]

"Fifi" Stahlschmidt, 3 Sep. 42

Author's Note: This combat took place on 3 September 1942 when fighters of I/ JG 27 attacked a formation of bombers escorted by P-40s of 2 and 4 SAAF, 64th and 57th FG USAAF, and Spitfires of No. 145 Sq. with 260 Squadron flying medium cover. After a long dogfight, Marseille and Stahlschmidt were able to get away only after both being hit by enemy fire. Wing Commander James "Stocky" Edwards is likely responsible for damaging one of the Messerschmitts.[16]

Another Marseille Confrontation

"On the 6th [September 1942] the squadron next encountered the enemy when we were briefed to fly as top cover on an interception patrol of the front line. We had hardly reached our objective when little black specks appeared on the horizon, Me-109s. About 2,000 feet higher than us they were obviously heading our way and intent on attacking. Initially we turned away and started climbing for all we were worth. We needed more time to meet them on their own level.

"It was to no avail, they were coming too fast. Attack being the best form of defence we turned to meet them head-on. Still lower than they were and at a distinct disadvantage, we pulled our noses up and opened fire but

Two photographs of Marseille's 137th victim, PO Dick Dunbar, shot down on 6 September 1942. *Both Courtesy of Michel Lavigne*

they were too clever to fall for that. They just climbed a little more and passed over the top of us. Head-on confrontations were not to their liking, or ours for that matter, but we had to put up some kind of a fight despite our inferior position.

"Before we had much time to think they were down on us. Steep turns into their attacks were the best method of defence, hoping against hope that their cannon fire would miss. Attack after attack continued as we put up a desperate defence.

"Inevitably it happened – someone was hit. Smoke poured from his engine as he started down in a tight spiral. As best we could we watched for him to bale out but it was not to be. Either wounded or killed there was no sign of a parachute. Shortly there was a violent explosion on the desert floor some 10,000 feet below. On return to base we knew that P/Off Dick Dunbar was missing. He was one of our more experienced pilots, a reserved fellow who neither drank nor smoked."[17]

Ron Cundy

Author's Note: Dick Dunbar was Marseille's 137th victory. An interesting note to this day's combat is that in addition to 8 Kittyhawks of 260 squadron and Tomahawks of 5 SAAF, it appears that American P-40Fs of the 64th FS were encountered for one of the first times. In addition to Dick Dunbar, Marseille claimed victories 138 through 140.

The Curious Case of 15 September 1942

One aspect of aerial combat that cannot be underestimated is the case of over claiming. This was common among all nations during the war. No Air Force or service was immune. There are of course any number of reasons for this, most of which I believe are unintentional. Eighth Air Force bomber gunners, for example, claimed some 6,259 enemy aircraft destroyed, 1,836 probable kills, and 3,210 damaged.[18] Are these numbers accurate? Probably not. Often, large claims were accepted when the actual numbers of aircraft destroyed were known to be much less. Does this mean these men were all liars? Absolutely not. Although some men certainly claimed victories that were not theirs, as a burning German fighter fell through a formation of bombers being fired upon by dozens

Marseille with wingman, Rainer Pöttgen. *Courtesy of author*

of men, undoubtedly many claimed that aircraft as "their" victory. It is only natural, since more than one gunner likely hit the same aircraft. The same is true in fighter-to-fighter combat when more than one aircraft may have attacked an already damaged plane, or where two or more fighters fire almost simultaneously at the same airplane. Why would each pilot not suspect, or hope, that it was their fire that brought the airplane down? Just look at Captain Thomas Lamphier and Lieutenant Rex Barber, who until their deaths still argued over bringing down C-in-C of the Combined Fleet Admiral Isuroku Yamamoto's aircraft.

Does this mean intentional over claiming does not occur? Certainly not. For whatever purpose, over claiming can have a significant political and moral advantages. For example, during the Battle of Britain the British claimed 144 aircraft destroyed on 18 August 1940. In reality only 69 aircraft were destroyed, while the Germans admitted to losing 36. The Germans in turn claimed 147 British aircraft destroyed, whereas only 68 were lost, and the British admitted to 23! On 15 September 1940, a date still celebrated as Battle of Britain Day, the British claimed both 185 aerial victories and a defining victory over the *Luftwaffe*. In fact the Germans lost closer to 60 aircraft destroyed or damaged beyond repair. As former U.S. Secretary of State Dean Acheson once remarked "...propaganda is that branch of the art of lying which consists in very nearly deceiving your friends, without quite deceiving your enemies."[19] When asked about the lack of forensic evidence strewn about the English countryside during the Battle of Britain to support RAF Fighter Command's claims, the expedient answer was that the German aircraft must have crashed in the Channel.

> "After the war, I became a friend of Erhard Braune, an ex-commanding officer of III/JG 27. In discussion with him on tactics, etc., I asked him why the claims of some *Luftwaffe* pilots appeared unrealistic as they didn't add up with our known losses. He told me that these high claims helped the morale of the German population."[20]
>
> Bobby Gibbs

In all honesty, high claims as described earlier in this chapter most certainly helped the morale of any country making the claim, just as minimizing one's own losses also helps. If over claiming did occur, and it did, it was in no way limited to the Germans. For the historians still wanting to question Marseille's claims, the phenomenon of over claiming still cannot entirely account for his success in North Africa.

In the case of Marseille during the summer of 1942, there may have well been other factors at work. Although I do not believe there was any intentional over claiming done by Marseille, I believe it is possible that being fueled and encouraged by his previous successes, he felt as though he had perfected his tactics to such a degree that he, and those pilots surrounding him, believed any time he fired his guns, an enemy aircraft was destined for Valhalla. Although it is certain the majority of claims by most German pilots, on either front, can be confirmed through existing records, there are of course those situations that cast serious doubt on pilots' victory claims. Marseille is not immune from this uncertainty.

In Russell Brown's excellent and preeminent study of Australia's Royal Australian Air Force (RAAF) fighter contributions in the desert campaign, *Desert Warriors*, he explains in great detail the strange occurrence of 15 September 1942 where, among other pilots, Marseille claimed to have shot down seven aircraft in eleven minutes. Below is Russell Brown's excellently researched discussion of this air battle, which saw many aircraft destroyed in a very hectic fight.

> "As explained in the text, unintentional over claiming by pilots off *all* nations was common, and was brought about by a number of factors. . . . Nevertheless, there were numerous occasions in the Desert war when *Luftwaffe* victories could not be verified by documented Allied losses. They are discussed in the text when Australian pilots were involved.
>
> "The most spectacular of these occurred on 15 September 1942, when JG 27 claimed a total of nineteen Allied aircraft in a combat which began some time after 1715, when the three Gruppen of JG 27 took to the air to escort a Stuka raid. Marseille's biographer, Franz Kurowski, listed the following claims.
>
> I Gruppe: 11 victories
> II Gruppe: 1 victory
> III Gruppe: 7 victories
>
> "Details from *Fighters Over the Desert* suggest that twenty claims were made, matching claims to names, several of which are omitted by Kurowski, who awarded Marseille seven kills in six minutes. (Actually 11 minutes)
>
> "The true facts of this engagement are rather different. Sgt. Des Cormack of 250 Squadron took off at 1736, leading a section of 250 Squadron as top cover to 112, 3 and 450 Squadrons. PO Keith Kildey of 3 Squadron was airborne at 1725, leading eight aircraft. His combat report shows that the engagement began at 1800, at an altitude of 12,000. Both pilots were heavily involved in the battle, submitting claims for a probable (later confirmed) and a damaged respectively, and both coming under attack from German fighters.
>
> "There was a total of 36 Kittyhawks in the 239 Wing formation. *Six* failed to return, and of these, 112 Squadron records show Sgt. Young was shot down by friendly AA fire! Even if this is mistaken, a discrepancy of fourteen can not be adequately explained. Keith Kildey almost certainly ended up as a little white bar on someone's rudder after he brought home his aircraft with cannon damage to the tail Sgt Ken Bee probably shard the same fate, returning with wounds in a damaged aircraft. 250 Squadron lost two aircraft, 3 Squadron two, 450 one and 112 one.

"Keith Kildey and Des Cormack were both interviewed as part of the research for this book, and both expressed shocked disbelief, followed by laughter, when told of the German claims.

"The circumstances of this combat cast serious doubts on assertions that the *Luftwaffe's* system of dealing with the confirmation of claims was so reliable. . . .

"Marseille made five claims on 2 September (only 3 of which are valid) taking his total to 126 and was awarded the Diamonds on the same day with 126 noted as his total at the time of his award.

"Clearly, in the combat of 15 September, there could not have been seven accurate eyewitness reports, let alone *twenty*, but Marseille's seven victory claims were apparently accepted without question. "After this outstanding victory, Marseille had brought his account up to 151 kills, meaning that he had reached third place in the absolute record list – behind Hermann Graf and Gordon Gallob."

"Authors working in the 1990s have access to squadron records, and Chris Shores, writing in 1969, made it quite clear that 239 Wing's losses on 15 September 1942 totaled six."[21]

Author's Note: Once again, keep in mind that over claiming in the desert was not limited to the *Luftwaffe*. In Michel Lavigne's book, *Kittyhawks over the Sands: The Canadians and the RCAF Americans*, he mentions the air battle previously discussed where Marseille was credited with his 32nd victory when he shot down Sergeant Malcom Canty S.E. of Tmimi. Following that particular combat, Marseille witnessed *Feldwebel* Franz Elles' 109 going down. It eventually crash-landed and Elles became a prisoner of war. In this combat, Elles' 109 was the only Messerschmitt actually shot down, although members of No. 250 Squadron claimed five victories.

Marseille's Final Victory

26 September was the final combat where Marseille was able to bring down an enemy aircraft. On this day, in two separate encounters, he claimed a total of six Spitfires. In the morning, he claimed three 92 Squadron Spitfires over el Daba, and in the late afternoon, a further three Spitfires over Hammam from an as of yet unidentified British unit. His final victory was a dogfight lasting almost twelve minutes (victory 157 - 1658 and victory 158 - 1710) in what has become an almost legendary dogfight. Unfortuately the pilot's name who nearly fought Marseille to a draw is lost to history. Whoever this unknown pilot was should be commended.

"Almost I thought it would be my last fight; but is seems, that time has not yet come for me."[22]

Hans-Joachim Marseille
After his last victory, 26 September 1942

"That was the toughest adversary I've ever had. His turns were fabulous."[23]

Hans-Joachim Marseille
(after his final victory 26 September 1942)

The following three photographs show Marseille next to a downed Hawker Hurricane. Note the wooden propeller on this aircraft. *Courtesy Bundesarchiv Bild 101I-440-1313-03*

Above: *Courtesy Bundesarchiv Bild 101I-440-1313-07* Below: *Courtesy Bundesarchiv Bild 101I-440-1313-09*

German Rules For Confirming Aerial Victories

"Without a witness, a *Luftwaffe* fighter pilot had no chance to have his victory claim confirmed. Such a claim, even if filed, would not pass beyond group level.

"The final destruction or explosion of an enemy aircraft in the air, or the bail-out of the pilot, had to be observed either on gun-camera film or by at least one other human witness. The witness could be the German pilot's wingman, squadron mate, or a ground observer of the encounter.

"There was no possibility, as with some RAF and USAAF pilots, of having a victory credited because the claiming officer was a gentleman and a man of his word. The German rule was simply, "no witness – no kill."

"The German system was impartial, inflexible, and far less error-prone than either the British or American procedures. German fighter pilots had to wait several months, a year, or sometimes even longer for a kill confirmation to reach them from the German High Command."[24]

Author's Note: Although idealistic and theoretically impartial in its approach, evidence suggests that in practice, this method was not faithfully followed in the field. When you consider all 57 of Marseille's claims upon his return to the desert at the end of August were "confirmed," it is apparent the German system made exceptions for at least some of its highest profile and most prolific aces.

Marseille's Hurricane

These three photographs (pp 66-67) show Marseille next to a downed Hawker Hurricane. Note the wooden propeller on this aircraft. Not being an expert on this type of aircraft, I once again wrote a short note to my friend, Aussie historian Russell Brown, and asked him about his thoughts on this aircraft. Below is what he wrote:

"Dear Rob,

The photo you sent shows the aircraft to be a Hurricane IIb: in other photos the outer wing isn't visible. Here we have two extra machine guns, unique to the IIb.

I have a book about RAF Fighter squadrons, which details exactly what marks the various units were using, and at what time. Of all the desert Hurricane units, only 30 and 274 Squadrons were using the IIb in February 1942. I've chosen February for a good reason. On 12 February '42, H-JM shot down four 274 Squadron Hurricanes over Tobruk. One pilot baled out, two others went into the sea, and one, Sgt. Henderson, crash-landed south of Tobruk.

You mention no Knight's Cross [on Marseille], so the time is right. The N visible (Photo 1 on fuselage just aft and below the cockpit rail) suggests 274 Squadron, and back during the '41 Tobruk fighting, 274 were using Mk.I Hurricanes (no extra guns), so it couldn't have been then.

Therefore, Cull used a photo which was not from that time frame, and Scutts, who says 213 squadron in Feb.'42 is probably half right.

Another STRONG possibility is 8 February, when he [Marseille] shot down two 274 Squadron Hurricanes over his own field at Martuba. (These were victories 37 and 38). One flown by F/Sgt. Hargreaves crash-landed. A good photo opportunity, the aircraft crashing so close, and I guess that they would be likely to remove the fuselage fabric for decoration of mess tents etc.

I think that the emblem under the cockpit is probably a personal decoration rather than a Squadron one. The RAF fighter's book shows all the squadron badges, and none of the desert Hurricane units had a badge even remotely like the one shown, nor were they in the habit of using them on their aircraft, whereas most pilots who used personal emblems or names, etc, had them applied under the cockpit. 274 Squadron DID sometimes apply a lightning bolt design around the fuselage roundel, which would be a great prize for the mess, and this Hurricane has certainly been well stripped.

After his 96th to 101st air victory in June 1942 in North Africa: *Hauptmann* Marseille has just landed, after he had shot down 6 opponents in an air fight (dogfight) of about 12 minutes. The men came from all directions to lift him up on their shoulders in triumph. *Courtesy of Paul Upton*

Take your pick, but I'm supporting 274 Squadron, F/Sgt. Hargreaves, on Marseille's own airfield, all this assuming that February, before award of KC, is the right month."

Russell, thanks again for your input.

Das Reich

On 27 December 1942, German newspaper *Das Reich* had a full two-page article about Marseille. The article included several photographs of Marseille and his aircraft. The more interesting photos were a series of four that showed Marseille returning from his mission on 17 June 1942, where he had just gained his 101st aerial victory. It is after this mission that Edu Neumann has been quoted as saying that he could tell Marseille was at the end of his rope and that his hands shook uncontrollably while he was trying to light a cigarette. This is when Neumann told Marseille he was "done," and was to return to Germany to receive the Oak Leaves and Swords from Hitler himself. These photographs have been reproduced in many different books and articles, but these scans come directly from the newspaper itself. Considering this issue is almost 65 years old, the quality of the photographs is still quite remarkable. I want to thank Mr. Paul Upton for providing the newspaper. I would also like to thank Mr. Frank Struppek for translating the photo captions for this section.

Marseille's Rudders

Keeping score of one's achievements in aerial combat was widespread throughout the Second World War. Different air forces had various methods for their pilots to keep track of their scores. While some painted victory marks of various types underneath the cockpit, the *Luftwaffe* practice was to place the victory marks on the rudders of their aircraft. The following photographs are some of the varying examples of Marseille's ever-growing victory total. It should be interesting to note that in interviews with Friedrich Körner, he stressed to me that in his *Gruppe* (I/ JG 27), victory marks were only carried on the left side of the rudder. As he put it, so the "pilot could see them" as he climbed into his aircraft. Whether this practice was standard throughout the *Luftwaffe*, I do not know. It does, however, explain why you will likely not see any photographs of I/ JG 27 aircraft with victory marks on the right side of the rudder. I myself have not.

When he opened the cockpit of his Me, his face was marked by the enormous strain of combat in such a noticeable way, which I had seldom seen before on a pilot. His smile seemed forced and his movements, like when he wiped the sweat off his face, were still of hasty nervousness. *Courtesy of Paul Upton*

They stood around him in silence and patience for about a minute. This short time was enough to let his young and healthy body regain its strength and calmness. The shadows from his face disappeared, and immediately the cheerful smile appeared which his comrades liked so much on him. *Courtesy of Paul Upton*

Three minutes after landing he was so fresh and alert as if nothing had happened, and he reported how he shot down five of six opponents over a British airfield and demonstrated with spirited gestures of his hands how he opened up his lightning fast successful attacks. *Courtesy of Paul Upton*

Marseille poses in front of his rudder displaying 48 victories. His 48th victory was 3 RAAF pilot FO Briggs, shot down on 15 February 1942. *Courtesy of E & C Collection*

This page and following: On 21 February 1942 Marseille scored victories 49 and 50 to become the leading ace in the desert. This was a lead that he never relinquished. All *Courtesy of E & C Collection*

W. Nr. 8693

W.Nr. 10059 displaying 68 victories. The last three victory marks were 4 SAAF Kittyhawks downed on 31 May 1942. *Courtesy of E & C Collections*

W.Nr. 10137 with 101 victories. Upon his return to North Africa, Marseille's rudder markings were changed to a wreath surrounding the number 100 and one additional victory mark. See photograph in the chapter "Enemy Perspectives." *Courtesy of E & C Collection*

Two excellent photographs of W.Nr. 8673 displaying 130 visible victory marks. It is likely there are at least two marks hidden in the shade. This is because Marseille finished 3 September 1942 with 132 victories. The external braces characteristic of the Bf-109F-2 variant are clearly seen in both photographs. *Both Courtesy of E & C Collection*

W.Nr. 8673. On 5 September, Marseille downed four Curtiss type fighters near El Alamein and Imayid, Egypt, to bring his total to 136. *Courtesy of author*

Below: W.Nr. 8673 with 150 visible victory marks. *Courtesy of E & C Collection*

An unidentified squadron member holds up the late Marseille's rudder showing all 58 kills. Behind the airman is a derelict Bf-109 E. *Courtesy of E & C Collection*

Photo of Marseille's rudder from the Marseille-Kaserne museum. *Courtesy of author*

5

Personality

In addition to Marseille's unquestioned tactical acumen, renowned flying skills, and superb marksmanship, I believe most endearing was his infectious personality and seemingly honorable character. Sometimes termed brash, aggressive, undisciplined, and cocky, other times he was considered polite, gentle, carefree, and charming. From an alleged one-time raging womanizer to a young man who dearly loved his mother, sister, and fiancée, Marseille's personality appears to be a study in polar opposites. Though some people disliked and were undoubtedly intimidated by the often-undisciplined Berliner, Marseille, for the most part, was loved by the people he came into contact with. Although obviously disruptive in terms of his attitudes toward authority and leadership, in relation to a strong work ethic and desire to excel, Marseille was a focused perfectionist.

As a significant historical figure, especially for a German soldier of WWII, I believe it is his personality and character that made Marseille so unique and set him apart from most of his contemporaries. While many technically proficient people in their field remain aloof and unapproachable, Marseille was neither of these. He kept his openness to his colleagues and tried to help them whenever possible. Although his temperament was initially difficult to contain, Marseille became the ideal squadron mate. Like many men, Marseille's one true weakness was his obvious fondness for the opposite sex, especially early in his career. This alone made him a pariah among the more conservative and traditional of his peers. But let us look at what others say about Marseille and his interesting personality.

Discipline

> "He had to be spoken to after every mission, so that he would stay close to the formation, so that he wouldn't become a lone wolf."[1]
>
> Herbert Ihlefeld

An excellent photograph of Marseille, his fiancée Hanne-Lies Kuppers, and his mother. *Courtesy of author*

Marseille with his mother during his summer leave, 1942. *Courtesy of author*

Another fine photograph of Marseille and his mother. *Courtesy of E & C Collection*

A Knight's Cross wearing Marseille poses with a squadron mate before his summer leave of 1942. *Courtesy of Paul Upton*

"Finally, I told him, Marseille, I really can't work with such an undisciplined fellow. He was transferred to Africa and was very successful there. And the secret of his success was the fact that there were no girls in Africa!"[2]

Johannes "Macky" Steinhoff

"Marseille was in my wing, 4/JG.52, just before the Battle of Britain and was there shortly after it started. I was his squadron leader, and I watched him. I knew he was a brilliant guy, very intelligent, very quick and aggressive, but he spent too much time looking for the girls, and his mind was not always on operations. He actually had to be taken off flight status on more than one occasion because he was so exhausted from his nights on the town, if you know what I mean."[3]

Johannes "Macky" Steinhoff

"Showed bravado and played pranks while under training. . . Committed offenses in contravention of flying regulations. . . a flying obscenity."[4]

Comments from Marseille's personnel file

"You are only alive because you have more luck than sense. But don't imagine that it will continue indefinitely. One can overstrain one's luck like one can an aeroplane. You have the makings of a top-notch pilot, but to become one you need time, maturity and experience – certainly more time than you have left if you go on as you have been doing."[5]

Edu Neumann

"He was the perfect playboy, but a real fighter. But he was an individual, not a team player. He had seven victories when I fired him, not because he was not good, but because he was shot down four times while getting those victories. He had no concept of *Rottenflieger* [i.e., a wingman's responsibility], and many men did not want

Oberst Herbert Ihlefeld. Scored 132 victories in over 1000 combat missions, including 15 four-engine bombers. He was Marseille's first commander in LG 2. *Courtesy of author*

Fine photograph of Marseille's commander, Eduard "Edu" Neumann. *Courtesy of author*

to fly with him as their wingman, which is very bad for morale. I thought the best thing for him was to transfer him away from the women, and he became a legend in North Africa, of course, winning the Diamonds [to the Knight's Cross] and scoring 158 victories. He was a true character and was the epitome of the First World War fighter pilot, but we were not fighting the First World War."[6]

Johannes "Macky" Steinhoff

"Marseille could have been a problem character or a very great fighter pilot. At first his individuality – and his lack of discipline – alienated his comrades."[7]

Edu Neumann

"I consider that he (Marseille) is at the point to get ready for himself. This man wishes to be taken in earnest and for others to believe in his own rules for tactical air fighting."[8]

Edu Neumann

"I think he will be all right from now on. He seems to have a premonition of what will happen, of some kind of decisive moment. You will understand that he has no limits. He is serious and he wants us to believe him, to have respect for his ambitions. Be firm with him but take him seriously."[9]

Edu Neumann

"In our neighboring Staffel there was a certain Ofhr. (Oberfährnrich) Hans-Joachim Marseille who, by devising his own tactics, gradually became famous. Nevertheless, in the early months of this campaign, his Staffelkapitaen, Oblt. Homuth, was much more successful. I don't know what the differences were in their victory scores, but what really set them apart was their personalities. Marseille was a difficult subordinate with an independence which, in military life, could not be tolerated."[10]

Friedrich Keller

"Homuth, Marseille, Schroer and Stahlschmidt were very good pilots. Marseille in particular was magnificent, looked after by the gods, though he was a little rascal and an impertinent lad. . . . When he arrived, his hair was too long, and his jacket was shabby. . . . It was said that he kept the company of film actresses and he was not considered suitable to be an officer. His Staffelkapitaen was (Gerhard) Homuth who was serious and intellectual, the opposite of Marseille, and Homuth did not like him. I kept a tight rein on Marseille and he trusted me."[11]

Edu Neumann

Marseille "hand flying." Gerhard Homuth stands with his back to the camera on the far right. *Courtesy of Paul Upton*

"I couldn't imagine a better relationship between superior and subordinate. I never had any discipline difficulties with Marseille. He behaved in a very orderly fashion, a very military way and he never drew attention to the fact that he was the famous 'eagle.'"[12]

Edu Neumann

Appearance

Much has been made of Marseille's unconventional appearance. Unlike the stereotypical Aryan officers portrayed in Hollywood, Marseille was as opposite that image as possible. From his un-regulation long hair, baggy uniform, and his non-issue scarf and sandals in which he often flew, the skinny kid with dark green eyes that dominated his slender face certainly made a striking image while in the desert.

"He used to wear a 'bum-freezer' uniform which was so faded and crumpled that it looked rather like a jeans jacket today. His hair was too long and he brought with him [to the desert] a list of disciplinary punishments as long as your arm. Of the 7 kills he had claimed fighting along the English Channel, four had not been confirmed - a large percentage. On top of it all, he was a Berliner."[13]

Edu Neumann

"Marseille's magic sparkled. It lay in his jaunty, cavalier personality, in his very unmilitary behavior and in his unconventional dress. His headgear was hardly "regulation"- certainly no infantry officer would have been seen wearing a hat styled like his."[14]

Werner Schrör

Marseille relaxing in his tent. *Courtesy of author*

"He wore his hair long. His way was the way of the Bohemian. His lean, handsomely chiseled features made him a favorite with the girls. Since Marseille liked female company, during this period he was more a lover than a fighter."[15]

Raymond Toliver

"Marseille was not robust, he was the exact opposite, somehow gentle. His blood vessels shone through his skin and I was always amazed by the strength he had when he flew in an air fight."[16]

Edu Neumann

A very young looking Marseille early in his North African career. Notice his slightly "slovenly" appearance. His hair is obviously too long and his shirt is hanging out. Not the epitome of the classic German officer. Marseille wears the early style kapok-filled life jacket. *Courtesy of author*

Character

Character has been described as "what you do when nobody is watching." Of course it is more than that, and it also embodies one's nature, temperament, disposition, spirit, and moral fiber. In general, one's character is what drives a person to either succeed or fail in their daily tasks. What we see about Marseille's character is that while he had a rather high sense of ethical conduct and behavior, at other times he was as far from that as possible. Too often we see our enemy as heartless and coldblooded killers. We seem to intentionally fail to take into account the humanity of our enemy. Below is a letter Marseille penned to his mother the day he scored his first aerial victory on 24 August 1940 over Kent during the Battle of Britain:

> "Dearest Mother,
>
> Today I shot down my first opponent. It does not set well with me. I keep thinking about how the mother of this young man must feel when she gets the news of her son's deaths. And I am to blame for this death. I am sad, instead of being happy about the first victory. I always see the face of the Englishman in front of me and think about his crying mother."[17]
>
> Jochen 24.08.40

Following this first victory, the "excitement and awareness" that Marseille fought to the death with another man for the first time almost paralyzed him. Although proud to be the victor in combat, it is said that he felt like someone who had killed his best friend.[18]

In the words of a long time Marseille family friend, Heide d'Alquen told me, "That 'Abschuss' (his first victory) must not have made him into an instant pacifist. There were plenty of mothers later, but it is very good to know that he had a decent conscience."

Although there can be no doubt that Marseille strove to be recognized as the best fighter pilot in the *Luftwaffe*, being an incredibly sensitive young man, he certainly paid a price for it in terms of his humanity. Although he "officially" shot down 157 more aircraft, this letter, along with stories of his continued nightmares and sleepless nights, showed that he took no pleasure in the taking of life even though that was requisite in achieving his greatness as a fighter pilot. Following the receipt of the Knight's Cross on 22 February, for example, some pilots in the squadron reported that it was the first time in quite a while that any of them had seen Marseille smile. Likewise, squadron mates reported that Marseille would remain close-lipped, uncommunicative, and quiet for extended periods of time as though he was one who felt he had nothing more to lose and therefore could afford to risk everything. Although vehemently denied by Marseille, one squadron member said that Marseille acted as though he didn't "give a damn" about anything anymore.[19]

Marseille's Early Development

The following comments from one of his teachers give insight into his early character development.

"When I taught Marseille, it was in the Quarta, well-known as the 3rd Class, and after some days at the Gymnasium, many teachers had already lodged complaints about his conduct. So I had a serious conversation with him about suitable students and the other ones, the undesirables. And he seemed to understand what I meant. I won't say that he was an exemplary student after this talk but I well remember that, from then on, there were no more complaints about Marseille. He was at that time at the collegial section Real.

"He was a good companion among the other students, liked by everyone, including most of his teachers even though he loved to play jokes on them. His serenity was so abundant that we could not be truly hard with him. When he arrived at the Gymnasium, Hans was short and light in body. Like other small men, and because he liked physical exercise, he was determined not to be beaten by this fact. He always succeeded in staying in the best of physical condition. In class, he was not working especially harder than the others but he learned easily. Seen from the outside, he always seemed calm, having charming manners, and was happy and jovial. His self-respect made a great impression on me. During these years I constantly witnessed the good influence made by his good education. I'm happy today to have been right in this judgment."[20]

Professor Dr. Poetzold

"When Jochen came to us from the 12th *Volkshochschule* in Berlin, he was a noticeably tender and pale young boy. Because of his interest in physical training he developed in build and soon belonged to that group who were always the center of focus – even though he was still one of the smallest and physically weakest in the class. This was one of his characteristics which I very quickly noticed: he only felt comfortable when he was at the center of things; he wanted the attention and praise of his schoolmates.

"Jochen learned rapidly and within a quarter of a year easily made up what he had missed the preceding year. The older he grew the more noticeable his good development became. The most remarkable thing about him was his straight and dignified bearing. His social graces were skilled, his manners courteous and winning. In addition to this, he manifested a composed, controlled demeanor and a bright and cheery temperament.

"In his graduation certificate I wrote: 'His Character, which of course is still in development, promised to be good. Particularly noticeable is his refined sense of honor.' I'm pleased to note that I didn't err with Jochen."[21]

Professor Dr. Paetzold

"The relationship with his real father is probably one of the keys to Hans-Joachim's character. He had refused for three years to visit his father, although Inge, his sister, had done so and had been won over by the General's charm. The young boy felt loyal to Reuter [Author's note: his stepfather]. . . . he felt that the General and the other woman had wronged the family. . . . The son finally thawed enough to agree to visit his father in Hamburg a few months later. The days there were not very happy ones; Hans was still very defensive about his stepfather. The

From *Der Adler*, a photograph of Marseille running through some scrub brush. *Courtesy of author*

conflict was heightened when during the visit the General apparently decided that his son, in certain respects, had been much too sheltered by his mother and sister. He took Hans-Joachim to a few bars and introduced him to some women. What kind of women seems fairly clear, and the boy, his sensitivities outraged, returned home shortly afterwards. He never saw his father again."[22]

Michel Lavigne

Marseille as a comrade

"He was an exceptionally kind man, very, very friendly and solicitous towards subordinates as well; towards the ordinary soldiers in the army. Whenever they needed help, he helped them. That was his most striking characteristic."[23]

Edu Neumann

"Hans-Joachim Marseille was a young daredevil, and what was especially impressive was that with all the success he achieved, he remained a kind and friendly comrade."[24]

Friedrich Körner

"In the Desert, his sense of fun and his charm were engaging. He had a free and easy attitude to life. He did not allow rules to inhibit him. He listened to the Allies' radio stations which were very much taboo. He said he preferred their music."[25]

Werner Schrör

"Marseille's was a personality which was familiar in any German or Allied fighter squadron in World War II. The colour; the flamboyance and the little affectations; the gaiety and the humour; the infectious friendliness; the mildly arrogant disregard for convention – and yet, despite it, the unwavering loyalty to Service, squadron and cause."[26]

Werner Schrör

16 April 1942: To celebrate one full year in the desert, members of I/JG 27 celebrated with a day of relaxation. Marseille sits in the front row and the far left (marked by an "X"), enjoying what appears to be a magic show. Marseille's friend, Hans-Arnold "Fifi" Stahlschmidt, with the watch on his wrist (57 kills before his death), also sits in the front row. He too is marked by an 'X". *Courtesy of Paul Upton*

Marseille, wearing the pith helmet at the far right, chumming with squadron mates in 1941. *Feldwebel* Franz Elles (5 kills) stands in the center holding the flare gun. Note the Bf-109 E in the background. *Courtesy of Paul Upton*

"Few knew that on many nights, Marseille lay on a bed in his tent with every nerve taut and rarely experienced an undisturbed deep sleep. But in the morning, when he climbed into his Messerschmitt, his comrades saw only the smiling young blond pilot."[27]

Heinz Nowarra

"On 7 September, Marseille claimed his 142nd victory, but on the same day, Stahlschmidt was shot down. The loss of his friend hit Marseille particularly hard, and it was said that afterwards he was never quite the same. Outwardly he remained friendly, but he said little and looked drawn and tense."[28]

Jean-Louis Roba

"Flying, swinging through the heavens towards the sun, it is all I wish for myself."[29]

Hans-Joachim Marseille

A very tired looking Marseille in the summer of 1942, just three months shy of his 23rd birthday. *Courtesy of E & C Collection*

"I'm putting on my good jacket for this occasion."[30]
Field Marshall Erwin Rommel on meeting Marseille

As a squadron mate and friend, Marseille was characterized as loyal, honest, and caring. Although apparently affected by the constant death all around him, he was still considered cheerful and sociable. It was said that "no force in the world" could drive him away psychologically or physically from the circle of friends and comrades he had in the desert, no matter how much fame he acquired.[31] In fact, the more fame he obtained, the more Marseille was willing to bring his men in to share in his "limelight." He never considered giving up his friendships because of his fame, and it was his refined sense of honor and respect for people that he never let his fame get the better of him. He would listen to the worries and problems of his men regardless of who they were or where they came from.[32] Even Edu Neumann could not escape the Marseille charm. After hectic days of flying and fighting, Neumann would often look toward Marseille for that relief from the tension of the day's combat. It appears that all the men in the unit not only needed Marseille's guns to bring them through the day, but they needed his cheerful disposition as well to cope with the stress of desert life.

"So whenever I had problems which bothered me, I took the car and drove over to Marseille's tent. There was a sofa made out of sand bags filled with sand and covered with horse blankets. So I used to sit down there and flip through the old newspapers which I had already read and in this way I let the atmosphere of the Marseille squadron wash over me."[33]

Edu Neumann

Insecurity

As with many high achieving individuals, there is something in their personality that drives them to succeed; in many instances to over achieve. Insecurity and the desire to be accepted at all costs is a normal culprit in such an individual. It is exactly those insecurities that, when properly channeled, help spark the impetus to succeed. Marseille was no different. Although clearly a first rate pilot, there continued to be that aspect of his personality, especially upon his arrival in the desert, that required him to be in the limelight. Marseille desired, indeed craved, to be recognized as the best, and to become famous like the heroes from both the First World War and the early war years.

Comments from his teacher Dr. Poetzold showed Marseille's propensity for this behavior early in his youth when he was among the smallest and physically weakest students in the school. Whether a young man in school or a full-fledged fighter pilot in North Africa, it seems to have taken a while for Marseille to outgrow this tendency. It can be argued, even following his greatest successes, he may never have fully put this part of his personality behind him.

"When Marseille came to JG-27 he brought a very bad military reputation with him, and he was not at all a

Preparing for another sortie. *Courtesy of E & C Collection*

sympathetic fellow. He tried to show off, and considered his acquaintance with a lot of movie stars to be of great importance.

"In Africa, he became ambitious in a good way, and completely changed his character. After some time there, it became a matter of some importance to movie stars to know him.

"He was too fast and too mercurial to be a good leader and teacher, but his pilots adored him. He thanked them by protecting them and bringing them home safely.

"He was a mixture of the fresh air of Berlin and French champagne-a gentleman."[34]

Edu Neumann

"On his way to a better image he didn't hesitate in emphasizing that he not only had a number of young women, but had also won over a famous actress. This was purely a boast. When telling these stories he couldn't check himself. He was too temperamental and unbridled. He was what one would nowadays call a playboy."[35]

Edu Neumann

"He was inclined to show off, but this was probably to compensate for some kind of complex; he wanted to feel he was in the circle of important officers. In trying to create an image, he wasn't averse from talking about the many girls he had been to bed with, among them a famous actress. He was tempestuous, temperamental and unruly."[36]

Edu Neumann

"He was an intolerable boaster, proudly displaying his publicized adventures with famous actresses. . . . Once he had been given the chance to prove himself fully, it became obvious that his behavior had been mainly due to an over-sized inferiority complex, but until that time he was closely watched by his commanders"[37]

Christopher Shores/ Hans Ring

Humor

Marseille was known for his sense of humor and fun loving ways.

"Shortly after I became General of the Fighters I made a visit to JG-27 in North Africa, commanded by

Marseille and 3 *Staffel* personnel surrounding a captured Allied Jeep. Lt. Jost Schlang, Marseille's replacement following his death, is on the far left. Marseille is on the far right. *Courtesy of Michel Lavigne*

Eduard Neumann. Marseille was one of his squadron commanders.

"The airstrip was located on top of a hill and the squadron was nestled in a small valley not far away. As I approached Marseille's bivouacked squadron in a jeep with Neumann, we began to see small signboards, nailed on trees and hung on bushes, which pointed the way to 'The World's Best Fighter Squadron.' They were all humorous or semi-humorous, but they indicated the high morale of Marseille's unit.

"He greeted me with grace and enthusiasm, and it was not long before I felt the full impact of his charm and recognized his natural bent for leadership."[38]

Adolf Galland

"We talked far into the night. I told him that I needed to perform a vital natural function before I could have a nightcap and go to sleep.

"Marseille immediately produced a small spade and said: 'Proceed sixty paces straight away from the tent, then turn right twenty paces, and use the spade, sir.' I duly followed his instructions.

"In the morning upon awakening, I stepped out of my tent to use the spade again. I was flabbergasted to find signs pointing the way now. One final sign had a huge, downward-pointed arrow and said: 'At This Spot, on 22 September 1942, the General of the Fighter Arm Answered Nature's Call.'"[39]

Adolf Galland

"Jochen was a practical joker; he was forever playing pranks. He came to see me and my squadron - No. 2 *Staffel* - one day in his colorful Volkswagen jeep. He called it OTTO. After a talk, a cup of sweet coffee and a glass of Italian Doppio Kümmel, he got into his jeep and drove it straight at my tent flattening everything. Then he drove off with a grin stretching across his face."[40]

Werner Schrör

Marseille's Rebellious Spirit

Marseille possessed what might be called a rebellious spirit. Others behind closed doors might have simply said he was a jerk. We have read how he once landed his airplane on the Autobahn when he was going through basic flight training. The 1957 movie suggests he did this to look for directions, while other sources claim it was to take care of a biological necessity. Whether true or not, many of us have also read how he once strafed the ground near his commander's tent when denied the opportunity to fly on patrol. Regardless, through his actions and contained within the words of the men that knew him best, Marseille seemed to openly and willingly contravene normally accepted behavior at nearly every turn. When reading the words of his teachers, commanders, and comrades, it is apparent that Marseille was an intelligent young man with a refined sense of honor, and as such, I would argue that he did few things without knowing the repercussions and reactions his positions would create. It has been written that Marseille also had a keen sense that let him identify a bad person and, once identified, Marseille usually made quick work of him by dismissing him altogether. Whereas many people see the entire

Marseille and squadron mates clown around in his *Kubelwagen* "OTTO." *Courtesy of author*

world in shades of gray, apparently Marseille did see many aspects of the world in black and white, right and wrong.

With this in mind, there are two areas that I feel need further investigation. Although both of these areas have been written about and described superficially, I believe they are another window into the complex Marseille personality. One of those areas is the acquisition of the black South African prisoner of war, Corporal Matthew P. Letuku "Matthias," and the other is Marseille's reported love of Jazz music. On the surface, both of these areas might appear insignificant and quite ordinary. Under closer examination, however—one not filtered through 65 years of historical refinement, but rather through the eyes of a very repressive 1940s German National Socialist regime—I believe these two areas further define the character of a socially refined German officer. I do not believe that the whole story of Matthias is simply, "he was a black guy Marseille knew." Nor do I believe the extent of Marseille's love of Jazz/ Swing music was simply "Marseille liked jazz." Although that may be the case, I do not believe so. There is more to it than that, and within the next few pages I will look into these two areas. I believe Marseille's most admirable character trait was that he seemed to openly reject National Socialist propaganda surrounding blacks and Jews. These areas will be looked at in closer detail.

The Unique Case of Matthias

When analyzing German National Socialist views on race, there can be little doubt that blacks were considered undesirable and inferior to the Aryan. Marseille and all the men of his unit were certainly aware of this. Upon Marseille's return to the desert on 23 August 1942, squadron members proudly displayed the new "bar" they had built while he was on leave. It consisted of a bar

Corporal Matthew P. Letuku, "Matthias." *Courtesy of Paul Upton*

and sofas made out of burlap sacks and other available materials. Upon entering the bar, Marseille remarked, almost in the vein of *Casablanca*, that they needed a "Negro" behind the bar wearing a white jacket.[41] Shortly after this, Marseille drove to the squadron with Matthias sitting in the passenger seat next to him. According to Fritz Dettmann, *Oberleutnant* Schlang had discovered Matthias in a military hospital where he was pedaling the drill for a dentist. Marseille promptly went out and brought him back to his squadron. There Matthias, the German speaking native of the Transvaal, became the personal batman of Marseille. Matthias would cook, clean, tend the bar, and help out around the squadron whenever possible. Following Marseille's death, Matthias stayed in that capacity until the end of the war. What started out as an oddity soon became an unlikely friendship between the two men.

Blacks, along with Jews and other undesirables were considered unfit for the noble German society, and although there was no systematic plan for the physical liquidation of blacks within the Reich as with the Jews, the Nazis made their positions clear on the subject of race and did, however, institute a program of forced sterilization of mixed race children within Germany.

The history of the anti-black psychology originated with German colonial influences in Africa. More recently with the National Socialists, however, it began with the occupation of the Rhine area after WWI by French black colonial troops dictated by the Treaty of Versailles. This situation brought the subject of blacks in Germany to the forefront of National Socialist thought. The occupation by these black troops was called the *Black Horror on the Rhine*, and as one can imagine, strict views on race and race mixing remained one of the lynchpins of National Socialist thought.

Within Nazi views, blacks were considered "sex crazed perverts performing outrages against German women, men, and children."[42] Blacks were also viewed as uncontrolled and wild by nature.[43] The SS itself took a much more proactive view and, obviously angry that France had enlisted the help of black troops in 1940, in their own journal, *Das Schwarze Korps*, wrote that blacks were "beings who derive cultic joy from murder and mutilation. . . who stand on a level of development not much higher than the gorilla." Echoing the memory of the black occupation after WWI, an article dated 31 May 1940 showed a photograph of black soldiers in France with the caption, "Today France has again let loose the cruel black beasts from the jungle against us, and again they have given free rein to their animalistic instincts."[44]

There is little doubt that while many Germans bought into this propaganda, many, including Marseille, did not. It is not clear exactly what Marseille's motivations were for befriending Matthias other than what has been quickly mentioned in *My Friend Marseille*. But there can be no doubt that he knew the act of taking Matthias from the hospital and bringing him into his squadron would certainly cause consternation among the more ardent followers of National Socialist doctrine. It is also evident that Marseille cared less what people thought about his actions.

When looking at Matthias' reactions following Marseille's death, it is obvious the two men had developed more than just an "I'm the boss" type of relationship, and a friendship of sorts had developed between the two. Even following Marseille's death, Matthias' presence was so welcomed that he remained with the squadron through the end of the war. It is apparent the majority of pilots had no problem with Matthias' skin color either, again casting some doubt on some very standard German stereotypes from the time. Even years following Marseille's death, Matthias was welcomed and attended functions honoring his old friend. If Marseille had been anything but a true friend and respectful to the South African POW, it is doubtful whether Matthias would have continued participating in such events.

Once again, the friendship between these two men may seem minor, or just an interesting footnote to those of us today, but when looking at those dark times through the turbulent and unforgiving eyes of 1940s Nazi Germany, I believe Marseille's relationship with Matthias and the obvious political statement it made again speaks volumes, and Marseille's unique character and personality once again shines through.

During the research for this book I contacted historian and author, Rafael Scheck. He is an Associate Professor and Chair of the History Department at Colby College in Waterville, Maine, and is the author of *Hitler's African Victims: The German Army Massacres of Black French Soldiers in 1940*. His book deals with the murder of black colonial troops by German soldiers during the Spring of 1940 as the *Wehrmacht* rolled through France. As an acknowledged expert on race issues and theories within the Third Reich, I asked if he would be kind enough to respond to some questions dealing with Marseille and Matthias. I posed several questions to Mr. Scheck. His responses follow:

Matthias stands in front of a Messerschmitt G model. Following Marseille's death, Matthias remained with I/ JG 27. *Courtesy of the Seattle Museum of Flight*

Even after JG 27 relocated to Germany for the defense of the Reich, Matthias stayed with them. Here Matthias poses with a young German girl. *Courtesy of author*

"Dear Mr. Tate,

Here are my thoughts:

1: What do you think the general attitude would be toward Matthias among ardent Nazis or those who at least believed in certain National Socialist racial attitudes?

Answer: There is no question that belief in Nazi ideology would have mandated keeping one's distance from a black man. Nazi racial theories placed blacks at the low end of the racial value hierarchy. Some theorists even argued that blacks and Jews were related to each other.

2: Do you (in your professional opinion) find Marseille's behavior odd?

Answer: I do not find it odd because I am accustomed to seeing many nuances among the Germans of the Third Reich. But his behavior would probably be startling for many other researchers.

3: From your experience, what were the general attitudes of average Germans towards black individuals? Do you think most Germans would have disapproved of Marseille's actions?

Answer: Nazi propaganda and discriminatory laws depicted blacks as dangerous polluters of the Germanic gene pool. We know of many German citizens of African descent (or partial African descent) who faced public shame and ostracism. Marseille's actions would have appeared questionable to many Germans - albeit by no means to all.

4. Does Marseille's "acquisition" of Matthias tell you anything about Marseille or his personality?

Answer: Hard to say without knowing him any better.

5. Did this type of action occur often? Do you know of other instances?

Answer: I know of the camp commandant of the concentration camp of Mauthausen, who held a black man as his personal servant. This was done out of disrespect, however. I do not think that aspect was relevant for Marseille."

Regardless, it is obvious to me that Marseille was not bound to the racial hatred espoused by National Socialist doctrine. As a hero of the German nation, Marseille risked much in his pursuit of his fair and ethical treatment of Matthias. His strength in this area is commendable.

Jazz and Swing Within the Reich

Beginning in the 1920s, the American Jazz phenomenon began to make its mark inside Europe. With its non-traditional sounds and sexy rhythmic dance, as well as performances by black and Jewish artists, it wasn't long before the National Socialists saw this form of music and dance as an affront to their vision of acceptable behavior for young Aryan boys and girls. As its popularity grew, reaching its German peak between 1924 and 1928, so did eventual attempts to outlaw and squash this new form of "degeneration." Jazz music, rooted in non-Aryan traditions, was looked down upon by the National Socialists because of its decadent and unacceptable American and British influences. The images of young boys and girls enjoying the light-hearted music, dancing with one another in a fashion contradictory to preferred waltzes, were too much for many.

One of the more well-known photographs of Matthias while in North Africa. *Courtesy of E & C Collection*

Until 1935, however, Jazz and eventually Swing music were not an official target of Propaganda Minister Josef Goebels. The Nazis felt that banning this form of music would be too difficult, rather opting for negative campaigning to influence youngsters that this form of music and dance were unacceptable. The National Socialists felt cooler heads would prevail, and with the strict and proper training of children from age 10 through organizations like the Jungvolk, Hitlerjugend, Arbeitsfront, and SA and SS, they would eventually eradicate this problem. As part of this plan, some more acceptable forms of Jazz were actually played on state run radios until 1935 when an attempt to ban this music failed. Much of the Nazi problem with their failure to "outlaw" Jazz came from the fact that there was no clear definition of what Jazz was. There was Jazz created by black and Jewish entertainers, and then there were Aryan Jazz professionals.

What about Swing? Swing, generally recognized as that music played by big bands such as Benny Goodman, Tommy Dorsey, and Glenn Miller, was almost altogether different, and began to grow in popularity by the early 1930s. These bands, tolerated by the Nazis for a short time, were considered to be "good dance music," and thought to be a "cultivated replacement of the old wild Jazz."[45] In other words, the more "primitive" music performed by black entertainers was less desirable than music even performed by Jewish artists. By failing to adequately define their "enemy," the Nazis were woefully unable to completely stamp out the Jazz "menace."

Swing music was often played throughout Germany, reaching its peak in 1936 at the time where it was openly played at the Berlin Olympics.[46] However, by 1937 the National Socialists again attempted to tighten their grip on "undesirable" music within the Reich. The Nazi authorities considered the Swing scene a particular menace. Swing was viewed as a very dangerous foreign import, because it too was rooted in immoral Black "jungle music" with accompanying allusions to wild, indiscriminate sex. Even worse, as far as the Nazi officials were concerned, Swing was a deliberate product of Jewish media moguls in America that, if spread to Germany, could contaminate the blood of its own youth. The Nazis believed that youngsters caught up in a possible invasion of Swing would revert to more primitive forms of African-inspired behavior. Their blood would become contaminated as they bred babies of uncertain parentage as a result of sexual relations with multiple Aryan as well as non-Aryan partners. Although non-German musicians, singers, and songwriters were eventually arrested, Nazi attempts to squelch the music itself failed.[47] As with any endeavor of its kind, those with the will and the means to indulge in "unacceptable" behavior will normally succeed in their quest.

Swing Kids

From within the ranks of those who professed to listen and dance to Jazz/ Swing music, several groups of youths emerged inside of Germany. These groups were the Swing *Jugend* (Swing Kids) and the *Edelweiss* Pirates. The Swing *Jugend* were upper class and upper middle class adolescents, while the Pirates were more from middle and working class areas. These groups that sprang up throughout Germany, in particular the Swing *Jugend*, were not necessarily "anti-Nazi" in any political sense, but rather by their mere actions were deemed anti-political and non-conformist. They openly welcomed their counter culture identities, looked fondly toward the dress and music of Germany's wartime enemies, and often openly accepted Jews into their groups. After all, many of the better-known Swing performers were Jewish.

The Swing movement flourished in certain parts of Germany while major cities such as Hamburg, Kiel, Stuttgart, Frankfurt, Dresden, and of course Berlin had large groups of Swing *Jugend* and their clubs as well. These middle and upper middle class Swing *Jugend*, from their dress to their "abhorrent" behavior, openly welcomed this form of entertainment. Since these kids certainly had access to more money than most, they were able to afford the more "chic" looking American and English clothes and had more access to the "forbidden" music.

As for the appearance of these Swing *Jugend*, they looked similar to the Swing kids found in the U.S. and in Britain at the time. This is because their influence came directly from the Western movies they saw in Germany, and reflected the styles they witnessed on their favorite Hollywood actors and actresses. Although there were distinct differences in their appearance from city to city, neither group's appearance was considered acceptable to the National Socialists.

1. Hair – As with adolescents from almost any generation, hair is often used to make the most profound statement of rebellion against authority. This was no different among the Swing *Jugend*. The men tended to rebel against the short military, *Hiterjugend* hair style by wearing their hair very long. Sometimes they sported "whips" of long hair, from their foreheads, that were combed backward with "Brilliantine or sugared water."[48]

2. Dress – This varied greatly from city to city. Within Marseille's hometown of Berlin, in the attempt to capture the "dead smart look," the Swing *Jugend* tended to wear double-breasted baggy suits with ties or flies underneath a variety of overcoats that included civilian trench coats, camel-hair coats, and even "teddy bear" fur coats.[49] These "flies" are often described as shawls or scarves. In addition to this look, Swing *Jugend* were also often seen with the obligatory "Shag Pipe."

Swing Behavior

As "offensive" and unconventional as the appearance of the Swing Kids may have been, it was their oftentimes "vulgar" behavior that caused the most reason for concern among the National Socialists. It was not just the sexually provocative dance steps that these youths practiced, but it was the sexual practices associated with the movement that was reason for the greatest concern.

> Hamburg Swing Festival, February 1940:
>
> "The dance music was all English and American. Only swing dancing and jitterbugging took place. At the entrance to the hall stood a notice on which the words 'Swing Prohibited' had been altered to 'Swing requested'.

Without exception the participants accompanied the dances and songs by singing the English lyrics. Indeed, throughout the evening they attempted to speak only English; and some tables even French.

"The dancers made an appalling sight. None of the couples danced normally; there was only swing of the worst sort. Sometimes two boys danced with one girl; sometimes several couples formed a circle, linking arms and jumping, slapping hands, even rubbing the backs of their heads together; and then, bent double, with the top half of the body hanging loosely down, long hair flopping into the face, they dragged themselves round practically on their knees. When the band played a *rumba*,* the dancer went into a wild ecstasy. They all leaped around and mumbled the chorus in English. The band played wilder and wilder numbers; none of the players was sitting any longer, they all 'jitterbugged' on the stage like wild animals. Frequently boys could be observed dancing together, without exception with two cigarettes in the mouth, one in each corner. . ."[50]

Author's Note: Keep in mind that while in the desert, Marseille's favorite song was *The Rumba Azul*.

"Dance music gave way to hot jazz; steps as learned in dancing classes gave way to free, spontaneous rhythmic movement, erect posture and tidy dress gave way to 'jitterbugging', hair 'down to the collar' . . . and a cult of 'slovenliness' and 'sleaziness.'"[51]

"The sight of some three hundred dancing people thrashing about was absolutely horrid. No one can describe the dancing because no one danced normally. Indeed, this was the naughtiest of Swing dancing that can be imagined. Sometimes two boys danced with one juvenile girl, and at other times several couples locked themselves into a mass embrace and just hopped around. Many couples hopped together while holding hands and bent over wildly, so that their long hair flew across their faces and whipped their thighs as they spun. You had to worry about the sanity of some of them. The scenes that happened on the dance floor were fit for a lunatic asylum. Even the most hysterical and primitive Black jungle warrior war-dance would have paled in comparison to what happened here. Everyone jumped about like crazy while they mumbled English musical gibberish. The Band increased the tempo faster by the minute. No member of the band was sitting, because they were all getting hotter and wilder as they also succumbed to the jungle beat on the stage. You often saw boys dancing together with other boys, always with two cigarettes dangling from each corner of the mouth."[52]

Hitlerjugend Patrol Report on a Hamburg Swing Dance,
August 2, 1940

Equally disturbing to the National Socialists was the penchant for increased sexual promiscuity among the members of these groups. Descriptions abound of "drunken free-sex affairs," boys and girls engaging in sex with multiple partners, "dance orgies where teenagers 'swung' and 'got hot.' Swing, with its unrestrained zeal and lust for physical exertion, seemed to be either a manifestation of serious mental illness or downright primitive Negroid hysteria."[53] Likewise, "Reporting about the Swing groups, the Nazi authorities stressed the incident of promiscuity, group sex, sexual intercourse involving minors and above all, unabashed pleasure in sexuality which was denounced as moral decency."[54]

Exaggerated? Likely, however, it does not alter the fact that the prevailing sexual attitudes and behavior of these adolescents were not what German authorities deemed acceptable for the nation's youth. These groups were so appalling to Nazi leadership that Heinrich Himmler at one point wanted to put the "ringleaders" of the swing movement into concentration camps for "at least two or three years of beatings, punitive drill and forced labor."[55]

Marseille's Jazz/ Swing Connection

Without definitive corroboration, I am not willing to claim that Marseille was definitely a member of the Berlin Swing *Jugend*

A tired and gaunt Marseille in the summer of '42. Notice Marseille's "shag pipe" in his pocket. *Courtesy of author*

Marseille badly in need of a haircut, as usual. This photograph was taken before his summer leave of 1942. Note he is only wearing the basic Knight's Cross. *Courtesy of Paul Upton*

movement. However, as I have read the instances of Marseille's behavior in relation to the conduct of the practitioners of Swing within the Reich, if Marseille was not an actual member, his actions, dress, conduct, and attitudes at a minimum showed a definite empathy for them and their counter culture, anti-National Socialist ways. From the words of those that knew him best to the many photographs of Marseille with his shawl, long hair, and shag pipe, this is what I clearly see within his personality:

1. Appearance – There is little doubt that Marseille, at least in some measure, dressed the part. Several photographs and video clips of Marseille clearly show him consistently brushing a long "whip" of hair off his face and combing it back over his head. This long hair style, clearly out of regulation, is consistent with the styles worn by the Swing *Jugend* not only in his hometown of Berlin, but throughout Germany as well. In addition to the length of his hair, even from his earliest days in the desert he was almost always photographed wearing his unmilitary, non-issue scarf, or shawl as one person described it. This again is consistent with the dress of members from this group. There are also several photographs of Marseille carrying a "Shag pipe" in his pocket.

> "He was marked by his long hair, a shawl which he always wore, and by his predilection for jazz, a form of music frowned on by the authorities at that time. . . ."[56]
>
> Christopher Shores and Hans Ring

Author's Note: "Frowned on by authorities at that time" is quite the understatement. Music almost entirely dominated by blacks and Jews was certainly not what the National Socialists wanted for their young people.

> "Individualistic in dress, a devotee of jazz, the latest dance steps and girls, he could have been a major disciplinary and morale problem."[57]
>
> Edward H. Sims

2. Behavior - In addition to Marseille's unmilitary dress and appearance, there is the issue of his, shall we say, overly promiscuous behavior. As described earlier, this was a blatant characteristic of the Swing *Jugend* movement. This does not necessarily imply that these kids were morally bankrupt, but this was one avenue they had to express their disdain for a government regime that continued to limit their rights and freedoms.

> "Marseille was extremely handsome. He was a very gifted pilot and fighter-but he was unreliable. He had girl friends every where, and they kept him so busy that he was sometimes so worn out he had to be grounded. His sometimes irresponsible way of conducting his duties was the main reason I fired him. But he had irresistible charm."[58]
>
> Johannes "Macky" Steinhoff

3. The Music – There is no doubt that Marseille was a dedicated fan of this type of music. From Jazz to Swing, and even to Cuban and Latin Rumbas, Marseille was a "devotee" of not only this type of music, but the corresponding dance as well. Indeed, Marseille's favorite song was a saucy Cuban Rumba by Ernesto Lecuona and the Lecuona Cuban Boys titled *The Rumba Azul*. Regardless of whether other officers around him liked this music or not, Marseille obviously cared less. Once again, as a brilliant young man, he had to know that his preferences for this music and dance had to have a negative effect on certain people around him. Chalk up yet another form of rebellion.

The significance of Marseille's Jazz/Swing connection may be nothing at all. But once again, I believe that looking at his actions, behavior, appearance, and his dress, Marseille was likely, if not a member of this Swing movement, at least in some way partial and empathetic to it. He loved the look; he loved the music; he loved the dance. At a minimum, he clearly enjoyed the consternation his behavior created among the established leadership. As for Marseille, I believe his adherence to this type of music and dress was a deliberate and calculated effort to demonstrate to those around him that he would not bow down to Nazi ideals. For a young German officer with his highly popular and public status, this form of rebellion is interesting. Even in photographs where he met Field Marshal Erwin Rommel in September 1942, the young and impetuous 22 year-old Captain can be seen wearing his "unauthorized" scarf.

Taken together with Marseille's relationship with Matthias, I believe we get a much clearer picture of a young man not restrained by ideologies that ran contrary to his highly sophisticated belief and value systems, one that was willing to stand up for what he believed, and one of many young soldiers that simply refused to fall into the archaic and oppressive Nazi mindset that pigeonholed people into differing categories based on harsh and restrictive subjective criteria. I think if Marseille was a member of this group, it does nothing to diminish his greatness, but rather enhances what we may think about his character and personality.

Final Thoughts

In addition to Marseille's obvious physical talents, it remains his personality that I find so engaging. Not only was he an excellent pilot, I believe it was his personality that set him apart from not just his peers, but more importantly, through the years will continue to distance him from the stereotypical German officer of WWII. Not all German soldiers were bad men, and Hans Marseille clearly epitomizes that reality.

"He spoke in excellent German with a light Berlin, touch. Light, like the people in Berlin. Because he was born in Berlin it was normal that you could hear a little touch, a Berlin touch in his speech. But it was very clear and accentuated or so."[59]

Friedrich Körner

An excellent study of "The Star of Africa."
Courtesy of author

6

Enemy Perspectives

As in any theater of operation, men of the *Luftwaffe* and DAF fought and died competing to become the best fighter pilot in the desert and, not surprisingly, both sides produced exceptionally skilled pilots equal to those in any theater. There can be no doubt that men like "Killer" Caldwell, "Stocky" Edwards, and "Screwball" Beurling were in many respects the equal of any pilot in any theater. As Marseille's legend continued to grow after the war, however, pilots and historians tried to make sense of his staggering claims. How could he have possibly destroyed seven times the number of aircraft as the highest scoring DAF pilot? Beliefs ranged from

Left: Undoubtedly one of the finest fighter pilots to fly in North Africa. Canadian James "Stocky" Edwards of 260 squadron was credited with 22 total wartime kills, including the downing of German ace Otto Schulz (51 victories) on 17 June 1942, the same day Marseille claimed his 100th victory. An excellent pilot and superlative marksman, few pilots on either side of the conflict were better than Edwards. *Courtesy of Michel Lavigne* Right: German ace Otto Schulz, downed by Canadian James "Stocky" Edwards. *Courtesy of E & C Collection*

awe, to questioning doubt, to outright disbelief that any pilot could possibly have shot down the number of Western flown aircraft Marseille claimed. Perhaps more important, however, is that pilots and historians could not, and to a degree still cannot fathom the method in which Marseille achieved his victories. Although many pilots from other countries had on occasion demonstrated the ability to down multiple aircraft on a single sortie, no other pilot had shown the propensity to repeatedly accomplish this feat against Commonwealth pilots during the time Marseille operated in North Africa. Below is a table showing some notable achievements in the rapid destruction of aircraft on single sorties. This table is only an attempt to show that on many occasions pilots from various nations were able to replicate the feats of Marseille:

Name	Date	Location	Victories
Cdr. David McCampbell, USN	19-06-44	Marianas	7
	24-10-44	Leyte Gulf	9
Major William A. Shomo	11-01-45	Luzon, Phillipines	9
Colonel Neele E. Keary, USAAF	11-01-45	Wewak, New Guinea	6
Major Erich Rudorffer, Luftwaffe	09-02-43	North Africa	13 in 17 Minutes
	06-11-43	Russia	8
Pilot Officer Charles Harold Dyson, RAF	11-12-40	Libya	7 in 15 Seconds

Questions and Doubts About Marseille's Success

There are several valid reasons for disbelief concerning Marseille's claims. As other fighter pilots who fought in North Africa, men infinitely familiar with the conditions in the desert were themselves unable to achieve such fantastic feats, so how could any other pilot have achieved such things? The destruction of so many aircraft in such little time could not possibly be true. 17 aircraft in one day? Impossible. Eight aircraft in ten minutes? Preposterous.

Likewise, there is certainly some ethnocentric bias involved. To be fair, ethnocentrism swings both ways. Whereas many Allied pilots and historians readily discredited the achievements of Marseille and labeled them as absurd Nazi propaganda, others willingly accepted all of his claims regardless of any evidence. The truth? It lies somewhere in between, with the evidence supporting most, but not certainly all of Marseille's successes. Regardless, look at what some enemy pilots had to say, both positive and negative, about Marseille and his victories.

"Be that as it may, there is the interesting if perplexing case of Hans-Joachim Marseille. Fighting over the Western Desert he is reported to have shot down 61 RAF aircraft in the period 1 – 7 September 1942, with 17 British aircraft downed in a single day (1 September). RAF records show that there were no losses that day in the areas the claims were made. Marseille was killed in a flying accident (as reported from German sources) on 30 September 1942. His total score by then was 158; 150 of them claimed over the Western Desert. It appears that his claims were accepted at face value and forwarded to the German High Command by the Jagdgeschwader concerned."[1]

W.G.G. Duncan Smith

Group of 260 Squadron pilots. From left to right: Sgt. Lionel Sheppard (RAF), F/Lt. Ron Cundy (RAAF), Sgt. James Stocky Edwards (RCAF), F/O Geoff Fallows (RNZAF), and F/O Nelson Gilboe (RCAF). *Courtesy of Ron Cundy*

Flying Officer John Lloyd Waddy from Sydney, Australia. Waddy served with Nos 250, 260, 4 SAAF and 92 Squadrons in the Western Desert flying Tomahawks, Kittyhawks, and Spitfires. Waddy became the third highest scoring Allied pilot in the African Campaign with 15.5 victories. *Courtesy of Michel Lavigne*

> ". . . it was while I was flying Spifires that Marseille was reported to be operating. I believe his claims were largely figments of his imagination and I have also been led to believe that he claimed to have shot down more Spitfires up to the time of his death than we ever had in the Middle East at that time. We struck him on several occasions in the air and not once did he shoot down one of our fighter aircraft."[2]
>
> J.L. Waddy

> "I have found it possible to make a detailed check of some of the claims of a well-known German who has been called 'the unrivalled virtuoso of the fighter pilots.' His greatest day in the Western Desert was on 1st September 1942, when he claimed seventeen victories, eight of them in the space of ten minutes. But our own records show that, on this day, we lost a total of only eleven aeroplanes, including two Hurricanes, a type which the German pilot did not claim. In fact, some of our losses occurred when he was on the ground."[3]
>
> John E. 'Johnnie' Johnson

To be fair, many post war comments such as these have since been found to be quite inaccurate. This is in no way meant to slander the men making these statements, but for whatever reason, many of the facts at the time of their claims may have not been available. For example, we can immediately dismiss Group Captain Duncan Smith's statements as incorrect. When Marseille left Libya for leave on 17 June 1942, he had amassed 101 total victories. After his return to Egypt on 23 August, he gained another 57 total kills with his final victory coming on 26 September. During the period mentioned by Smith (1-7 September), Marseille actually claimed 38 victories, not 61 as claimed by Smith. Although quite impressive, Marseille's totals nonetheless were nowhere near those stated by Duncan Smith. Likewise, although some over claiming may have occurred during this period, the German practice of confirming kills, albeit certainly imperfect, remained quite rigid.

As for Group Captain Waddy's (third highest scoring DAF pilot with 15.5 kills) comments about the number of Spitfires in the Middle East, Marseille claimed a total of 15 Spitfires during his 18 months in the desert. Records indicate Marseille claimed 4 Spitfires over Bir Hakeim on 4 June 1942, another on 17 June, and one more on 31 August, 1 September, and 3 and 6 September. Four days before his death on 26 September, he then claimed six more Spitfires on two sorties. If you consider Marseille's claimed Spitfire victories while operating in the desert came from 45 Sq., 601 Sq., and 92 Sq., there were certainly more than 15 Spitfires in the North African theater of operations, unless of course each squadron only consisted of five aircraft each. In total, five squadrons flew the Spitfire in the Middle East, and Marseille's first desert Spitfire claim was not until 10 June 1942. He made no Spitfire claims before their arrival in the desert.

In addition to Waddy's incorrect assertion of a lack of Spitfires, an analysis of Marseille's claims where the victim can be identified include no less than 14 aircraft downed from the squadrons where Gp. Capt. Waddy operated. The claim that Marseille "not once" shot down one of his squadron's aircraft is altogether incorrect. Whether Waddy was airborne or assigned to that particular squadron at that time is immaterial. Marseille did clearly shoot down aircraft from squadrons where Waddy was or had been assigned.

Finally, regarding the comments of Air Vice-Marshal "Johnnie" Johnson, it is easy to see where his comments may have originated. Even after further analysis, the hectic air fighting that took place on 1 September in support of Rommel in the Battle of Alam el Halfa left a lot of confusion. Many of the initial claims of Marseille's victories being erroneous came from early reports about total DAF losses that day and statements mentioning Marseille was on the ground while much of the combat took place. Christopher Shores and Hans Ring, in *Fighters Over the Desert*, have done much to quell most of the doubts about this day. Their research confirms that DAF losses that day included 9 Hurricanes, 4 Kittyhawks, 4 Tomahawks, 2 Spitfires, and 2 Beaufighters. Also, 1 USAAF P-40 F was destroyed. In all, the Germans claimed 26 victories while actual Allied losses were 20 single-engine fighters, one two-engine fighter, and several more that were badly damaged, but were able to limp back to friendly territory.[4] Marseille's claims that day were 5 Hurricanes, 1 Spitfire, and 11 Curtiss fighters. Although only 8 Curtiss fighters were downed, Marseille, like many German pilots, was notoriously bad at identifying enemy aircraft, and in all likelihood misidentified one or more of his victims.

It is also possible, indeed highly likely that one or more of Marseille's claims that day, although hit and damaged, may have actually made it back to base. This would account for a claim on the German side but registering as only a damaged on the Allied side. If there can be one criticism of Marseille's tactic of short but accurate bursts, it is that many of the aircraft he hit were not completely "blasted" out of the sky. Many pilots, like Erich Hartmann, opted for short range attacks and holding down the trigger until the enemy aircraft exploded or broke apart in mid-air. In becoming the consummate sharp-shooter, Marseille may have unwittingly allowed definite kills to escape and limp back to base or crash land in the desert. Regardless, Marseille's 17 claims, as well as total *Luftwaffe* claims are reasonably consistent with the number of DAF aircraft lost or damaged that day over Egypt.

Enemy Encounters With Marseille

On more than one occasion, Marseille found himself on the receiving end of another pilot's guns. In particular, one Free French pilot, Sous-Lt James Denis, DFC, was able to best Marseille on two separate occasions. Here is what Denis reported after his encounters with Marseille. This first combat took place on 23 April 1941.

> "I was well-trained and a confirmed fighter. What's more, I was considered an elite shooter. I knew my job well, and it explains why during my fight with this pilot, presumably Marseille, I was patient enough to act as if I hadn't seen him, wait until the last second and skid, avoiding his bullets which passed very close to my right. I saw them well."[5]
>
> Sous-Lt James Denis

During this combat, it was reported that Marseille narrowly escaped getting killed. Sous-Lt Denis' shooting was so accurate that thirty-some bullets hit Marseille's cockpit and engine area. Two bullets barely passed behind his head when he leaned forward, one bullet apparently nicking his flight helmet and two more bullets passing just in front of his eyes. His plane was disabled, and he was forced to put down in the desert.

Author's Note: This battle took place on 21 May 1941, and describes the second encounter between Denis and Marseille. Once again, Denis emerged as the victor.

> "With Pompei and Ballatore I went to Sidi Barrani for a supply-line attack. During take-off, Ballatore [V7429] touched a water tank and damaged his propeller, so I went with Pompei only. Instead of flying very low, as we usually did, I decided to take some altitude. When we arrived near the target, I dived quite steeply and realized my wingman was following shyly. Pompei was a very good pilot but had never trained as a fighter pilot. Worried to see he was following so far behind, I kept looking back and noticed a ME109 attacking him. Having no radio, I could not warn him. He was hit and then the ME109 flew in my direction. I acted as if I hadn't seen him, but never stopped watching, and when he was within range I throttled back violently and skidded to the left. Since I was going very fast, my Hurricane [V7859] reacted violently. I saw the hail [of bullets] pass on my right, and the ME109 could not slow down and flew in front of me. We then started a dogfight, for which the Hurricane was quite good due to its maneuverability. At that moment my plane was flying nose up, hooked to its propeller, when I saw the ME109 in the sun. I fired a burst so close that we almost collided. I noticed my bullets enter its fuselage."[6]
>
> Sous-Lt James Denis

In the chapter *Victories*, RAAF pilot Ron Cundy discusses Marseille's downing of Pilot Officer Dick Dunbar on 6 September 1942. Immediately following that engagement, Ron Cundy encountered an overly aggressive *Luftwaffe* pilot. He relates that story below.

> "It was on this occasion that I had one of the greatest fights of my life. Uncharacteristically, the German fighters rarely took us on and engaged in close combat. Aircraft were milling all over the sky. One virtually needed eyes in the back of one's head to avoid being shot down or colliding with another aircraft. As I eased out of one very tight turn I saw a Me-109 crossing in front of me from my right and perhaps 200 feet higher. I had washed off a lot of speed during the steep turn and knew I had little chance of hitting him but could not resist the temptation. Ramming the throttle fully open I pulled my nose up, laid off as much deflection as possible and opened fire. My Kittyhawk immediately stalled and went into a spin. By the time I stopped the spin I was down to a thousand feet. On recovering I rammed the throttle open (having closed it during the spin) and pulled around into a left-hand steep turn with a quick glance over my left shoulder. There sitting on my tail was a 109. He had obviously followed me down looking for an easy kill. I tightened the turn a little more until I was just over the stall. I could see the flashes of his guns as he opened fire. As well as turning as steeply as possible, with the help of a little flap, I began to gain what height I could.

From the way the German was handling his aircraft it was obvious I was dealing with a very experienced pilot. I had a horrible feeling that he would probably shoot me down, so provided he didn't kill me I needed as much height as possible in order to bale out.

"I never took my eyes off him. For what seemed like hours but in reality was probably only about fifteen or twenty minutes he kept at me, every now and then pulling his nose in a little tighter and opening fire. Every time he did this a funny tingling feeling ran up and down my spine. I could clearly see the flashes of his guns. Eventually he either ran out of ammunition or patience and disappeared from sight. Still in a steep climbing turn I glanced to my right and there he was again, level with me and not far off my right wing tip, his face clearly visible. He nodded, saluted and disappeared. What a relief. I could hardly believe I had survived.

"Since I was now alone in my piece of sky, I tried to call up the other pilots but found I could not speak. Unconsciously, during the engagement, my mouth was open and apparently I was huffing and puffing the whole time. My mouth was completely dry, absolutely no saliva. Looking back on this incident, I sometimes wonder whether the attacking pilot was the famous Hans-Joachim Marseille the German ace. . . . I read somewhere after the war that on one occasion he expressed admiration for a pilot who had eluded him. Was I that pilot?"[7]

Ron Cundy

Marseille In The Theater

How well known was Marseille to DAF personnel in the desert? Apparently not so well. Although there is little indication that some Allied pilots may have heard of Marseille, this information did not readily make its way down to individual squadrons. Fanciful stories abound of how pilots knew of one another and hoped to duel with each other in the skies. This was more than likely not the case. Without any significant markings or exceptional paint schemes, most DAF pilots were too concerned with surviving to

Formal photograph of the dashing Ron Cundy, (DFC, DFM, MID) *Courtesy of Ron Cundy*

Excellent color photograph of a tired looking Marseille taken during September 1942. *Courtesy of author*

notice individual aircraft numbers painted on the Messerschmitt fuselages. In the desert not too much differentiated one German fighter from another. Unlike Erich Hartmann's black tulip on the nose of his Messerschmitt or von Richthofen's blood red aircraft, there was absolutely nothing unique or distinguishable about any of Marseille's aircraft except for the growing victory tally on his rudder.

> "Marseille is the best the Germans have here. He flies a Bf 109 like the others, but he flies better than they. Always in the forefront. He attacks with only a few machines. Do not allow yourself to become involved in wild dogfights. Make your attacks quickly. You must see that you can attack him frontally or from the side before he is in a position to maneuver. . ."[8]
>
> British Communiqué

Author's Note: This communiqué, if accurate, is interesting, in that it hints at the German use of the *Rotte* and *Schwarm* to attack the larger DAF formations. What is missing, however, is any indication of how a pilot is to know he is in the presence of "The Great One."

> "We did not hear much about the German pilots, or rumours that some of them were building up large scores, but we did hear of Marseille as their leading pilot, although we were not aware of meeting him in the air other than to vaguely wonder if a particularly tough opponent had been he."[9]
>
> N.F. Duke

> "I don't recall ever having heard the names of any of our opponents in the Desert or anything about them personally in fact, though I guess my feeling was a very impersonal one altogether."[10]
>
> G.C. Keefer

Interesting photograph of Marseille. He wears the Knight's Cross with Oak Leaves and Swords, and yet the rudder clearly shows 101 victories. This photograph was likely taken immediately upon his return to the desert following his summer leave. *Courtesy of author*

Believe it or Not

"Among Marseille's opponents was a British Wing Commander who had formerly been based on Malta. Shot down by Marseille, he told the Germans after his capture: 'I had just come from Malta and he was all I heard about. They told amazing stories about him in the officer's mess and I longed to meet Marseille. Finally I declared high-spiritedly: Want to bet that I can get him? After all I was one of the best Royal Air Force pilots stationed on Malta. A few days later I got my chance. I took off with a squadron to attack German airfields. The devil knows, we were at about 4,000 meters, when one of my people reported: 'Germans from out of the sun!' And then they were upon us.'

"There was a wild dogfight. My adjutant shot down a Messerschmitt. The pilot swung to earth beneath his parachute. I heard the voice of another of my men: 'There he is. .! Watch out. . ! Mar. . .' There was a crash. I felt my stricken aircraft lose height and I saw Marseille sitting behind me. A thought raced through my head: If he fires now I'm finished. But the fellow didn't fire. He just sat behind me, as if he would have enjoyed seeing me simply fly into the ground. For what could I do in this situation?'

Suddenly I saw him rock his wings. Now he's going to tear my wings off, I said to myself. More instinctively than deliberately, I threw back the cockpit hood and climbed out. At that moment I saw Marseille pull up. He circled round me a few times, waggled his wings again – I even think he waved – and then I landed. Yes, and now I'm here.'

"The Englishman took a deep breath. 'A damned fair lad. He could easily have killed me. . .but he didn't do it.'"[11]

British Wing Commander, unknown

Author's Note: This story, although interesting to read, is highly unlikely, and probably the product of wishful thinking. This account is made without any supporting data, dates, locations, or names, and as previously stated, without a significantly different paint scheme on his Messerschmitt, how was a DAF pilot to know Marseille was in the opposite formation? If this British Wing Commander's statement that he was one of the best RAF pilots stationed in Malta is true, it is likely this story helped ease the pain being bested in aerial combat. After all, if you were almost shot down and thought of yourself as a better than average pilot, would you rather claim to be shot down by an unknown pilot or by the best the *Luftwaffe* had to offer? I like to think this story fits in the category of interesting story but needs more information to verify. One of my good Commonwealth friends was not so generous in his opinion, and said that this story was pure "Twaddle." I do not believe the proper American translation is printable here.

7

Stories

As with any legendary figure, true, fanciful, and embellished stories abound regarding their alleged deeds and actions. Marseille is of course no exception. As the saying goes, "When legend and history contradict one another, print the legend." There are numerous stories surrounding Marseille that have helped make his legend grow. Although many of these stories are unfortunately unsubstantiated, they still give us a glimpse into Marseille's personality and life values. For example, there is the story of Marseille coming to the aid of an elderly Jewish woman being bullied by a group of Hitler Youths in Berlin, as well as the unverified accusation that Marseille may have tried to run away with his fiancée Hanne-Lies after being confronted with Hitler's

Marseille discusses tactics with Gerhard Homuth. *Courtesy of E & C Collection*

Marseille following another sortie. Not many photos show Marseille with his sleeves rolled down. *Courtesy of E and C Collection*

plan for the Jews during his summer leave in 1942. Other assertions, such as his airplane never skidding in a turn or his airplane never being hit by enemy fire, are simply untrue claims.

Yet there remain other stories, those that are substantiated, which do serve to bolster our perceptions of Marseille. There is the story of Marseille "calling his shot" during a conversation with members of his squadron in which during the hectic month of June 1942, Marseille was in a race to reach the 100 victory milestone. In this conversation Marseille, like Babe Ruth pointing to the upper decks with his bat, boldly claimed he would shoot down his 100th airplane on Wednesday, 17 June 1942. He didn't fail.

Likewise, there have been stories witnessed by dozens of people surrounding his flying acumen. Spectators claimed he picked up handkerchiefs suspended from poles with the wingtip of his airplane, cut a ribbon with the tail of his airplane while flying inverted only feet above the ground, and awed his squadron mates with aerial demonstrations above the airfield. On 8 February 1942 Marseille was attacked by 5 Hurricanes of 274 Squadron while he was trying to land at his base in Martuba. Turning to face his attackers alone, Marseille downed two Hurricanes and drove off the remaining three while the entire contingent of JG 27 stood below and watched the incredible display of airmanship.

In addition to the already legendary combat stories, there are more personal and insightful glimpses into Marseille's character. During one of the many interviews I conducted with Herr Friedrich Körner, one conversation centered around the death of *Oberfeldwebel* Hermann Förster (2/ JG 27, 7 victories) who, after being shot down near Tmimi, Libya, on 14 December 1941, bailed out and was killed while in his parachute. Following his death, pilots of I /JG 27 gathered together in order to discuss reprisals, if any, against Allied pilots. Friedrich Körner said, "Yes, this was real wide in the squadrons. There were some who said that one should consider this. If they do it, why shouldn't we? I think Neumann, no Woldenga [Major Bernhard Woldenga, JG 27 Kommodore: 23 June 1941 – 7 June 1942], he said no further discussion. We don't do it. It is not our, uh, it is not the way we act. No further discussion went on and this was never done. I never heard of a single action like that."[1] When I asked if Marseille was part of these heated discussions, he said that Marseille, like most of the unit's pilots, vehemently refused to shoot pilots in their parachutes, no matter what orders may have been handed down.

Each of these stories, the unsubstantiated as well as Fritz Körner's recollections, illustrates the honorable mindset of Marseille. Of all the "unsubstantiated" stories surrounding

Marseille, however, there is likely no other episode in the desert war more endearing than the following. When I say unsubstantiated, I say this because Wing Commander Geoffrey Morley-Mower, a British tactical reconnaissance Hurricane pilot with 451 Squadron RAAF, tells an intriguing story that to date has not been reported from the German side. This leaves the reader wondering if the German pilot in question was indeed Hans Marseille. I believe Marseille is the pilot in this story because no other German would have had the incentive to do what this pilot did. There is no doubt the following event occurred. Witnessed by many and reported by a credible source, the only question is whether Marseille was actually involved.

In the late afternoon on 13 September 1941, Flight Lt. Pat Byers took off in his Hurricane IIC to reconnoiter an area where earlier in the day Erwin Rommel's forces had taken a severe beating. Flying alone without a wingman, Byers headed directly into the setting sun to locate Rommel's *Panzers*. Unknown to Byers, Marseille and Rainer Pöttgen were prowling the skies on a *Freie Jagd*. Although specific details of the ensuing combat are unknown, it has been confirmed that Marseille shot down Byers and, although severely burned, Byers was able to parachute to safety. Below is the event as written by one of the men who watched this entire event unfold. This story is repeated in its entirety with the permission of the late Mr. Morley-Mower from his book *Messerschmitt Roulette*:

"There was great tension in the Squadron all day. Groups of pilots sat in the mess tent drinking tea and discussing the non return of the two Australians. My reaction was to steer clear and keep busy. I volunteered for any flying that was going and spent the rest of the afternoon delivering a Hurricane for its routine inspection at our base landing ground at Qasaba and fetching back a serviceable one. It must have been six O'clock when I taxied in, handed over the kite to a servicing team and walked up to the mess for a drink. Wizard, Doc Reid, Molly, Hugh Davies and Pat Byers were in session, looking serious. Wizard who was on the outskirts of the group, spoke to me.

"Horrocks (Brigadier B.G. Horrocks, 13 Corps) wants a late sortie. Rommel has turned back and seems to be crossing the wire again. (Author's Note: The Wire was a long barbed wire fortification that marked the frontier between Libya and Egypt) But it may be a feint. The old soldiers at Corps Headquarters don't trust the bugger. I've been objecting to a late sortie because it's too dangerous with the *Luftwaffe* out in full force. Unnecessary too because Rommel's taken a tremendous pounding all day and is obviously going back with his tail between his legs. But Horrocks pulled rank. Pat Byers has volunteered to do it.

Yellow 14 ready for combat. *Courtesy of E & C Collection*

From *Signal*, September 1942. Field Marshall Erwin Rommel, the *Desert Fox*. *Courtesy of author*

"'I can't see how a couple of squadrons of medium bombers could possibly stop a tank force of that size,' I said. 'Maybe Horrocks is right.'

"Wizard laughed and made an ironical victory sign.

"'The Marylands caught them refueling. Absolute luck. Ed Kirkham says there was black smoke a mile high. Carmichael's just come in and says they may have lost half their armor. They're toddling off home now. I don't see the necessity for another sortie.'"

"It was extraordinary, I thought, that Rommel had not coordinated his refueling with the Messerschmitt squadrons. Or maybe he had, but our fighters had driven them off. We didn't know. We were the eyes of the army and knew nothing of our own fighter and bomber operations at all. Beyond, of course, what we could actually observe for ourselves. Later on I became very uncomfortable about this.

"Ray Hudson, who had been detailed to cover Pat, came in, his handsome face set in frustration.

"'My kite's unserviceable,' he said. 'The sergeant's going to get another checked and re-fueled. It'll take twenty minutes.'

"'I've got to go,' said Pat.

"'But you can't go without me,' said Ray, pleadingly. 'For Christ's sake, it can wait twenty minutes, can't it?'"

"'I'm going now. A cover won't be much help.'

"Pat was leaning forward in his canvas chair, talking quickly in his characteristic splutter. His round face red with sunburn.

"'We've all done a sortie today,' he said. 'You can't see a bloody thing out there when the sun gets low. A cover wouldn't do much. I'd have as good a chance on my own.'

"'If it's going to be tricky out there, you need two covers not one,' I said. 'Wait a bit and I'll come too.' I didn't mean my offer very seriously. I was just arguing for safe procedures. Pat stood up, smiled, waved his hand at us and walked out of the tent.

"Pat took off at six twenty for a sortie that should have taken thirty minutes at most, for the column was less than forty miles from our landing ground. Ray Hudson took off in pursuit a quarter of an hour later. By 7:30 neither had returned and Wizard came into the dining tent where I was eating to ask me to fly a back up sortie. Horrocks was adamant that the Army Commander must know the position and direction at nightfall.

"'Don't kill yourself to count anything,' he said, apologetically. 'Just check that he's on his way home. I wish I'd stopped Pat from going without a cover.'

"'Easier said than done,' I replied. 'Pat was in a dramatic mood.'

"I took Ken Whalley with me, thinking that if two Australians had gone to their eternal reward, it might be equitable to offer a couple of Englishmen. I was full of morbid thoughts, feeling like an understudy who is informed at very short notice that he is to play *Hamlet*.

[Author's Note: 451 Squadron RAAF consisted of pilots from most of the Commonwealth countries. According to Mr. Morely-Mower, at times there was quite a bit of animosity and lack of trust between pilots from the different countries. He often felt compelled to uphold the honor of the Englishmen amid his tough and courageous Aussie counterparts.]

"The problem of a late evening sortie in good weather was that the position of the sun, low down on the horizon, made it difficult to see the fighters. They could hang up in the sun and have a good view of intruding aircraft while being invisible themselves. Staring into the sun was counterproductive. My logbook entry reads, 'Evening TAC/R 1 hr 15.' And my penciled annotation 'Jerries return to wire.' The comparative length of the flight, from a landing ground only fifty miles from the Libyan border, shows the caution with which I approached it. What I did was to pierce the wire well south of the area of reconnaissance, get up sun as far as I reasonably could in the empty desert, and then fly back towards the column down the well worn track called the *Trigh Capuzzo*. The sun was by this hour so low on the horizon that I had a fairly good view of the western sky in the fading light. I stared anxiously into the blankness for fighters but could see nothing. Perhaps they were satisfied with shooting down Pat Byers. Was the show over just as the understudy was entering stage left? Underneath me the desert was dark purple and I could see the column, a long pink-tinged dust cloud to the north, still heading west towards the frontier. In the distance it looked like a giant slug undulating across the vast lonely landscape. I approached gingerly, still fearing the deceptive quality of the evening light.

"'I don't' see any fighters, do you, Ken?'

"'They've all gone home, sir.'

"Whalley was inconsistent in his form of address. With a civilian disregard of military convention he sometimes called me 'Geoff' and at other times 'sir.'

"I flew by the column to make a count. There were sixty-four tanks among the more numerous soft-skinned vehicles and I saw again, at closer quarters, the long barrels of the 88mm guns, drawn by stubby tractors. With the host in such turbulent motion I didn't expect to be shot at and they seemed to take no heed of our presence overhead. Close up, I could see that they were strung out in several straggly lines and many of the trucks were following independent paths.

"Color was leaking away from the scene and the sun no longer tinged the dust they threw so abundantly into the air. The leading tanks were just riding up to the faint line of the Libyan frontier. Rommel's probe was over. I turned steeply towards the darkened east and made for home.

"It became almost dark as we flew back. I turned on my navigation lights so that Ken Whalley could see me. Slow on the uptake, he didn't respond by turning his own on.

"'Turn on your nav lights, Ken,' I said.

"'OK, Geoff.'

"His lights flicked on, looking very bright and close. Six oil flares had been laid out to mark the landing path and we got on the ground without fuss. Few lights were showing on the base. Most people turned in when it became dark.

"When I swung down from the cockpit Hugh Davies was there with his staff car.

"'Glad to see you made it," he shouted. 'Is it still heading west?'

"'Yes. It's just crossing the wire, heading for Capuzzo. I've marked the position on my map.'

"'Thank God for that. I'll get on the blower to the Corps.'

"'Did Pat get back?'

"'No. Ray Hudson went after him but couldn't find him. Ray got back about an hour ago.'

"Wizard, Molly, Doc Reid and a few other anxious souls waited up in the mess tent, hoping to hear the engines of Pat Byers' Hurricane overhead and chewing over the day's excitements. We all knew he'd been shot down, though. There had been a strange atmosphere about his sacrificial gesture, as if he'd foreseen his own fate and seized the opportunity to prevent the involvement of another pilot.

"Two days later, just as dawn was breaking, I was awakened by the sharp crack of a Bofors anti-aircraft gun situated fifty yards away. I scrambled out of my tent to see two Messerschmitts motoring in to our strip as if to make a landing. They were below 50 feet, flying slowly. The other seven guns of our airfield defenses opened up a second later at these sitting targets. MEs could not be mistaken for friendly aircraft. They were smaller than any plane we flew and typically screamed across the sky with a high-pitched engine noise that was quite distinctive. On this occasion their noise was muted and they lost height steadily, heading straight into our landing area. Gunfire petered out when they were too low to attack without risking damage to our parked Hurricanes. Half way up the strip a dark object fluttered to the ground. The MEs opened up their engines and snarled off, weaving violently, followed by a pattern of Bofors shells whose white puffs curtained the dawn sky.

"The squadron commander's car drove slowly down the strip and we saw Wizard get out and pick up the package. I ran across to the mess where the cooks were already active, dishing out mugs of weak tea to the assembled officers. Seeing the dainty shapes of these gnatlike aircraft flying slowly through our Bofors fire to drop something that did not explode was beyond our comprehension. We hardly exchanged a word, staring at Wizard's distant figure in the half light.

"When he eventually drove over he was all smiles, holding a handwritten sheet of paper over his head in ironical imitation of our least popular politician.

"'You won't believe this, gents,' he said. 'I feel like Mister bloody Chamberlain bringing peace in our time! I'll read it out to you. It's signed by the Messerschmitt flight commander.'

"However, when Wizard began to read the message his face became grave and his voice, more Welsh than ever, took on the cadences of a chapel preacher.

WE ARE SORRY TO REPORT THAT LT. BYERS WAS SHOT DOWN ON SEPTEMBER 14 BY AIRCRAFT OF THIS SQUADRON. HE WAS BADLY BURNED WHILE ESCAPING FROM THE COCKPIT. HE IS NOW IN DERNA HOSPITAL AND WE HAVE HOPES FOR HIS RECOVERY. WE WISH TO EXPRESS THE REGRETS OF THE LUFTWAFFE.

"A cheer went up. There were some expressions of amazement. Then we dispersed in a subdued manner to our bivouacs. We all feared burning above every other disaster.

"A couple of weeks later, when I was away from the unit, the message-bearing Messerschmitts returned. I wish I could say that our anti-aircraft defenses held their fire in homage to a chivalrous foe, but the guns were under orders and belted away at the slow flying targets. Another package was dropped and the Messerschmitts disappeared (to everyone's relief) unharmed. This time the message was that Pat had died of his injuries and to once again present the regrets of the *Luftwaffe*.

"The affair left the squadron stunned. It was such an extraordinary courtesy, almost medieval in character. It made nonsense of our built-up hatred of the Germans. It even made hard feelings impossible. World War I was fought in the infancy of the flying era, when merely taking to the air was an adventure and every landing in those unstable early biplanes a threat to life and limb. Out of that conflict a tradition of respect for the enemy's courage and skill had grown up between the German and British air forces. Only the most daring spirits turned up for those first tourneys in the sky; and when a pilot fell to earth the victor did not triumph over him. When Baron von Richthofen was shot down on April 20 [21], 1918, his body was buried with full military honors, six RAF pilots bearing his coffin on their shoulders. As late as September, 1941, this feeling was clearly not dead.

"We did not realize, nor did the Germans, that September, 1941 was to be a turning point in the war. Hitler was saying that England's neck was to be wrung like a chicken, and many Germans may have felt secure enough in the final outcome of the war to harbor genuine sympathy for their British cousins. When the Americans declared war in December, the balance of forces changed so dramatically in our favor that it is unlikely such a gesture could have been repeated.

"Of all the episodes in my war this remains the most amazing, and over the years I have tried to imagine the face and bearing of the *Luftwaffe* officer who risked his life and the life of his wingman on two occasions simply that Pat Byers' fate should not become a mere statistic. Whoever he was, I thought, he was determined to personalize the conflict and to put his own imprint on the passing tragedy.

"In 1992 while examining a copy of *Fighters Over The Desert* by Christopher Shores and Hans Ring, I was finally able to identify the messenger. . . In the appendices of the book Hans-Joachim Marseille's extraordinary career of 158 victories, 151 of them in the Western Desert, is recorded. He was twenty-one and a *Hauptman* in the famous Messerschmitt squadron I/ JG 27 when he shot down Pat Byers. [Authors Note: Actually he was still a *Leutnant* at this time] A year later he was dead. I am pleased to be able to add this grace note to his history, for it is a moral certainty that it was Marseille who dropped the messages. Not only was he crazy enough to fly through our anti-aircraft defenses, who else would have had the motive for delivering a message about Byers except the man who had destroyed him?

[Author's Note: Remember Marseille's words to his mother in the letter dated 24-08-40.]

"The feelings of brotherhood expressed here do not aspire to the level of Marseille's quixotic missions, but he was no ordinary pilot and no ordinary man. . . .

"His greatest deeds, only revealed by the patient work of scholars and the accident of my own involvement as an eye witness, were almost private and purely compassionate. He must have had an easy shot at Pat's lone Hurricane, diving out of the sun, steady in the

Marseille in June 1942. *Courtesy of E & C Collection*

evening air. As he watched the aircraft go into its blazing descent to earth and the struggles of the pilot to extricate himself, he must have felt both guilt and compassion. Did he visit Pat in his bed at Derna Hospital? I think so. Did something in Pat's deplorable condition or the courage of his responses touch him so deeply that he felt obliged to act as he did? We will never know the details, but the facts as they stand do him more honor than his 158 victories in the air."[2]

Geoffrey Morley-Mower

Mr. Morley-Mower, English professor at James Madison University, died in 2005.

Author's Note: There is something intriguing about this story. When reading the words other men used to describe Marseille, this story makes perfect sense. Comments like "bravado," "exceptionally kind," "refined sense of honor," and "a mixture of the fresh air of Berlin and French champagne – a gentleman," all further place Marseille's behavior and attitude in a class of his own. Although to my knowledge there are no German records to verify Mr. Morley-Mower's story, there is no reason to doubt the event occurred. And if Marseille was one of the pilots who flew over the enemy airfield to drop a note expressing the regrets of the *Luftwaffe*, what better tribute to him than these words of a former enemy?

"It may be difficult for most people to understand today that the British flyers always enjoyed our respect and sympathy. This is more conceivable if one knows that in all German pilots' messes in peace time the old veterans of World War One always spoke of the British pilots, of air combat with them, and of the British fairness in the most positive way. Many German pilots could speak English better than any other foreign language and were thus always quickly on good terms with captured pilots."[3]

Edu Neumann

The following story comes from the war diary of RCAF fighter pilot Nelson E. Gilboe. It is an interesting read, and the background for this story is that F/Lt Gilboe claims that during an air-to-air confrontation on 3 November 1942, he had a midair collision with the 109 flown by Marseille at which time he was killed. Pay close attention to the final paragraph of the narrative. This chapter has been reproduced with the permission of Mr. Gilboe's widow, Mrs. Betty Gilboe:

"Chapter 19: Two's a Crowd

The battle at El Alamein had been raging for more than ten days. It was apparent now that the Axis forces

451 Squadron RAAF, November 1941. In this photograph are five of the people mentioned in this story. 1. Stan "Doc" Reid. 2. Ray Hudson, the pilot scheduled to fly with Byers, but was unable due to a broken aircraft. 3. Ed Kirkham (holding the dog), reported the destruction of much of Rommel's armor. 4. Squadron Leader R.D. "Wizard" Williams, retrieved the note dropped by Marseille. 5. Geoffrey Morley-Mower, author of the story. *Courtesy of Geoffrey Morley-Mower*

PO Nelson Gilboe, author of the poem "The Ace" seen in the front of this book, and the pilot who was informed by a German officer that it was his plane that killed Marseille in a mid-air collision on 4 November 1942. *Courtesy of Michel Lavigne*

would have to pull back. There was no longer any resistance from the German army and the Luftwaffe had almost disappeared from the skies. In the last few days, although we had been flying two and three sorties a day, we were encountering fewer and fewer enemy aircraft. The coastal road running between El Alamein and Mersa Matruh was solid with German utility vehicles and walking troops making their way back to the west. What had started as an organized retreat was turning into a full-scale rout.

"At 0600, on the morning of November the third, we took off on what was to be a routine sweep of the coastal road to harass the retreating German and Italian troops. Since there was no longer much resistance from the German *Luftwaffe*, our Squadron Leader Devonish elected to lead this mission himself. He led the four Warhawks on the bottom flight while Edwards [Canadian James "Stocky" Edwards] took lead of medium cover. I had my section of four on top cover again. Normally, in these early morning attacks, we would fly a short ways past our selected target then make a 180 degree turn and attack from west to east along the coastal road. In this way, although we would be flying into the sun as we concentrated on our target, we would have a clear view of what might be behind us if we ourselves became the attacked.

"However, on this occasion and no one will ever know why, S/L Devonish picked out a target on the road in front of us and ordered the squadron to begin their descent. To watch out behind us we looked directly into the rising sun, so it was almost impossible to be sure we were safe. The leading section of four had already reached a level close to the road, with Edwards' section about five hundred yards behind them. My section brought up the rear about the same distance behind Edwards. Suddenly, events that had seemed to be routine, took a dramatic change. Within the time space of about two or three seconds, a German pilot would lose his life, and mine would forever be changed.

"There had been no warning from anyone that 'Rats' were in the vicinity. I happened to glance straight up and sitting there about a hundred feet above me and a little ahead of me was a single Messerschmitt 109 who was making a diving attack on Edwards in the section ahead of me. At the instant that I saw him, he was seen also by Edwards who looked back and saw a large white spinner of a 109 sitting right on his tail. Edwards screamed into the radio:

"'Turnabout right, turnabout right, go! go! go!'

"But it was too late. I had already started up, firing as I went, to intercept the 109 before he could fire his 20 mm cannon. As Edwards started to turn, the German turned with him and in doing so, he came directly into my line of flight. I saw the black crosses on the bottom side of his wings and I knew that I was going squarely between them. There was a soft sound of a 'whoomf' as my left wing cut through his fuselage, neatly cutting his plane in half while at the same time shearing off most of my own wing on that side. The 109 went straight down into the ground, while I continued in an upward direction with the help of the speed at which I was traveling before the accident happened. My aircraft was now tumbling upwards completely out of control. I glanced quickly outside the cockpit and when I saw the wing was gone, I knew that all was lost. I then rolled back the canopy and once again I released myself from my harness and was thrown violently out of the cockpit by an invisible centrifugal force.

"I felt no pain as I left the aircraft and a broken antenna wire slid along my thigh inflicting a deep gash in my upper leg. When I pulled the ripcord and the 'chute opened I first looked down to see how close I was to the ground. Not very far! Then I noticed my torn pant leg was covered with blood and I wondered how badly I was hurt. Maybe my leg was broken. What would happen when I hit the ground? My mind raced with all the possibilities.

As I looked down towards the spot where I would likely land, I saw an Italian soldier calmly set aside the pan in which he was preparing his breakfast, and he picked up his rifle as he waited for me to arrive. Other soldiers were also running toward the area. This possibly would be the end for me. They had to be upset with us. We had been strafing them every hour or two for the past week. They would not be happy to see me.

"In a few moments I had hit the ground and there being no wind the 'chute collapsed around me. I was immediately surrounded by a half dozen Italians who had their rifles pointed at my head waiting for someone to make the next move. Almost immediately, a German staff car appeared on the scene, and a German officer approached all the while shouting orders at the soldiers who surrounded me. The German took off my shirt and wrapped it tightly around my bleeding leg. An Italian took off my shoes and I never saw them again.

"The German then pointed at a nearby truck and ordered me to be put into the passenger seat. He then designated a driver from the group and sent the others away to continue with whatever they had been doing before I had arrived. Then he went on his way as well.

"Now things were quieting down a little and I began to get my wits about me. I was in a GMC stake truck which the Germans had probably captured on a previous campaign. I had an Italian driver who spoke no English but had been ordered to take me to a nearby field hospital. There was only one problem. This Italian had never driven a truck or any other vehicle and was completely dumbfounded as to how to proceed. With the use of some sign language, and physically helping him to shift the gears, we did manage to get the vehicle started and rolling in one of the lower gears. Then he steered us wildly around various obstacles until we arrived at the Red Cross tent about a mile from where we had started. When we stopped. I patted him on the back and thanked him over and over again. Not so much for bringing me here, but for not killing us both in doing so.

"Some orderlies took me from the truck and laid me on a stretcher. There were wounded men lying on stretchers all around the tent. I was taken directly inside where I saw two parallel rows of operating tables with a man's body on each one. A basket, partially filled with body parts was near the door. Doctors and orderlies moved swiftly from one table to the other checking on the progress of each patient. I was soon on one the tables myself and again I began to wonder what was going to happen to me. I still felt no pain. Could my wound be so serious that I would be put ahead of all those I saw outside lying in the sun? A doctor came over to my table and had an orderly remove my shirt bandage. He then cut away the torn parts of my pant leg to get a better look at how bad the situation was. It looked bad to me. All I saw was torn flesh and white parts of a bone . I closed my eyes and looked away.

"The doctor asked me if I spoke German. I told him: 'Nein' He had noticed the 'Canada' patch on my shirt and asked me in French: 'Parlez-vous Francais?' 'Oui' I answered, glad now that we would at least be able to converse. 'Your wound is very bad' he said in French, 'and it is very high on your leg. It has also been covered with sand and flies for some time. There is a very good chance for an infection. It would be my suggestion that we remove the leg now before gangrene sets in, because if that happens, we possibly could not save your life.' I must have paled at that suggestion. I could not imagine myself without a leg. 'No' I said. 'Please leave the leg and do what you can without taking it off. I will take my chances with an infection.' He shrugged his shoulders and said 'Well, it's up to you, I am too busy to argue about it.'

"With that he ordered me to be given a sedative, which put me to sleep for a short time. When I awoke, I was still on the table, but my leg had been cleaned of all loose flesh and they had dusted it heavily with sulfur powder. They then put a dry bandage over the wound and wrapped it loosely with a gauze tape. The orderlies then went about other business and I did not see the doctor again. Before I was removed from the hospital tent, a German officer accompanied by two NCOs came up to me and introduced themselves. They asked me if I knew of *Hauptmann* Joachim Marseille. I said that I did not. They then told me that he had been killed when my aircraft had collided with his. I offered my condolences and they went away. It was not until I had reported this incident to the authorities in the prison camp that I learned that he was one of the *Luftwaffe's* leading aces with more than 150 victories to his credit. It was later reported by the German press that Marseille had been killed when his aircraft caught fire in the air and his parachute had failed to open. The real truth will probably never be known. But I think it was strange that a German officer with two of his men would have taken the time to come and report this to me when they must have had many more important things to do."[4]

Author's Note: The end of Mr. Gilboe's diary states the following:

"1942 - Assigned to duty in North Africa flying RCAF P40F. He had two kills to his credit when his P-40 mid-aired Germany's top ace flying an ME109, killing HANS JOACHIM MARSEILLE and bailing out with minor injuries to himself. He was officially credited with 3 enemy planes including Marseille. Gilboe was 19 years old at the time.

"The action against Marseille took place in Nov. about the 3rd (the German report of September is inaccurate; also Marseille's ME109 exploded, so the German report of the ace's parachute failing to open, is true in the respect that Marseille never had a chance to pull the rip-cord.)"

Undoubtedly this is an interesting claim. History shows us that personal accounts are often times blurred through the sands of time. Although there can be no doubt that N.E. Gilboe did collide with a Bf-109 during air combat, official documents show that this being the aircraft flown by Hans Marseille is highly unlikely.

In Canadian historian Michel Lavigne's book *Kittyhawks Over the Sands: The Canadians and The RCAF Americans*, he discusses in some detail the air combat described by N.E. Gilboe. Lavigne states that this combat actually took place on 4 November and involved the Messerschmitt 109 G-2 flown by Horst Schlick. Following the collision, like Gilboe, Schlick was able to get out of his aircraft and survived the collision. The website containing this account likewise claims the "German report of September is inaccurate," but all documents to include Marseille's death certificate, Neumann's accident report, and Marseille's burial in Derna on 2 October clearly point to the date of his death more than a full month before the Gilboe incident.

There can be no doubt of the gallant service provided by F/Lt N.E. Gilboe, and absolutely no reason to doubt the late Mr. Gilboe's recollection of this event. I believe these Germans likely did approach him and mention Marseille in the manner in which they did. I also believe they were lying or simply spreading misinformation. I don't believe it possible for any German soldier in North Africa in the summer of 1942 to have not been made fully aware of Marseille's death on 30 September, not 4 November.

Star of Afrika

Smoke in the cockpit,
Have to get out.
Make the quick call:
I can't mess about.

Canopy jettisoned,
Dive over the side.
Smash in the ribs,
with the tail collide.

Pain in my body,
Falling through space.
A terrible end,
for the world's greatest ace.

It was always so good:
I'm known far and wide.
I'm young and I'm handsome
and awesome besides.

How could this happen,
Especially to me?
My God, I'm too good,
On that all agree.

Farewell my 3rd *Staffel*
and JG 27.
Farewell my dear comrades,
As I plummet through heaven.

No Tommy could beat me,
In the skies over sand.
The best of the best
Eyes, head, heart and hands.

No Hurri or Kittyhawk,
Put a round through my skin.
It took Yellow Fourteen,
...to do poor Jochen in!

Courtesy of Barrett Tillman

PO Nelson Gilboe. *Courtesy of Michel Lavigne*

8

Death

Now more than 60 years removed from the end of the Second World War, we continue to attribute subjective and sometimes irrational characteristics and values to those who fought in the war. It is true that we often intentionally demonize our enemies and give them characteristics contrary to reality. It therefore makes it easier to hate them while we can freely justify our own actions and objectives. For example, when we watch war movies depicting that period, the Germans are usually portrayed as heartless, ruthless killers, hell bent on destroying everything and everybody in sight. We lose sight of the fact that many of these soldiers were nothing more than reluctant young men, doing a job that their counterparts from other parts of the world were also required to do. The

After nearly 18 months of continuous combat in the desert, the once handsomely chiseled features of Marseille began to give way to the haggard countenance of a young man who has endured too much, too early. This photograph, taken in September 1942, shows evidence of this. It is hard to imagine that Marseille is only 22 years old in this photograph. Many felt that Marseille could not continue going at his current pace. Something had to give. *Courtesy of the author*

German soldier in many respects was no different than the Allied soldier he fought in the sky, on the ground, or at sea. The corrupt regime they fought for was undoubtedly evil, worthy of defeat, and without question, units existed within the German military that had shameful histories. Those units were the exception to the rule. It is on a personal level, however, where many of these young men had the same hopes, fears, and dreams as did their enemy counterparts.

As Marseille continued his fight in the desert, he often suffered greatly with the constant thoughts and reminders of death and killing, such that he often slept little and spent many nights alone in the desert thinking. As the strain of constant combat tore at him physically, spiritually, and emotionally, his features began to show the haggard countenance of a man who had seen too much war; too soon. Keep in mind that Marseille may have been the top scoring pilot in North Africa, but at the time of his death, he was still only 22 years of age. As the tactical, operational, and personal pressures mounted, sizeable cracks in his external façade became more evident. *The Star of Africa* was only human after all.

"What are you thinking about, Jochen?" asked Stahlschmidt quietly.

"About that last Tommy I shot down today," answered Marseille, his voice sounding completely unnatural. "I was just thinking how it feels when you're plummeting down in your crate; maybe still conscious, knowing that it will soon be all over."[1]

Hans-Joachim Marseille

"I am flying, then suddenly it gets dark all around me. I know I'm falling, but I don't feel anything. And before I hit the ground, it's already over."[2]

Hans-Joachim Marseille

"If fate had not caught up with him near El Alamein, it's a fair bet he would have been killed later attacking the Americans' four-engine bombers."[3]

Werner Schrör

These are the two last known photographs of Marseille alive, taken Tuesday night, 29 September. In the first candid photograph, the strain of September's combat and the death of his best friend Hans "Fifi" Stahlschmidt is clearly evidenced in his face. By the time the second photo has been taken, Marseille's countenance has returned to normal, his young face cheerful and playful. There would be no more live photographs of one of the most photographed men in Germany. *Courtesy of the Bundesarchiv Bild 101I-445-1872-03 and 101I-445-1872-02*

30 September 1942

At the height of both the desert war in North Africa and the career of young "Jochen" Marseille, tragedy struck the *Luftwaffe* such that they would never again be a serious threat in North Africa. Scheduled to fly a new Messerschmitt Bf-109 G-2, W.Nr. 14256, Marseille was called upon to once again escort the painfully obsolete Stuka dive bombers against ground targets in Egypt. At 1047, Marseille took off on his final sortie. After completing the escort mission, Marseille and his squadron were directed to intercept a flight of enemy aircraft sighted south of Imayid, Egypt. No contact with the enemy fighters was made, and the flight of Messerschmitts set a course for home.

At 1135 Marseille indicated that he had smoke pouring into his cockpit, and it was becoming difficult to either breathe or see. Other members in the flight urged Marseille to remain with his aircraft for another couple minutes since they were still over enemy-held territory. By 1139 smoke in the cockpit was now unbearable, and Marseille was forced to leave his airplane. Marseille's last radio transmission was, "I've got to get out now. I can't stand it any more."[4] Now over German territory, at approximately 10000 feet, Marseille rolled his aircraft inverted in a standard maneuver to prepare for bailout. Suffering from probable spatial disorientation, possibly toxic hypoxia, as well as being blinded by the smoke in the cockpit, Marseille's aircraft entered an inverted dive with an approximate dive angle of 70 to 80 degrees. At a speed of approximately 400 knots, Marseille left his smoking aircraft. Momentarily hung up on the aerial mast, Marseille's body finally broke free, but unfortunately, the left side of Marseille's chest and groin area struck the tail of his airplane, either killing him instantly or incapacitating him to the point where he was unable to open his parachute. As the other members of Marseille's squadron watched in horror, Jochen's body landed face down 7 km South of Sidi Abd el Rahman, an unfitting end to the "African Eagle" and a foreshadowing of things to come for the *Luftwaffe*.

The Fall of Marseille

> "I've got to get out now. I can't stand it anymore."[5]
> Hans-Joachim Marseille's last words

> "He fell. Fell like a stone."[6]
> Rainer Pöttgen

> "I was at the command post myself and listening to the radio communication between the pilots of the No.3 Squadron. I realised immediately that something serious had happened. I knew while they were still in flight that they were trying to bring Marseille over the lines into our territory while his plane was emitting a lot of smoke. And when it finally got to the point where they told him 'alright, you can get out now', he presumably turned the plane over onto its back, but with the engine at a sharp downward inclination. As he got out, he fell against the tail unit and the whole of his groin area on one side was torn open. We always assumed that this was what caused his death, or if not, that he was unconscious and not even able to make an attempt to open his parachute."[7]
> Edu Neumann

The saddest photograph of all. Following his collision with the tail of his Bf 109 G-2, Marseille plummeted to the desert floor with his chute unopened. Witnesses state that his body impacted the desert floor face down in a prone position. The damage to Marseille's body verifies this claim. A close inspection of the photograph also reveals evidence across his hip indicating the damage from the initial collision with the tail. *Courtesy of Bender Publishing*

Damage to Marseille's skull is clearly evident. *Courtesy of Bender Publishing*

"The pilot lay on his stomach as if asleep. His arms were hidden beneath his body. As I came closer, I saw a pool of blood which had issued from the side of his crushed skull; brain matter was exposed. I then noticed the awful wound above the hip. With certainty, this could not have come from the fall. The pilot must have been slammed into the airplane when bailing out.

"The parachute rested a few meters next to the dead man. The pack which still contained it was torn abut 40 centimeters along its side. White parachute silk spilled out like intestines. The release handle for the parachute had buried itself deep into the sand right next to the dead man. It was still on 'safe'.

"I carefully turned the young pilot over onto his back. The finely cut features of his face below a high forehead were nearly undisturbed. It was the countenance of a tired child.

"I opened the zipper of his flight jacket, saw the Knight's Cross with Oak Leaves and Swords and immediately knew who this was. The paybook also told me: in front of me lay *Hauptmann* Marseille.

"I glanced at the dead man's watch. It had stopped at 1142 hrs.

"I left to get help in order to recover the body. When I returned with some Italian engineers, two of the dead pilot's comrades were already on the scene."[8]

Oberarzt Dr. Bick

Author's Note: Although it doesn't appear in the photographs that Marseille was wearing a flight jacket when he died, Dr. Bick's observations remain sobering.

The Effect of Marseille's Death

"The dangers of allowing one pilot to become such a legend can be seen when Marseille was killed, the death of this one pilot so damaging the morale of a complete Gruppe that it had to be removed from the area for nearly a month."[9]

Christopher Shore and Hans Ring

"This is also mentioned in the book when Marseille was killed in [the] accident. And when he was brought back to the squadron. Captain Franzisket, he took the action, I think Neumann had asked him, because all pilots were down, completely down. Because everybody had seen him jumping out and hitting by his own aircraft. And the parachute didn't open. And Franzisket, brought him back. And in order to overcome this, very dangerous psychological situation, he ordered to put the record, what Marseille liked most, on the recorder. And then he told to the pilots of the number 3 squadron, 'it is useless, life goes on and remember Marseille the best way it is possible. But never let it influence your reaction.'

"I have forgotten the name of this famous record. Marseille was crazy on one of these records. He had listened in Italy and had brought back I think it was in the Bari and he bought the record. And the record was continuously played when Marseille was in his tent. And it, I think it is very well recognized by Franzisket. He said, 'I'll get it. Remember, that was his favorite song. I'll put on the record and so, the situation was softened.'"[10]

Friedrich Körner

"The members of the flight sat at the table in silence. Matthias, Marseille's batman, had disappeared. From the kitchen where he usually worked no sound could be heard. Not until evening did he return from some hiding place or from out of the desert. He was carrying a necklace of shells. He handed it to Poettgen.

"'What is that Matthias?'

"'Fifty-seven shells, sir. Fifty-seven victories since I came to the Captain at the end of August. I have looked for them all one by one. Sometimes it was a long time before I found one that matched, white and beautiful.'

"Matthias was proud but the tears ran down his black cheeks. 'Lay the chain in his grave,' he said, as he turned away and left the tent."[11]

"Nevertheless, all of us had the feeling that our lives were over."[12]

Ludwig Franzisket

"Morale was so low that we needed a personality, someone like *Oberstleutnant* Franzisket and it was he, incidentally, who recovered the body from the desert. In the evening he drove into the camp and gave the order to play the 'Rumba Azul' record. It was Marseille's favorite record. Psychologically speaking, he did the right thing. You pulled yourself together, you covered up your worries and your anger and your fear. You were young, after all, and you could handle the problem. But there was no getting away from the fact that Marseille was the last great 'eagle' of the squadron that was utterly exhausted and really in no condition to put in more service on the front."[13]

Edu Neumann

"When Richthofen was killed in World War 1, they said, 'The front stopped breathing.' And this is what you had to say too after the death of Hans-Joachim Marseille. It touched us all very deeply, incredibly deeply, no matter whether we were army or navy, Italian or German."[14]

Edu Neumann

"His loss was a bitter blow to his compatriots on JG-27 but a blessing to those of us on the other side."[15]

Ron Cundy

Following Marseille's death, *Geschwaderkommodore* Edu Neumann published the following Order of the Day:

"On 30 September 1942 *Hauptmann* Marseille died a pilot's death, unvanquished by the enemy.

Marseille's body lies on a cot beneath the German flag. *Courtesy of Bender Publishing*

Above: A German honor guard stands watch over Marseille's body. *Courtesy of Bender Publishing* Below: Another German honor guard watches over Marseille. *Courtesy of E & C Collection*

One of the lynchpins in 260 Squadron was RAAF F/L Ron Cundy. Cundy had 5 confirmed kills with 2 shared victories. Here he is pictured with his father in the summer of 1942. *Courtesy of Michel Lavigne*

> "It is difficult for us to accept that this bright, cheerful and brave fighter pilot of our *Geschwader* will no longer be with us.
>
> "His victories against our most bitter enemies – the English – are one of a kind. We should be both happy and proud to have counted him among us.
>
> "These beautiful words cannot express what this loss means to us.
>
> "He leaves behind for us our duty to emulate him as a person and a soldier. His spirit will forever be a model for this *Geschwader*."[16]

Burial

> "The burial service took place in the cemetery at Derna, a dignified but at the same time simple affair under the conditions of war. Field Marshal Kesselring spoke first and then it was my turn."[17]
>
> Edu Neumann

> "*Hauptmann* Marseille is fallen. Unbeaten. With his passing, a heroic individual, a marvelous colleague, an artist in the air and the best fighter pilot in the world is gone from our ranks forever."[18]
>
> Generalfeldmarschall Albert Kesselring

The Marseille Pyramid and Dedication

On 22 October 1989, the German Fighter Pilot's Association dedicated a unique tribute to Marseille. On the spot where he fell some 47 years earlier, a pyramid, one improved over a similar monument hastily built by the Italians in 1942, was erected as a lasting tribute to "The Great One." In attendance were many *Luftwaffe* veterans and many of the men who flew with Marseille in North Africa, such as Friedrich Körner and Edu Neumann. President of the Fighter Pilot's Association, Anton Weiler, presided over the ceremony. In part, Anton Weiler said that the Marseille pyramid had nothing to do with "hero worship," and that it was their "duty to remark that the German soldier did his duty with honor and courage."[19] It is a rare instance in these times for Germans to proudly stand before their war dead and make this claim.

The pyramid stands there today as a marker for one of just thousands of men on both sides of the conflict that died in the desert sands of Egypt, Libya, and Tunisia. The simple marker on the pyramid reads: "Here died *Hauptman* Hans-Joachim Marseille: Undefeated"

„**Er fiel unbesiegt.** Auf dem Weg nach Tobruk fanden wir auf dem gut erhaltenen deutsch-italienischen Soldatenfriedhof in Derna das Grab des unvergessenen Jagdfliegers Hans-Joachim Marseille. Als ‚Jäger von Afrika' wurde er seinerzeit zum Begriff für einen ganzen Kriegsschauplatz. Im Zeitraum eines halben Jahres erhielt Marseille die höchsten deutschen Tapferkeitsauszeichnungen und stieg vom Leutnant zum jüngsten Hauptmann der Wehrmacht auf. Nach 158 Luftsiegen erlitt sein Flugzeug Motorschaden. Marseille mußte aussteigen — aber der Fallschirm öffnete sich nicht . . ."

Marseille's grave marker at the Derna cemetery. *Courtesy of Penn Templeman*

This page and following: These three photographs were taken at Marseille's funeral at the German-Italian cemetery in Derna, Libya. *Courtesy of E & C Collection*

Courtesy of Seattle Museum of Flight

Courtesy of E & C Collection

Field Marshal Albert Kesselring. *Courtesy of author*

Final Thoughts

When I first proposed this tribute to Schiffer Publishing, my goal from the beginning was to honor my childhood hero, Hans-Joachim Marseille. As I have gotten older, and hopefully more mature, my study of Marseille has also become more objective, realistic, and honest.

In *Hans-Joachim Marseille: An Illustrated Tribute to the Luftwaffe's "Star of Africa"*, my goal was to introduce the reader to the *Star of Africa* from an angle hopefully not yet explored. Although several biographies have been written, once again I wanted to show the character, personality, and fighter pilot skills as seen, not only through my words and thoughts, but more importantly through the eyes of those that flew with and against Marseille in North Africa. I hope I have accomplished that.

There is one aspect of Marseille's career that I feel must be addressed before I can close out this project. As you have read my words, there can be little doubt that I believe Marseille to be one of the finest fighter pilots of World War II. Not only was he a superlative marksman and talented aerobatic pilot, but his boldness of spirit and tactical insight helped him overcome superior odds on an almost daily basis. Even with all of these facts present, there remains one undeniable truth as to Marseille's record in North Africa.

With the increasing amount of research and data continually making itself available, there can be little doubt that Marseille did over claim while he was in North Africa. Throughout this book I have discussed this phenomenon, and when viewed through the work of men like Michel Lavigne and Russell Brown, it seems rather highly unlikely that all of Marseille's 151 desert claims are valid. But this is where it becomes infinitely sticky.

For those that believe over claiming was strictly related to the *Luftwaffe*, there is much remedial re-thinking to be had. In Michel Lavigne's *Kittyhawks Over the Sands*, he lists the following kill

Postcard of Marseille's pyramid that I purchased at the Marseille-Kaserne in Uetersen in 1991. *Courtesy of author*

totals for P-40 DAF units in North Africa from June 1940 to May 1943 and their corresponding corroboration with German records:

Squadron	Aircraft claimed destroyed	Corroboration with enemy records
94 RAF	23 ½	Around 20
112 RAF	211	100 to 110
250 RAF	128	70 to 80
260 RAF	65 ½	Around 65
3 RAAF	170	90 to 100
450 RAAF	46	Around 35
2 SAAF	96	60 to 70
4 SAAF	56	35 to 45
5 SAAF	68	40 to 50[20]

Units of the 9th USAAF faired little better with the 57th Fighter Group (FG), claiming 128 kills with evidence of 90 to 100, the 79th FG claiming 29 against 20 in German records, and the 324 FG very close, with 28 claims against 25 matches in German records.[21] Note: Failure to corroborate does not mean a victory did not occur, only that a cross referencing of records, at this time, does not substantiate the claim.

As you can imagine, these records translate into inaccuracies among individual pilots as well. For the top six P-40 pilots, only Canadian James "Stocky" Edwards' record shows a verification of over 100 percent. In fact, according to Lavigne, Edwards is the only top ace of World War II whose claims are actually less than those verified by German records. Although his logbook only claims 17 aerial victories (plus several damaged and probable kills), German records show that he actually downed 22 aircraft. As for the other P-40 pilots in the desert, top scoring Australian Clive "Killer" Caldwell's record of 19 1/2 P-40 kills is only 50% to 60% verifiable. British ace Billy Drake's 16 victories are 70% to 80%, while Aussie John L. Waddy's 15 1/2 is respectable 70% to 80% verifiable, and Andrew Barr's 11 P-40 kills are 60% to 70% verifiable.[22] In all, the top scoring P-40 pilots' verification rates ranged from 30% to 90%, with most of them hovering around 40% to 70%. My Australian friend Ron Cundy came in at close to 100% verifiable for his 5 1/2 victories.

These victory rates are very telling, and go back to the statements made about confusion in aerial combat. From Michel Lavigne's research, almost every single pilot certainly over claimed while in the desert. It is very likely this data extends to all air forces and to all theaters during the war.

Where does this leave us with Marseille? When looking at his victory log in Appendix 1, if you count the names of pilots shot down where the pilot is known, we come up with 67 victories. If, however, we look at those victories where a squadron has been identified, we come up with 104. When you look at Marseille's 151 desert victories and in a worst case scenario say he actually only shot down 50% of his claims, he still ends up with 75 victories. 60% corroboration gives him almost 91, and 70% gives him over 105, while an almost unlikely 80% would give him just shy of 121 kills. If you consider the likelihood of most pilots over claiming at consistent rates throughout the theater, Marseille still walks away with over 7.5 times the kills of Caldwell and twice the number of Werner Schrör (both at 50% corroboration). Without a doubt, Marseille still reigns supreme as the most talented and deadly fighter pilot in North Africa. By looking at the data as presented in Appendix 1, however, it is more than likely that Marseille comes in at close to 65-70% corroboration. Keep in mind, the data in Appendix 1 is a compilation of information gathered from several different sources.

Even if Marseille did over claim, and the evidence certainly supports this, does it diminish his accomplishments in the desert? No. Still, it remains in the eyewitness accounts from both sides of the battle that clearly recognized the talent Marseille brought to the table. Whereas most *Luftwaffe* pilots avoided the long turning dogfights while greatly outnumbered, it was Marseille who continually reveled, and indeed succeeded in this environment unlike any other *Luftwaffe* pilot. He still averaged 15 rounds per kill, still awed his squadron mates with his flying and tactical acumen, and scored time and again when no other German pilot scored. Beyond that, however, I believe it still remains his unique personality, character, and sense of honor that set Marseille apart. Whether delivering messages to the squadron of a downed enemy pilot, refusing to shoot pilots in their parachutes, embracing the Swing counter-culture, befriending Matthias the black South African prisoner of war, or being a loyal comrade and devoted combat commander, when seen as part of the whole man, no matter how impressive Marseille's numbers were, it remains the effect on his men and his unit that is most telling about the *Star of Africa*. That is the true legacy of Marseille and the value of this tribute.

> "His motto was: 'Don't turn around, always look ahead.' Perhaps this best describes his character. I was and am proud of my boy, who so well suited the ideas of an officer as I pictured them when I held that tiny bundle of humanity right after his birth. Brave, decent and loyal. That was my Joachim."[20]
>
> Frau Marseille

Translation of the reports of the circumstances of the death of Hauptmann Hans-Joachim Marseille

> "*Jagdgeschwader* 27
> Kommodore In the Field, 3 Oct. 1942
> Re.: Crash *Hauptmann* Marseille
> To
> *Fliegerführer Afrika*
>
> At 1050 hours a Stuka wave passed over our airfield at 3,500 m. On course to the lines. I/JG 27 received the order to fly high cover for this Stuka unit. Hpt. (Captain) Marseille was one of them.
>
> After the Stukas had finished their attack I directed Hpt. Marseille over the R/T to an enemy formation of fighters which were spotted south of Imayid on a westerly

Auf der Höhe heldischen Einsatzes, vom Feinde unbesiegt, fiel am 30. September in Afrika für seinen Führer in festem, unbeirrbarem Glauben an Deutschlands Sieg unser über alles geliebter Sohn (aus erster Ehe), der

Hauptmann

Hans-Joachim Marseille

Inhaber des Eichenlaubs mit Schwertern und Brillanten zum Ritterkreuz des Eisernen Kreuzes, des Deutschen Kreuzes in Gold, der höchsten italienischen Tapferkeitsmedaille in Gold sowie anderer Orden und Auszeichnungen

im blühenden Alter von 22 Jahren.

In stolzer Trauer:
Siegfried Marseille, Generalmajor, z. Z. im Felde; **Charlotte Reuter-Marseille**, geb. Riemer; zugleich namens aller anderen Angehörigen

Berlin W 30, Schwäbische Str. 9

Der „Stern von Afrika" bekommt ein Denkmal in der Wüste

Kairo, 10. April
Dem bekannten deutschen Kampfflieger Hans-Joachim Marseille soll in Ägypten ein Denkmal gesetzt werden. Die Kairoer Zeitung „Al Achbar": Das hat die Bundesregierung beschlossen.

Das Denkmal für den Flieger, der den Beinamen „Stern von Afrika" trug, soll in der Nähe von El Alamein an der ägyptischen Mittelmeerküste entstehen.

Marseille wurde am 30. September 1942 bei El Alamein abgeschossen.

In der anschließenden Schlacht zwischen Generalfeldmarschall Rommel und der britischen 8. Armee unter Feldmarschall Montgomery starben 80 000 Soldaten.

Hans-Joachim Marseille wurde 1942 in Nordafrika abgeschossen

Following Marseille's death, newspapers and magazines across Germany mentioned his untimely death. These are three examples of articles discussing the death of a national hero. *Courtesy of Author and Paul Upton*

Unbesiegt den Fliegertod gestorben

Zum Tode des erfolgreichsten deutschen Jagdfliegers in Nordafrika, Hauptmann Marseille

Wie der Bericht des Oberkommandos der Wehrmacht mitteilt, hat Hauptmann Hans Joachim Marseille, Träger der höchsten deutschen Tapferkeitsauszeichnung, unbesiegt vom Feind, auf dem nordafrikanischen Kriegsschauplatz den Fliegertod gefunden. „Erfüllt von unbändigem Angriffsgeist, hat dieser junge Offizier in Luftkämpfen 158 britische Gegner bezwungen. Die Wehrmacht betrauert den Verlust eines wahrhaft heldenhaften Kämpfers."

Mit Hauptmann Marseille hat die deutsche Luftwaffe einen ihrer besten Kämpfer, die deutsche Wehrmacht einen der besten Soldaten verloren. Unbesiegt ist er nach mehr als einundeinhalb Hundert Siegen über den britischen Gegner den Fliegertod gestorben. Der Führer hat in seiner Rede in unvergeßlichen Worten der Taten unserer Soldaten, darunter auch der Taten unserer Jagdflieger gedacht. Seine Worte sind der ehrenvollste und würdigste Nachruf auf den tapferen Flieger. „Was aber die Schilderung an Leistungen im einzelnen umfaßt, das wird der großen Masse unseres Volkes gar nicht bewußt werden können. Es ist unmöglich, daß der einzelne genau weiß, was es heißt, wenn ein Flieger dreißig, vierzig, fünfzig Abschüsse zählt, oder wenn er gar achtzig oder hundert Abschüsse erzielt. Das sind nicht hundert Kämpfe, sondern dafür setzt er oft tausendmal sein Leben ein." Seine einmaligen Taten hoben Hans Joachim Marseille aus dem großen namenlosen Heere der Frontsoldaten hervorgehoben. Sein Name war jedem Deutschen bekannt und vertraut geworden. Das ganze Volk dachte seiner in Liebe und Verehrung und wünschte ihm neue Siege und neuen Ruhm. Begeistert verfolgte vor allem die deutsche Jugend seine Taten, deren Herz nun einmal für die Flieger und die Männer der U-Boote schlägt. Sein Name gehört zu dem ewigen Vermächtnis dieses Krieges. Seine Taten werden vor kommenden Geschlechtern von der Größe dieses Kampfes und der unerreichbaren Größe deutschen Heldentums zeugen. Sein Werk wird für immer Aufruf und Ansporn zu höchsten Leistungen und furchtlosem Einsatz sein.

Hauptmann Hans-Joachim Marseille wurde als Sohn eines Generalmajors am 13. Dezember 1919 zu Berlin-Charlottenburg geboren. In harten Luftkämpfen gegen die britische Insel errang er seine ersten sieben Luftsiege. Darauf kam er, noch Oberfähnrich, im Frühjahr 1941 nach Afrika, wo er Leutnant wurde. Mit unbeirrbarem Kampfeswillen stellte er seine Gegner und schoß einen nach dem anderen ab. Nach seinem 46. Luftsieg erhielt er, damals Flugzeugführer in einem Jagdgeschwader, am 22. Februar dieses Jahres das Ritterkreuz des Eisernen Kreuzes. Zum Oberleutnant und Staffelkapitän befördert, wurde er immer mehr der gefürchtetste deutsche Jagdflieger in Nordafrika. Nach seinem 75. Abschuß wurde Marseille Anfang Juni 1942 vom Führer durch Verleihung des Eichenlaubs zum Ritterkreuz ausgezeichnet. 11 Tage danach hatte Marseille ein weiteres Viertelhundert britischer Flugzeuge abgeschossen und der 101. Luftsieg war von ihm errungen. Dafür erhielt Oberleutnant Marseille das Eichenlaub mit Schwertern zum Ritterkreuz des Eisernen Kreuzes. Mitte August überreichte der Duce dem erfolgreichen deutschen Jagdflieger die italienische Goldene Tapferkeitsmedaille und sprach dem deutschen Fliegeroffizier herzliche Worte der Anerkennung aus. Am 2. September errang Marseille wie schon oben gesagt, seinen 125. Luftsieg. Nach Mölders, Galland und Gollob wurden ihm nun die Brillanten zum Ritterkreuz des Eisernen Kreuzes mit Eichenlaub und Schwertern als höchste Tapferkeitsauszeichnung verliehen. Außerdem wurde Oberleutnant Marseille zum Hauptmann befördert.

Für die herzliche Anteilnahme am Fliegertode unseres unvergeßlichen „Jochen" des

Hauptmann

Hans Joachim Marseille

sagen wir unseren besten Dank.

Carl Reuter, Hptm. a. D., als Pflegevater
Charlotte Reuter-Marseille als Mutter geb. Riemer
Hanne-Lies Küpper als Braut
Gertrud Riemer als Großmutter

Berlin W 30, im November 1942
Schwäbische Straße 9.

Service appreciation card sent to Marseille's family following his death *Courtesy of Penn Templeman*

Following Marseille's death, the rudder from his 109 F-2 Trop, WkNr 8673, along with other artifacts were sent to his mother in Berlin. These items are on display inside her apartment. Hanging from the rudder is the shawl (scarf) that Marseille always wore. *Courtesy of author*

course. Hpt. Marseille and the other pilots saw these enemy aircraft.

At 1130 hours I heard the report that an engine was burning, but I did not at that time know if the engine was one of our own or one of the enemy aircraft.

After this I heard until 1135 hours a conversation between Hpt. Marseille and his pilots. From this I gathered that Hpt. Marseille had his cockpit filled with smoke and was not able to see anything. He was directed by R/T over our lines. In the course of this his questions were: 'Are we over our lines yet?,' 'Am I flying correctly now?' etc.

At 1139 hours, the aircraft started to swim slightly at 3,000 m. It turned on its back and dived down at an angle of 70-80 degrees in inverted flight. After a dive of 100-300 m. Hpt. Marseille left the aircraft and fell to the ground without pulling the release cord, according to the statements of Oblt. Schlang and Feldw. Pöttgen, who had escorted Hpt. Marseille's aircraft.

I explain the circumstances of the accident as follows:

By the leakage or fracture of a glycol line (*Kühlstoffleitung*) the aircraft lost coolant, which entered the cockpit as smoke. Hpt. Marseille thought it was the smoke of a fire. After the loss of coolant had grown it seems possible that a fire broke out due to overheating of the engine. This caused Hpt. Marseille to leave his aircraft by parachute.

My opinion is confirmed by the following facts:

1. Oblt. Schlang, flying beside Hpt. Marseille, has the firm opinion, that the aircraft lost only coolant from the first report until shortly before the crash.

A very interesting photograph of an unidentified *Luftwaffe* member holding the rudder of what is obviously Marseille's final 109 F, WkNr8673 (an older F-2 model). The partially scrubbed rudder clearly shows the 100 victory wreath and 58 barely visible yellow victory marks. It is interesting to ponder why these markings were scrubbed, at least in part, from this rudder. *Courtesy of Paul Upton*

Luftwaffe fighter pilot's memorial in Geisenheim, Germany. *Courtesy of author*

2. Hpt. Marseille would not have been able to speak without fatigue in his voice for 9 minutes in the smoke of a fire.

Before baling out Hpt. Marseille intended to roll his aircraft on its back. Because of the poor visibility in smoke he was not able to judge the exact position of his aircraft, and crashed down at the angle mentioned above. The consequence of this was that he hit the tail-unit and was injured so baldly that he was either unconscious or unable to pull the cord.

I exclude the possibility of sabotage. It seems impossible to interfere with a glycol line in such a manner that the failure will happen 50 minutes after take-off."

Neumann
Major

"*Der Oberbefehlshaber* SUD
Headquarters, 8 October 1942
Flugunfalluntersuchungsstelle
u. *-Flugsicherheitsstelle*
AZ. 52.Br.B.Nr.270/42
Re: Type Bf 109 G-2, W.Nr. 14256. Markings:
Location of accident: Egypt, *ca.* 7 km. South of mosque Sidi Abd el Rahman on the telegraph track.
Date: 30.9.42, 1136 hours.
Pilot: *Hauptmann* Marseille, Hans-Joachim, *Staffelkaptitän*.
Unit: I/JG 27, 3 *Staffel*.

To:
Distribution:

I. *Circumstances*

Hpt. Marseille was forced to leave his aircraft as the consequences of an engine failure, crashed down with a closed parachute and was killed. The aircraft was destroyed by fire on crashing.

II. *Inquiries*

In the course of a *Freie Jagd* mission (during which there was no contact with the enemy) Hpt. Marseille reported over the R/T when at 3,000 m over enemy territory: 'My engine is burning!'and 'I cannot see anything!' At the same time his wing-men saw a small white flag of smoke which came from the engine mounting, but they saw no flames. During the return flight the aircraft lost no altitude. Hpt. Marseille asked after some minutes: 'Question, am I right? I cannot see anything,' and shortly afterwards: 'I will land in our territory.'

In the meantime the bright trail of smoke had intensified, and flames could now be seen on the engine cowling. About six minutes after the appearance of the trouble and immediately after crossing the German lines, Hpt. Marseille jettisoned the cockpit roof. Then the aircraft made a half-roll into an upside-down position and went into a steep inverted glide. After a loss of altitude of about 200-300 m., the pilot left the cockpit, but the parachute did not open, the body crashing in an almost horizontal attitude without any sign of efforts being made to ward off the impact, and hit the ground on the stomach.

Hpt. Marseille made his reports over the R/T until the end in a clear and steady voice. This seems to signify that the smoke in the cockpit can not have caused the pilot to faint. The jettisoned cockpit hood cannot have hit the pilot, because he was able to make a controlled roll on to his back and untie the safety harness. After the crash it was established that the release lever of the parachute had not been pulled. The body of the pilot had a severe wound caused by a blow across the left half of the chest, which was not explained by the wounds suffered when he hit the ground.

From this and from the lack of any reaction during the fall, we are of the opinion that Hpt. Marseille hit the tail unit with the left side of his chest when he left the aircraft. This rendered him unconscious and he was not able to pull the cord as a consequence. The reason for hitting the tail unit was that he left the aircraft when it had moved from inverted flight to a dive. The pilot was hindered by poor visibility in the smoke to realize this because otherwise it would not have been difficult to rectify.

Technical inquiries:

The aircraft type Bf 109 G-2, W.Nr.14256, Lizenzbau Erla, was ferried in a brand new state to the unit via Bari. The flight ending with the crash was the first mission of this aircraft. Due to the fact that various troubles with new ex-works aircraft had often been caused by serious defects, W.Nr. 14256 was checked especially carefully before take-off, including a full power test-run of the engine. No defects were found in the course of this, and during the ferry flight from Bari. The engine DB 605 A-1, W.Nr. 77411 was completely destroyed after the vertical crash from 3,000 m. On the connecting rod assembly no signs of overheating could be found. The guide surfaces of the pistons and bearings showed no points of corrosion. Therefore it is correct to say that the strong smoke during the last six minutes flying time at maximum speed could not have come from an important loss of coolant or lubricant, as this would have produced greater damage in the connecting rod assembly. Burning fuel is eliminated because the colour of the cloud of smoke was white or light grey. Over and above this, the heat would have been intolerable for a Bf 109 pilot. It turned out that there must have been a failure in the reduction gear before take-off. This failure was accompanied by the generation of considerable heat and led to a fracture of the casing and to the loss of lubricant at this point. The escaping lubricant ignited and was the cause of the smoke. It was impossible to investigate the starting point of the failure in the reduction gear because the destruction in the crash was too great. Certain signs point to teeth breaking off the larger gear wheel in the reduction gear.

III. *Results*

The accident was introduced by a failure in the reduction gear. The failure itself was the consequence of technical defects. The result was burning lubricant with strong smoke and poor visibility for the pilot. After leaving the aircraft *Hauptmann* Marseille was hit by the tail unit so hard that he lost consciousness and crashed down with a closed parachute.

The collision with the tail unit came about because the aircraft changed from upside down fight to a dive. Hpt. Marseille was not able to realize this or change it because of the poor visibility.

Sabotage or incompetence of other persons is eliminated.

For the *Oberbefehlshaber Sud*
The Chief of General Staff
I.A."
Schmidt-Coste
Oberstleutnant

Author's Note: This entire translation is reproduced form the book *Fighters Over the Desert*, by Christopher Shores and Hans Ring, pages 252-254.

9

Possible Marseille 109E4/E7

Several years ago, I wrote an article discussing the possibility of finding a previously unidentified Marseille desert "Emil." My wife and I came across Photograph A while rummaging through some old *Luftwaffe* books I had placed in storage. Until that time, the only place I had seen this photograph was in *Aircraft and Legends: Messerschmitt Bf-109*, published by Haynes Publishing Group in 1989. When my wife opened the book, it fell open to the page containing this photograph. She smiled, shoved the book in my face, and said, "Look." I replied that the pilot in the photograph was "the Great One," and then I said, "And he's climbing into a 109E!" I couldn't believe I had never noticed it before. Immediately bells and whistles started going off in my head. Could this be a "Yellow 14" desert Emil I was staring at? There is unfortunately precious little photo documentation of any of Marseille's desert 109Es, of which he lost several, even though several of his "Friedrich" models have been generously documented, photographed, described, and modeled.

The photo credit states: "The arrival of I./JG 27 in Libya soon put a stop to British air superiority (Bf 109 E-4)." Unfortunately the author, noted *Luftwaffe* historian Heinz J. Nowarra, didn't mention the name of the pilot or the possibility of the man in the photograph being Marseille. There is little doubt in my mind, however, that it is indeed Marseille. The pilot's noticeable long "whip" of hair hanging from beneath his flight cap, the distinctive hairline and

Photograph A *Courtesy of E & C Collection*

Photograph B *Courtesy of E & C Collection*

shape of the pilot's head, the barely discernable facial features and the general physical size and shape, leaves me to believe that the pilot on the wing of this Messerschmitt 109 can only be Marseille. The true historical significance of this picture remained in doubt, however, since Photograph A by itself raised as many questions as it gave us answers.

After publishing my article several years later in Barry C. Rosch's *Luftwaffe Verband* and Scott Rose's *Luftwaffe Resource Page*, I was fortunate enough to get several responses about the photograph in question. Once again Mr. Russell Brown from Great Western, Australia, came through and pointed out that both Photographs A and B could be found together on page 53 in *Luftwaffe Camouflage and Markings Vol. 2*, written by J.R. Smith and J.D. Gallaspy. It is obvious from the placement of the drop tank in the foreground to the rocks, crates, shadows, and scrub brush located in the two photographs that they were taken at the same time. Perhaps most important, however, was conclusive evidence that the aircraft in Photo A, unfortunately, was not Marseille's "Yellow 14."

When reading the caption between both photographs in *Luftwaffe Camouflage and Markings Vol. 2*, keep in mind this book was written in 1976:

> "One of only three known photographs (see also Page 82) of a Bf 109E-4/Trop with tan 79 (not yellow) upper surfaces. It is possible that this particular aircraft, of 3./JG 27, was repainted apart from the cowling which was left in the original yellow. The aircraft's individual number 6 was painted in yellow 27, and the badge of the first group, comprising a black map of Africa over which was superimposed a brown Negro's face and a yellow and black leopard, appeared on the nose. The spinner was half yellow and half white with the propeller blades black-green 70."[1]

In Jerry Scutts' book *Bf 109 Aces of North Africa and the Mediterranean*, Photograph B appears on page 73. The very different Scutts caption reads:

> "A scratched and stained drop tank rests on its 'dolly' awaiting attachment to the centerline shackles of 'White 6,' whilst another I. *Gruppe* machine comes in to land behind it at Ain El Gazala in October 1941. This E-7/Trop belongs to one of the last *Staffel* within I/JG 27 to transition onto the Bf 109F, a fact denoted by the Emil's overall tan colour scheme, which lacks the dapple green blotches applied earlier in the campaign to allow the aircraft to blend in with the camelthorn bushes found near the coast."[2]

In *Luftwaffe Colours: Volume 3, Section 3: War Over the Desert – North Africa June 1940 – June 1942*, both photographs can once again be found together in addition to an excellent color profile by artist Tom Tullis. In this book, the photo caption reads:

> "A Bf 109 E-7 Trop of 1./JG 27, 'White 6' at Gazala. Pilots who returned to Germany to collect new aircraft have remarked that the only external difference between their standard Bf 109s and those intended for North Africa was that the latter were fitted with a dust filter and it is assumed from this that such aircraft still retained their European schemes. Presumably, therefore, the new

Sand 79 paint scheme was applied in transit, probably in Sicily."[3]

Once again, neither author identified the pilot on the wing of the 109 as possibly being Marseille.

Although I proposed in my article that the pilot in Photo A was Marseille, it was now interesting to see the "White 6," not "Yellow 14," on the fuselage. Although the caption from Smith and Gallaspy states that this aircraft belonged to the 3rd squadron, which may very well be true for reasons that will be mentioned later, the markings themselves, however, make this difficult to ascertain. The problem identifying varying shades of color on a black and white photograph often makes positive verification difficult, although that is certainly not the case with these two photographs. It can be agreed that the nose of this airplane is indeed yellow. When comparing the shades, there appears to be significant variances between the nose and the number "6" on the fuselage.

By also comparing the color of the "6" to the yellow rudder, the two-tone spinner, the white Mediterranean Theater fuselage band, and the white in the I/ JG 27 emblem, it would seem that this aircraft, as also mentioned by Scutts, is indeed "White 6." Therefore it would appear that this aircraft actually belonged to 1 *Staffel* and not Marseille's 3 *Staffel*. Likewise, authors Smith and Gallaspy identify the spinner as being half yellow and half white. It is clear there is significant difference in color between the yellow nose of this aircraft and the two-tone spinner. More than likely the spinner, as depicted in Tom Tullis' color profile, is red and white.

So where does this leave us with the possibility Marseille is climbing into the cockpit of this "Emil?" In Photograph B, although a pilot is barely visible sitting in the cockpit, even under significant zoom, there are no clear features to positively identify him. Unfortunately, only part of a helmet and goggles can be seen. According to the caption found in the Kookaburra book, this particular paint scheme was rare on JG 27's desert birds. Not being an expert on *Luftwaffe* paint schemes, Jerry Scutts' explanation of this being a later paint scheme seems to make a lot of sense. The aircraft pictured in this article, according to Scutts, simply had a latter scheme that was similar to those found on the 109Fs that were beginning to replace the older E-4/7s. This may explain its scarcity in photographs.

Since the aircraft is clearly "White 6," does this necessarily mean this aircraft was not a part of Marseille's third squadron, and the pilot must therefore be a 1 *Staffel* member? Not necessarily. We know that I/ JG 27 started replacing their "Emils" for the "Friedrich" models in September 1941. As pilots were rotated back to Germany for conversion on the new planes, it is likely there became an excess of "Emils" within I *Gruppe*. Since 1 *Staffel* was the first to rotate out to get their "F" models, the 2nd and 3rd *Staffeln* would certainly have become the recipients of the better excess "White" aircraft. Some of these would likely have been flown before they had the honor of being repainted, if at all, in their new squadron colors. If Scutts' dating is correct, it is likely the "White 6" in this photograph falls into this category. There are several photographs showing a row of I JG/27 "Emils" next to each other on the flight line with aircraft carrying the colors of all three *Staffeln*. This likely illustrates the period of transition with excess "Emils" being used within one squadron. Once again, we are left with as many questions as we have answers. We have an aircraft with a "rarely photographed" paint scheme that has been identified as both an E-4 and an E-7 Trop. It has also been identified as both "White 6" and "Yellow 6." Perhaps most important is seeing this aircraft from different sides and angles. This fortunately gives us more detail and information than we had with just Photograph A. Together, these two photographs, if Marseille is indeed the pilot in the first photograph, give us an interesting historical record of a I/ JG 27 aircraft that likely started its career in one squadron and ended in another. Although this aircraft is clearly "White 6," we know for certain it is not, at least at the time this photograph was taken, "Yellow 14." As for one of Marseille's personal 109s or at least one he flew, the most overwhelming evidence is the image of the pilot seen in Photograph A. Even if this "White 6" did not become Marseille's personal aircraft, keep in mind that pilots sometimes flew aircraft that were not their own, so there should really be no surprise to see Marseille climbing into or out of an aircraft not marked with Yellow 14. On 19 March 1942, for example, Friedrich Körner shot down JG 27's 1000th aircraft while flying "Red 2" instead of his usual "Red 11."

I still believe the pilot in Photograph A is Marseille, and viewing the photograph under extreme enlargement convinces me even more. Whether this aircraft was later painted in 3 *Staffel* colors, Marseille's "Yellow 14," or Marseille just happened to fly it on this one occasion, we are still left with a bit of unique, albeit unanswered, Marseille aircraft history to deal with. Considering the photographic shortage of Marseille's desert "Emils," if the pilot is indeed "Jochen," it makes this aircraft even more historically significant, since we can actually identify another Emil flown by Marseille.

Author's Note: When I first decided to write this tribute, I had originally planned to have color profiles created for this chapter. These profiles were going to include Marseille's Battle of Britain 109E "White 14" featured in Nicolas Trudgian's *High Summer–High Battle,* Marseille's generously reproduced F models, as well as the G-2 he was flying the day he died. Although I do know a little bit about Marseille, I am in no way an expert on his aircraft. As fate would have it, during the writing of this book I discovered that two well respected authors and researchers, John Beaman and Jim Kitchens, were teaming up with aviation artist Tom Tullis to produce a comprehensive study of all the planes Marseille is known to have flown. This study will include new and highly accurate color profiles by Tom Tullis. With the depth of their research and knowledge of Marseille's aircraft, I felt that producing color profiles on my own would pale in comparison to the work of these dedicated historians, and similarly would add no new information from the color profiles already created in other books. That being said, if you are interested in Marseille's aircraft, there will be some very interesting information on the market very soon.

10

Marseille Artwork

If imitation is indeed the sincerest form of flattery, then the sheer amount of artwork surrounding Marseille and his aircraft suggests that he is indeed one of the most recognized and respected pilots of World War II. There are literally dozens of pencil drawings, watercolors, oil paintings, computer generated images, and at least one bronze statue depicting some aspect of Marseille. In this chapter, I have tried to compile a representative collection of just some of the artwork concerning the topic of "The Star of Africa." By no means is this collection to be considered "all inclusive." There were many more pieces of art from my personal collection, for example, that I would like to have included in this book, but was unfortunately unable to secure permission from the artists. Perhaps if there is a second edition I will be able to include more of these pieces.

As for the artwork presented here, I have to take my hat off to the artists that so graciously allowed the use of their work. Not to single out any artist in particular, but you will notice that there are many well-known as well as some unknown artists represented here. As for the quality of their work, you will see that each has his own distinctive style and unique way of presenting his thoughts on Marseille and his aircraft. As a collector, although I have to admit that I do have my favorites, it is generally my goal to acquire each Marseille piece I can in order to give a more completed and well-rounded view of Marseille and his aircraft. I respect each artist and thank each of them for their work. As you look at each piece, admire the artists' contributions and enjoy their representations of Marseille and his aircraft. All of these pieces form part of my Marseille art collection.

The Star of Africa by Jay Ashurst. *Image courtesy of Jay Ashurst*

Untitled work by Les Carter. *Image courtesy of Greg Dortch, friend of Les Carter*

The Star of Africa by Julius Cassani. *Image courtesy of Julius J. Cassani*

Untitled work by Mike Chappell. From the author's private collection. First seen in the book *Bf 109 Aces in the Mediterranean*. I had the opportunity to purchase this original painting several years ago. *Image from author's private collection*

The Star of Africa by Jerry Crandall. *Image courtesy of Jerry Crandall*

Hans Marseille by Tony Jackson. *Image courtesy of Tony Jackson, BA (Hons) Dip SIAD*

Star of Africa by Konley Kelly. Accomplished via computer graphics. *Image courtesy of Konley Kelly at www.shortfuse3D.com*

Stern von Afrika by Heinz Krebs. *Image courtesy of D. Stricker; Airport Galerie*

A Vivid Discussion by Alexey Linkov. I found this artist's work several years ago on EBay. He was selling his art, and I purchased the following pieces. *Courtesy of Alexey Linkov*

Apparition by Alexey Linkov. Courtesy of Alexey Linkov

Desert Eagle: Hans-Joachim Marseille by Alexey Linkov. *Courtesy of Alexey Linkov*

Desert Eagle: Jochen Marseille and His Bf-109 by Alexey Linkov. Courtesy of Alexey Linkov

The Enigma of Hans-Joachim Marseille by Alexey Linkov. *Courtesy of Alexey Linkov*

Home Free by Alexey Linkov. Courtesy of Alexey Linkov

Spirit in the Sky by Alexey Linkov. *Courtesy of Alexey Linkov*

Undefeated Ace: Hans-Joachim Marseille by Alexey Linkov. Courtesy of Alexey Linkov

Untitled by Alexey Linkov. Courtesy of Alexey Linkov

Star of Africa by Lonnie Ortega. *Image courtesy of Lonnie Ortega*

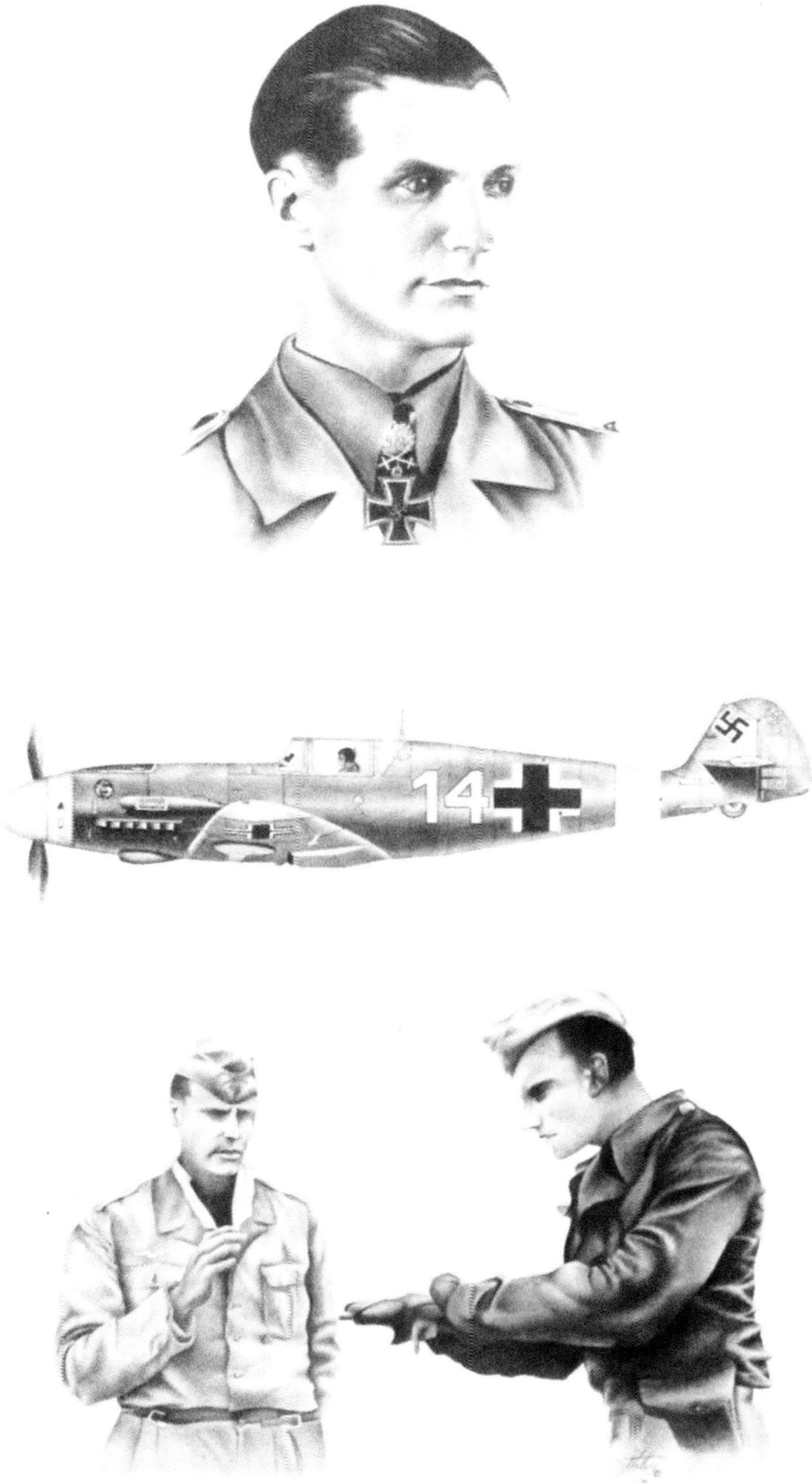

Untitled work by Mike Staley. More than ten years ago, when I was still in the Air Force, I had a friend of mine, TSgt. Mike Staley, draw this picture for me. He did such a good job that I decided to put it in the book. Unfortunately I have not had contact with Mike in ten years, but I hope he doesn't mind me showing his work, which resides in my private collection.

Yellow 14 by Stan Stokes. *Image courtesy of The Stokes Collection*

Cold cast bronze statue of Hans Marseille by Rick Terry. *Image courtesy of Penn Templeman*

Desert Victory by Nicolas Trudgian. *Image courtesy of Nicolastrudgian.com*

High Summer, High Battle by Nicolas Trudgian. *Image courtesy of Nicolastrudgian.com*

Marseille Over Dover by Nicolas Trudgian. I was fortunate enough about ten years ago to find this piece for sale. It is an outstanding addition to my collection, since it is an original pencil drawing depicting Marseille during the Battle of Britain. Although I hate to admit it, this piece is my favorite. *Image courtesy of Nicolastrudgian.com*

Marseille Portrait by unknown artist. My friend Frank Struppek had a Romanian artist at the Munich Kristkindle Market draw this image for me several years ago. The artist's full name and whereabouts are unknown. *Image courtesy of author*

Untitled work by Tony Weddell. *Image courtesy of Tony Weddell and the Seattle Museum of Flight*

Messerschmitt Bf 109 F-4 Trop by Friedl Wülfing. Image courtesy of Friedl Wülfing and Luftfahrtkunst.de

Appendix 1: Marseille's Victory Log

***Hauptmann* Hans Joachim Marseille's Reconstructed Logbook**

Victory	Date	Time of Action	Place of Action	Type of Aircraft	Squadron	Country	Pilot	Notes
1	24/08/40		Kent	Spitfire		RAF		
2	02/09/40		Southern England	Spitfire		RAF		
3	11/09/40	1705	S.E. England	Spitfire		RAF		
4	15/09/40		Thimse Estuary	Hurricane		RAF		
5	18/09/40		S.E. England	Spitfire		RAF		
6	27/09/40		London	Hurricane		RAF		
7	28/09/40		S.E. England	Spitfire		RAF		
8	23/04/41	1250	Tobruk	Hurricane	73 Sqdn	RAF		KIA[1]
9	28/04/41	0925	Tobruk	Blenheim	45 Sqdn	RAF		All KIA (5)
10	01/05/41	0915	18 km. S.Tobruk	Hurricane	274 Sqdn	RAF	PO Godden	KIA
11	01/05/41	0925	5 km. S.E. Tobruk	Hurricane	274 Sqdn	RAF		Crash Land
12	17/06/41	1715	N.E. Gambut	Hurricane	1 SAAF	SAAF		

Marseille with fellow Knight's Cross recipient and rival, Gerhard Homuth
Courtesy of author

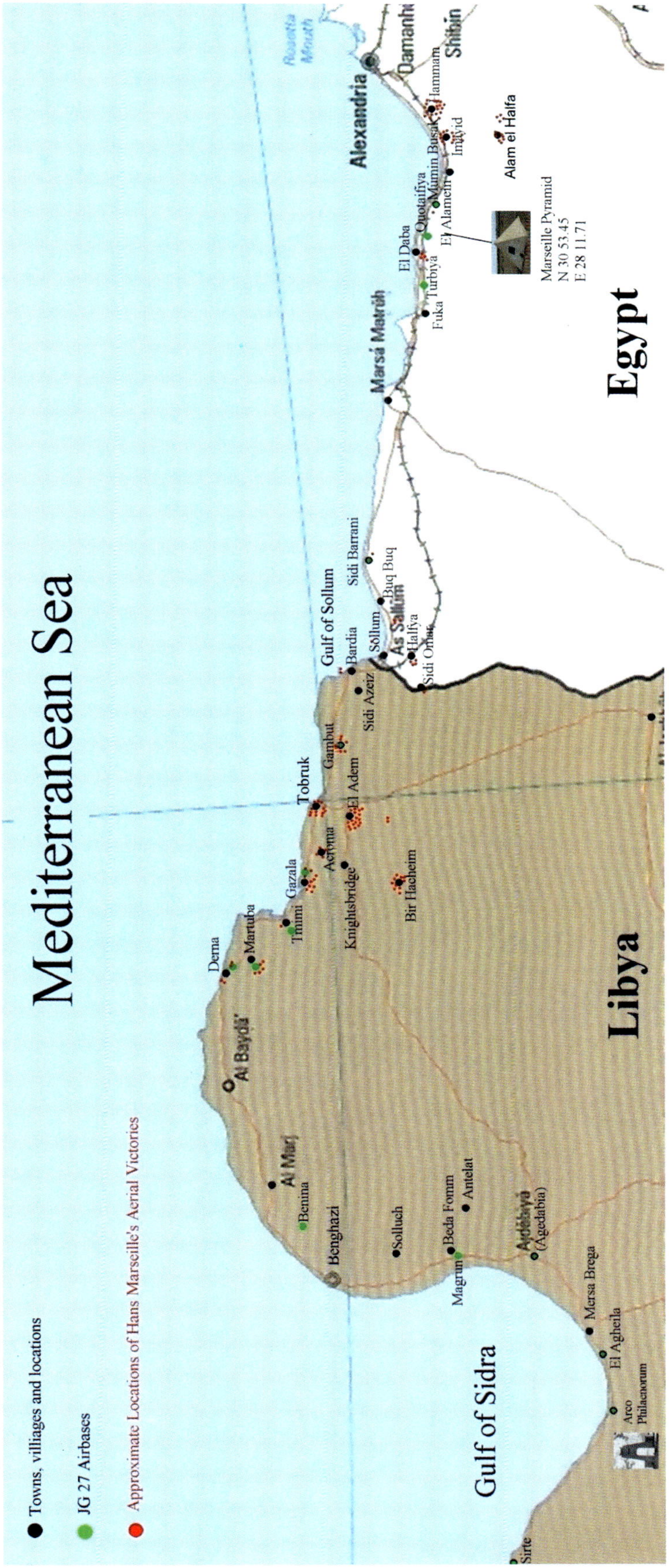

Map of the North African Theater of Operations. The map is marked with the approximate locations of Hans Marseille's 51 desert victories as well as the bases of I/ JG 27 during Marseille's time in the desert. *Courtesy of author*

Victory	Date	Time of Action	Place of Action	Type of Aircraft	Squadron	Country	Pilot	Notes
13	17/06/41	1845	15-20 km SE Sidi Omar	Hurricane	1 SAAF	SAAF		
14	27/08/41	1800	Sidi Barrani	Hurricane	1 SAAF	SAAF	Lt. Williams	[2]
15	09/09/41	1712	Bay of Sollum	Hurricane				
16	09/09/41	1718	S.E. Bardia	Hurricane	33 Sqdn	RAF		
17	13/09/41	1725	S. Bardia	Hurricane	451 Sqdn	RAF	Flt.Lt. Byers	POW[3]
18	14/09/41	1746	S. El Sofafi	Hurricane	33 Sqdn	RAF	Sgt. Nourse	Baled Out
19	24/09/41	1330	Bardia uber See	Maryland				
20	24/09/41	1645	Buq Buq	Hurricane	1 SAAF	SAAF		
21	24/09/41	1647	Buq Buq	Hurricane	1 SAAF	SAAF		
22	24/09/41	1651	Buq Buq	Hurricane	1 SAAF	SAAF		
23	24/09/41	1700	Buq Buq	Hurricane	1 SAAF	SAAF		
24	12/10/41	0812	Bir Sheferzan	Kittyhawk	3 RAAF	RAAF	FO Roberts	Crash Land
25	12/10/41	0815	Bir Sheferzan	Kittyhawk	3 RAAF	RAAF	Sgt. Scott	Landed/ Damaged
26	05/12/41	1525	S. Bir el Gubi	Hurricane	1 SAAF 274 Sqdn	SAAF RAF		1st Kill with 109F
27	06/12/41	1210	SSE El Adem	Hurricane	229 Sqdn	RAF		[4]
28	06/12/41	1225	S. El Adem	Hurricane	238 Sqdn	RAF		[4]
29	07/12/41	0930	20 km S. Sidi Omar	Hurricane	274 Sqdn	RAF	Flt.Lt. Hobbs	
30	08/12/41	0815	SW. El Adem	Hurricane	274 Sqdn	RAF		
31	10/12/41	0850	SE. El Adem	Kittyhawk	2 SAAF	SAAF	Lt. Enslin	BaledOut
32	11/12/41	0930	SE. Timimi	Tomahawk	250 Sqdn	RAF	Sgt. Canty	KIA
33	13/12/41	1600	Martuba	Kittyhawk	3 RAAF	RAAF	FO Trimble	Crash Landed
34	13/12/41	1610	Timimi	Hurricane	1 SAAF	SAAF	2Lt. Connel Lt.Meek	[5]
35	17/12/41	1110	SE. Derna	Hurricane	1 SAAF	SAAF		
36	17/12/41	1128	SE. Derna	Hurricane	1 SAAF	SAAF		
37	08/02/42	0822	Martuba	Hurricane	274 Sqdn	RAF	Flt.Sgt. Hargreaves	POW[6]
38	08/02/42	0825	Martuba	Hurricane	274 Sqdn	RAF		KIA[6]
39	08/02/42	1420	Derna	Hurricane	73 Sqdn	RAF		
40	08/02/42	1430	Derna	Hurricane	73 Sqdn	RAF		#1 Ace in Afrika
41	12/02/42	1330	10 km. NW. Tobruk	Hurricane	274 Sqdn	RAF	Sgt. Henderson	Crash Land[7]
42	12/02/42	1332	20 km. NW. Tobruk	Hurricane	274 Sqdn	RAF	Sgt. Parbury	Baled Out[7]
43	12/02/42	1333	23 km. NW. Tobruk	Hurricane	274 Sqdn	RAF	PO Kuhle	KIA
44	12/02/42	1336	35 km. WNW. Tobruk	Hurricane	274 Sqdn	RAF	Flt.Lt. Smith	KIA
45	13/02/42	0920	20 km. SE. Tobruk	Hurricane	1 SAAF	SAAF	Lt. Le Roux	Wounded Crash Landed
46	13/02/42	0925	23 km. ESE. Tobruk	Hurricane	1 SAAF	SAAF	Lt. Herbert	KIA[8]
47	15/02/42	1300	3 km. WSW. Gambut	Kittyhawk	3 RAAF	RAAF	Sgt. Reid (AK605)	KIA – Too low to bail out
48	15/02/42	1303	5 km. SW. Gambut	Kittyhawk	3 RAAF	RAAF	FO Briggs (AK594)	BaledOut
49	21/02/42	1210	10 km. W. Fort Acroma	Kittyhawk	112 Sqdn	RAF		[9]
50	21/02/42	1218	20 km. NE. Fort Acroma	Kittyhawk	112 Sqdn	RAF		[9]
51	27/02/42	1200	10 km. ENE. Ain-el-Gazala	Kittyhawk (AK689)	3 RAAF	RAAF	PO Hart	BaledOut
52	27/02/42	1212	10 km. ENE. Fort Acroma	Kittyhawk (AK665)	3 RAAF	RAAF	Sgt. Jennings	KIA 4th Ops Flight
53	25/04/42	1006	2 km. N. Gazala	Kittyhawk	260 Sqdn	RAF	Sqdn. Ldr Hanbury	Crash Land
54	25/04/42	1008	10 km. N. Gazala	Kittyhawk	260 Sqdn	SAAF	Sgt. Wareham	KIA[10]
55	10/05/42	0913	25 km. SE. Martuba	Hurricane	40 SAAF	SAAF	Capt. Cobbledick	
56	10/05/42	0915	25 km. SE. Martuba	Hurricane	40 SAAF	SAAF	Lt. Flesker	
57	13/05/42	1010	16 km. SE. Gazala	Kittyhawk (AL172)	3 RAAF	RAAF	FO Pace	KIA
58	13/05/42	1015	14 km. ESE. Gazala -- Bucht	Kittyhawk (AK855)	3 RAAF	RAAF	Sgt. McDiarmid	Baled Out
59	16/05/42	1805	20 km. E. Gazala	Kittyhawk (AL120)	3 RAAF	RAAF	Sgt. Teede	Crash Landed on fire

Victory	Date	Time of Action	Place of Action	Type of Aircraft	Squadron	Country	Pilot	Notes
60	16/05/42	1815	3 km. E. Fort Acroma	Kittyhawk (AK697)	450 Sqdn	RAAF	PO F.E. Parker	Baled Out[11]
61	19/05/42	0720	8 km. SW. Fort Acroma	Kittyhawk	450 Sqdn	RAAF		Force Land
62	19/05/42	0730	5 km. S. Fort Acroma	Kittyhawk	450 Sqdn	RAAF	Sgt. Ivan Young	Crash Land
63	23/05/42	1105	3 km. SE. Toburk	Baltimore	223 Sqdn	RAF		
64	23/05/42	1106	4 km. SE. Tobruk	Baltimore	223 Sqdn	RAF		
65	30/05/42	0605	1 km. NW. El Adem	Kittyhawk	250 Sqdn	RAF	Sgt. Buckland	KIA
66	31/05/42	0726	5 km. W. Bir el Harmat	Kittyhawk	4 SAAF	SAAF		
67	31/05/42	0728	8 km. W. Bir el Harmat	Kittyhawk	4 SAAF	SAAF		
68	31/05/42	0734	10 km. SW Fort Acroma	Kittyhawk	4 SAAF	SAAF		
69	01/06/42	1915	20 km. ENE. El-Cheimar	Curtiss				[12]
70	03/06/42	1222	3 km. W. Bir Hakeim	Tomahawk	5 SAAF	SAAF	Captain Pare	KIA
71	03/06/42	1225	5 km. W. Bir Hakeim	Tomahawk	5 SAAF	SAAF	2Lt. Martin	Crash Land
72	03/06/42	1227	5 km. W. Bir Hakeim	Tomahawk	5 SAAF	SAAF	Captain Morrison	Wounded[13]
73	03/06/42	1228	7 km. W. Bir Hakeim	Tomahawk	5 SAAF	SAAF	Lt. Muir	Wounded[13]
74	03/06/42	1229	10 km. W. Bir Hakeim	Tomahawk	5 SAAF	SAAF	2Lt. Golding	Wounded[13]
75	03/06/42	1233	7 km. W. Bir Hakeim	Tomahawk	5 SAAF	SAAF	Captain Botha	Force Landed
76	07/06/42	1610	SW. El Adem	Kittyhawk	2 SAAF	SAAF	Lt. Frewen	Baled Out
77	07/06/42	1613	10 km. NE. El Adem	Kittyhawk	2 SAAF	SAAF	Lt. Bernage	KIA
78	10/06/42	0735	5 km. NW. Mteifel Chebir	Spitfire	145 Sqdn.	RAF		
79	10/06/42	0741	6 km. NE. Mteifel Chebir	Spitfire	145 Sqdn	RAF		
80	10/06/42	0745	6 km. E. Mteifel Chebir	Spitfire	145 Sqdn	RAF		
81	10/06/42	0750	6 km. ENE. Mteifel Chebir	Spitfire	145 Sqdn	RAF		
82	11/06/42	1724	SW. El Adem	Kittyhawk	112 Sqdn	RAF	Sgt. Greaves	Baled Out
83	11/06/42	1734	18 km. NW El Adem	Hurricane				
84	13/06/42	0810	5 km. W. El Adem	Kittyhawk (AL127)	450 Sqdn	RAAF	Sgt. Halliday	KIA
85	13/06/42	1811	3 km. NW. El Adem	Kittyhawk (AK952)	450 Sqdn	RAF	Sgt. Stone	KIA
86	13/06/42	1814	2 km. NNE. El Adem	Kittyhawk (AL106)	450 Sqdn	RAAF	PO Osborne	Crash Land
87	13/06/42	1815	3 km. ENE. El Adem	Kittyhawk	112 Sqdn	RAF	PO Edwards	KIA[14]
88	15/06/42	1801	6 km. NW. El Adem	Curtiss				
89	15/06/42	1802	4 km. NNW. El Adem	Curtiss				
90	15/06/42	1804	8 km. NE. El Adem	Curtiss				
91	15/06/42	1806	3 km. NNE. El Adem	Curtiss				
92	16/06/42	1802	17 km. SW. El Adem	Hurricane	73 Sqdn 208 Sqdn	RAF		
93	16/06/42	1810	5 km. E. El Adem	Curtiss		SAAF		[15]
94	16/06/42	1811	5 km. NNE. El Adem	Curtiss		SAAF		[15]
95	16/06/42	1813	10 km. N. El Adem	Curtiss		SAAF		[15]
96	17/06/42	1202	5 km. W. Gambut	Hurricane	73 Sqdn	RAF	SdnLdr D.H. Ward	KIA
97	17/06/42	1203	3 km. W. Gambut	Hurricane	73 Sqdn	RAF	PO Wooley	KIA
98	17/06/42	1205	4 km. SW. Gambut	Hurricane	73 Sqdn	RAF	PO Stone	Baled Out
99	17/06/42	1208	6 km. SW Gambut	Hurricane	73 Sqdn	RAF	Sgt. Goodwin	Baled Out
100	17/06/42	1209	2 km. S. Gambut	Kittyhawk	112 Sqdn	RAAF	Sgt. Drew	KIA[16]
101	17/06/42	1212	SE. Sidi Omar	Spitfire				
102	31/08/42	1003	25 km. SSE. Alamein	Hurricane	213 Sqdn	RAF	PO Barnes	BaledOut
103	31/08/42	1004	26 km. SSE. Alamein	Hurricane	213 Sqdn	RAF		
104	31/08/42	1825	15 km E. Alam Halfa	Spitfire	601 Sqdn	RAF		
105	01/09/42	0826	18 km SSE. El Imayid	Hurricane	1 SAAF	SAAF	Lt. Bailey	KIA[17]
106	01/09/42	0828	20 km SSE. El Imayid	Hurricane	1 SAAF	SAAF	Maj. Metelerkamp	KIA[17]
107	01/09/42	0835	18 km SE. El Imayid	Hurricane	1 SAAF	SAAF	FO I.W. Matthews	Wounded[17]
108	01/09/42	0839	18 km SSE El Imayid	Spitfire	92 Sqdn.	RAF	PO Bradley-Smith	BaledOut[17]
109	01/09/42	1055	20 km. S. Alam el Halfa	Curtiss				[18]
110	01/09/42	1056	15 km. SE. Alam el Halfa	Curtiss				[18]
111	01/09/42	1058	10 km. SE. Alam el Halfa	Curtiss				[18]
112	01/09/42	1059	15 km. SE. Alam el Halfa	Curtiss				[18]

Victory	Date	Time of Action	Place of Action	Type of Aircraft	Squadron	Country	Pilot	Notes
113	01/09/42	1101	7 km. ESE. Alam el Halfa	Curtiss				[18]
114	01/09/42	1102	12 km. E. Alam el Halfa	Curtiss				[18]
115	01/09/42	1103	20 km. E. Alam el Halfa	Curtiss				[18]
116	01/09/42	1105	23 km. E. Alam el Halfa	Curtiss				[18]
117	01/09/42	1747	7 km S . Imayid	Hurricane	33/213 Sqdn	RAF		
118	01/09/42	1748	8 km S Imayid	Hurricane	33/213 Sqdn	RAF		
119	01/09/42	1749	6 km SE Imayid	Hurricane	33/213 Sqdn	RAF		
120	01/09/42	1750	9 km SSE Imayid	Hurricane	33/213 Sqdn	RAF		
121	01/09/42	1753	7 km SSW Imayid	Hurricane	33/213 Sqdn	RAF		
122	02/09/42	0916	25 SE. Imayid	Kittyhawk	2 SAAF	SAAF	Lt. Stuart	BaledOut
123	02/09/42	0918	30 km. SSE. Imayid	Warhawk	64 FS	USAAF	Lt. McMarrell	Crash Land
124	02/09/42	0924	10 km. S. Imayid	Warhawk				
				Kittyhawk	64 FS	USAAF		[19]
					2 SAAF	SAAF		
125	02/09/42	1518	20 km. SE. Alamein	Tomahawk	5 SAAF	SAAF	Lt. Lindbergh	KIA
126	02/09/42	1521	El Alamein	Tomahawk	5 SAAF	SAAF	Lt. Carman	KIA
127	03/09/42	0720	25 km. SW. Hammam	Spitfire	145 RAF	RCAF	Sgt. Powers	[20]
128	03/09/42	0723	27 km. SW. Hammam	Kittyhawk	260 RAF	RCAF	WO Stan Bernier	KIA[20]
129	03/09/42	0728	30 km. SW. Hammam	Kittyhawk	2 SAAF	RSAF	Lt. Ryneke	[20]
130	03/09/42	1508	Imayid	Curtiss				
131	03/09/42	1510	2 km. SW. Imayid	Spitfire				
132	03/09/42	1542	40 km. SSE. Alamein	Hurricane	7 SAAF			
133	05/09/42	1048	13 km. SE. Alamein	Curtiss		RAF		[21]
134	05/09/42	1049	SE Alamein	Curtiss		RAF		[21]
135	05/09/42	1051	SSE. Imayid	Curtiss		RAF		[21]
136	05/09/42	1100	SSE. Imayid	Curtiss				

Marseille's 128th victim, WO Stan Bernier. Killed by Marseille when his 260 Squadron Kittyhawk was shot down on 3 September 1942. *Courtesy of Michel Lavigne*

Victory	Date	Time of Action	Place of Action	Type of Aircraft	Squadron	Country	Pilot	Notes
137	06/09/42	1703	SE. Alamein	Kittyhawk	260 Sqdn	RAF	PO Dick Dunbar	KIA
138	06/09/42	1714	SSW. Alamein	Curtiss				
139	06/09/42	1716	SSW. Alamein	Curtiss				
140	06/09/42	1720	SSW. Alamein	Spitfire				22
141	07/09/42	1743	SE. Alamein	Tomahawk		5 SAAF	Lt. Cowen	23
142	07/09/42	1745	SE. Alamein	Tomahawk		5 SAAF	Lt. McCarthy	23
143	11/09/42	0740	15 km. SE. Alamein	Fghtr Bmbr		RAF		
144	11/09/42	0742	5 km. WSW. Alamein	Fghtr Bmbr		RAF		
145	15/09/42	1651	25 km. SW. Alamein	Curtiss				24
146	15/09/42	1653	28 km. SW. Alamein	Curtiss				24
147	15/09/42	1654	27 km. SW. Alamein	Curtiss				24
148	15/09/42	1657	26 km. SW. Alamein	Curtiss				24
149	15/09/42	1659	20 km. SW. Alamein	Curtiss				24
150	15/09/42	1701	18 km. SW. Alamein	Curtiss				24
151	15/09/42	1702	19 km. SW. Alamein	Curtiss				24
152	26/09/42	0910	12 km. SW. Alamein	Hurricane	213 Sqdn	RAF	PO Luxton	Crash Land
153	26/09/42	0913	14 km. SW. Alamein	Spitfire	92 Sqdn	RAF		
154	26/09/42	0915	14 km. SW. Alamein	Spitfire	92 Sqdn	RAF		
155	26/09/42	0916	15 km. SW. Alamein	Spitfire	92 Sqdn	RAF		
156	26/09/42	1656	SW. Imayid	Spitfire		RAF		
157	26/09/42	1659	10 km. SSE. Imayid	Spitfire		RAF		
158	26/09/42	1710	10 km. S. Hammam[25]	Spitfire		RAF		KIA

[1] 3/JG-27's first kill in North Africa. HJM also shot down by Free French pilot Sous-Lt. Denis.

[2] This victory conflicts with Woods, which lists this as the 28th. Ring/Shore show no combat on 28th.

[3] Severely burned, Derna Hospital, See "Stories" with the account of Geoffrey Morley-Mower.

[4] Victories came from one of these two squadrons, records cannot verify with 100% accuracy.

[5] One of these two men was likely Marseille's 34th victory.

[6] Victories 37 and 38 occurred over Marseille's airfield as he was trying to land.

[7] Neither saw Marseille, thought they were hit by FLAK. (FOTD, p. 93)

[8] During the fight with Lt. Le Roux, Marseille's aircraft was damaged by the explosion. The aircraft's engine quit, and Marseille elected to crash land the airplane. Marseille spotted Lt. Herbert's aircraft, shot it down, and continued his glide to a successful crash landing.

[9] During this engagement, "Fifi" Stahlschmidt likely shot down by Aussie pilot, Clive "Killer" Caldwell.

[10] Sgt. Wareham was a South African flying with the 260 Sqdn.

[11] After Pilot Officer Parker baled out of his burning Kittyhawk, the airplane flew into the aircraft flown by a Sgt. W.J. Metherall. Marseille did not claim the third Kittyhawk. (FOTD, p. 111)

[12] After 100 sorties as Marseille's wingman, Poettgen scores his first kill.

[13] The pilots from victories 72-74 are listed as wounded because records to this point do not indicate whether they baled out or crash landed, just that they were reported in Tobruk hospital with injuries. It is claimed Marseille used only 10 cannon shells and 180 bullets to destroy these six aircraft.

[14] Kill was allegedly made at just six feet AGL. (FOTD, p. 126)

[15] Victories 93-95 were from 2, 4, and/ or 5 SAAF; records are confusing and unclear.

[16] Shot down while trying to land at Gambut Airfield.

[17] These kills allegedly came with 20 Rounds of canon and 60 machine gun rounds per kill (80/240 total).

[18] Records indicate P-36s, but probably were P-40s. These kills represent an entire squadron of aircraft.

[19] This kill likely came from one of these two squadrons.

[20] During this running dogfight, Marseille's plane hit by fire. Probably fire from aircraft flown by Wing Commnder J.F. Stocky Edwards. Reports sketchy, but these three claims most likely shared with Stahlschmidt. (Lavigne)

[21] These victories were either Kittyhawks or Spitfires. Once again shows Marseille's poor aircraft recognition.

[22] Marseille claimed a Spitfire, but kill was probably a P-40 F from the USAAF 64th Sqdn. (FOTD, p. 174)

[23] During this combat, Gerhard Homuth also claimed one victory. One of these men may have been downed by him.

[24] See Section "The Curious Case of 15 September" in Victories chapter for detailed discussion of this engagement. Aircraft from 250, 112, and 450 Squadrons RAF and 3 RAAF all participated in this melee. RAAF pilots from 3 RAAF PO Donald baled out and was captured. Sgt Gordon Scribner was KIA. Sgt. Ewing of 450 Squadron was shot down as well. It cannot be ascertained whether Marseille was the confirmed victor in these engagements.

[25] 11 - 12 Minute dogfight. Marseille's last victory. See signed *Signal* card dated 26 September 1942

Sources Used:

1. *Fighters Over the Desert*, by Christopher Shores and Hans Ring.
2. *Kittyhawks Over the Sands*, by Michel Lavigne
3. *Desert Warriors*, by Russell Brown
4. *O.K.L. Fighter Claims: Chef für Ausz. Und Dizsiplin Luftwaffen-Personalamt L.P. (A) V Films and Supplementary Claims from Lists: Mediterranean and Southern Front 1941-1942*, compiled by Tony Woods.
5. *Hans-Joachim Marseille; German Fighter Ace*, by Franz Kurowski.
6. *Marseille: Ein Jagdfliegerschicksal in Daten, Bildern und Dokumenten*, by Walter Wübbe.
7. Correspondance with Russell Brown.

As I compiled this list of Marseille's victory claims over the past decade or so, several things became readily apparent. Combat pilots often state how complex and confusing dogfights can be, and this directly impacts objective attempts at researching victory claims. When comparing several sources for this list, for example, it became obvious that mistakes and contradictory information have been recorded through the years. And although I do not believe this to be an indication of any intentional dishonesty by Marseille, it is an indication of the confusing environment in which he operated. This being said, this list is in no way "all inclusive," and will definitely differ from similar efforts by other researchers. As I compiled this information there are at least five areas that I feel need a modicum of clarification.

1. Aircraft Types: From within these different sources, aircraft have sometimes been mislabeled as Kittyhawks, Tomahawks, or even Hurricanes. I have tried to list the aircraft type only where a known squadron took part in a combat. For example, if a squadron was not specifically identified, I simply listed the aircraft as a Curtiss instead of a Kittyhawk or Tomahawk. Even if Marseille claimed a Tomahawk, with his well-known poor aircraft recognition skills, I still refer to it as a Curtiss unless the squadron is known. If Marseille had a difficult time differentiating a Hurricane from a Curtiss, what are the chances he could tell the difference between a Kittyhawk or a Tomahawk? Likewise, in one or more cases where the squadron is known, if the aircraft claimed is incorrect, I list the correct aircraft type for that squadron. For example, if 5 SAAF was involved in the fight and a claim was made for a Kittyhawk, I changed the list to reflect a Tomahawk since sources show that was the aircraft this unit flew.

Courtesy of Paul Upton

2) Times: It is not uncommon or unusual for times to vary plus or minus several minutes between different records. After all, men marking these times were often more concerned with the battle raging around them than obtaining an exact time hack. Likewise, clerks transcribing times into official records may have incorrectly listed a time as well. If you look at some official records, there is often a time difference of exactly one or two hours between sources. This can be accounted for by the logging of local time as opposed to the logging of GMT (Zulu time) in the records. For the sake of continuity and standardization, all times in this log correspond with Tony Woods' compilation, *O.K.L. Fighter Claims: Chef für Ausz. Und Dizsiplin Luftwaffen-Personalamt L.P. (A) V Films and Supplementary Claims from Lists: Mediterranean and Southern Front 1941-1942*.

3) Locations: These lead to yet other interesting variations. Within these records, there is a wide mix of locations between sources. The areas mentioned where Marseille fought in Libya and Egypt were sometimes quite close to one another, and in one report, for example, a document claims Marseille shot down an aircraft SE of Gazala. In another report, this same claim states NE of Fort Acroma. Geographically, SE of Gazala and NE of Fort Acroma are identical. In several cases, the locations identified in *Fighters Over the Desert* were quite specific, and in those cases they were used. Other times, Tony Woods' compilation was used. Regardless, multiple sources were used to as closely pinpoint Marseille's victories as possible. Once again, the confusion of battle and trying to identify "15 km. SW. of El Alamein" as opposed to "17 miles SW. of El Alamein" could be almost impossible at best to clearly determine. This table presented in this Appendix was used to mark the approximate locations of Marseille's kills on the map found on page 161.

4) Multiple Victories: In cases where multiple victories are registered and the pilots' names are listed, this is in no way an attempt to necessarily verify that Marseille's victims fell in that precise order. For example, on 17 June, Marseille's first five victims were Ward, Wooley, Stone, Goodwin, and Drew. With the exception of Drew, who Ring and Shores identify as Marseille's fifth victim that day, the other four men may have actually fallen in any order. This is another limitation of this type of list. In other words, do not necessarily assume that Marseille's 98th victory was Pilot Officer Stone; for example, he may have actually been number 99 or 97.

Yellow 14 undergoing maintenance. *Courtesy of E & C Collection*

5) Squadrons and Personnel: A quick look at this victory list and you will immediately notice large gaps of information. This should not be surprising. In several cases, more than one and sometimes up to four enemy squadrons were all embroiled in a bitter dogfight. Since it may be impossible to determine with any certainty that one airplane was shot down from within a specific squadron, either the column was left entirely blank (see Marseille's second sortie on 1 September 1942), or in some cases if a known victory came from one of two squadrons, both squadrons were likely annotated in the graph. Also, this is a likely indication that at least some of Marseille's "victories" actually survived, since there may or may not be corroborating data from Allied records.

The bottom line when generating a table like this is that one could spend years trying to decipher all the details and still come up with missing, conflicting, or inaccurate information. Although compiled from several independent sources, this list is not only admittedly incomplete, but very likely contains some errors. But to the best of my ability, and in trying to propose an honest account, this list is a generally fair and relatively accurate representation of Hans-Joachim Marseille's aerial victories.

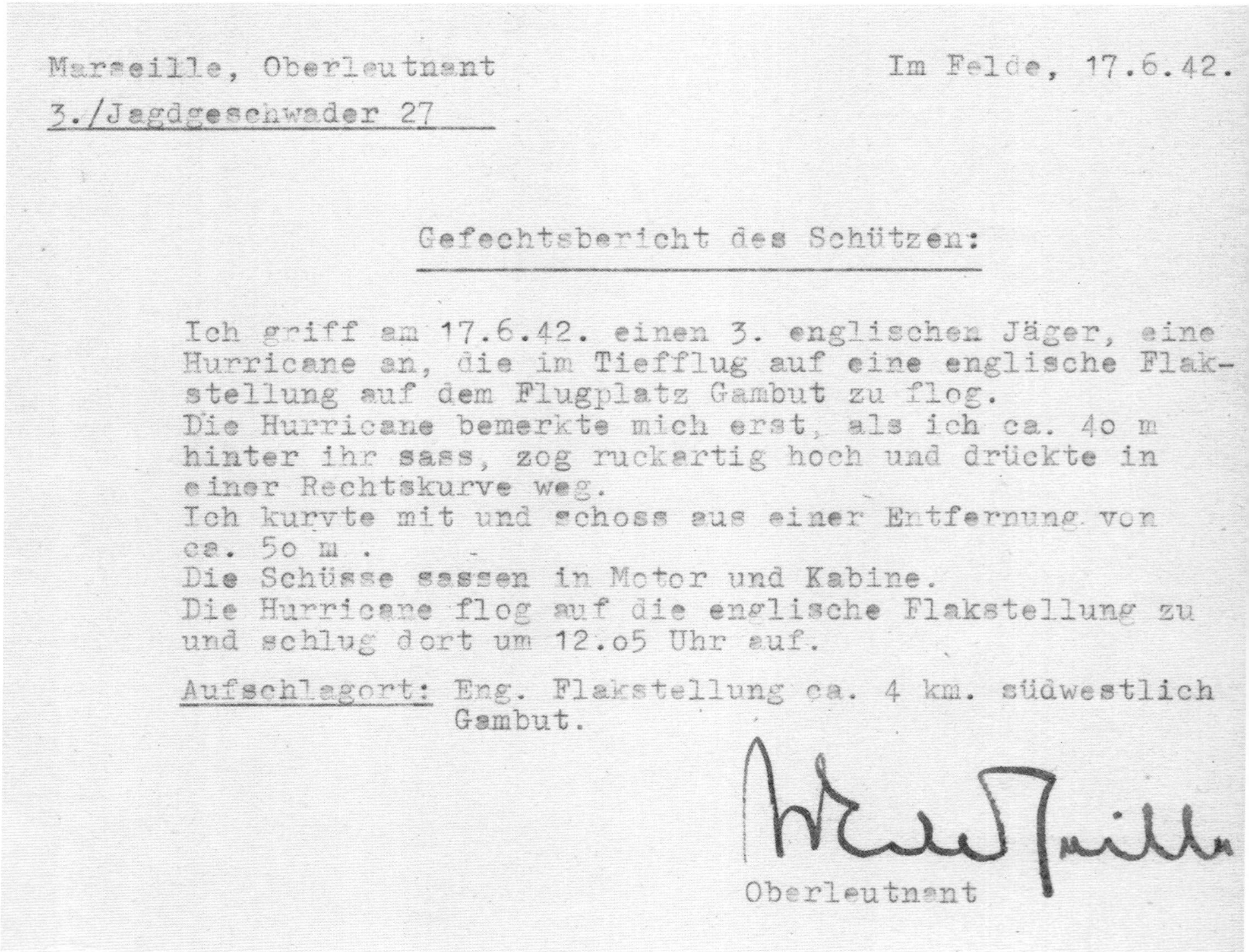

Marseille, Oberleutnant
3./Jagdgeschwader 27

Im Felde, 17.6.42.

Gefechtsbericht des Schützen:

Ich griff am 17.6.42. einen 3. englischen Jäger, eine Hurricane an, die im Tiefflug auf eine englische Flakstellung auf dem Flugplatz Gambut zu flog.
Die Hurricane bemerkte mich erst, als ich ca. 4o m hinter ihr sass, zog ruckartig hoch und drückte in einer Rechtskurve weg.
Ich kurvte mit und schoss aus einer Entfernung von ca. 5o m .
Die Schüsse sassen in Motor und Kabine.
Die Hurricane flog auf die englische Flakstellung zu und schlug dort um 12.o5 Uhr auf.

Aufschlagort: Eng. Flakstellung ca. 4 km. südwestlich Gambut.

Oberleutnant

Marseille's Combat report from 17 June 1942. It reads:

Im Felde / at the front Combat Report of the Gunner:
On the 17th June 1942 I attacked a 3rd British fighter, a Hurricane, which was flying at low level toward a British AA gun position at Gambut air field.
The Hurricane just took notice of me when I was 40 meters behind her, then immediately pulled up and then pushed away in a right turn.
I turned with her and shot from a distance of approximately 50 meters.
The shots hit the engine and cockpit.
The Hurricane flew toward the British AA gun position and impacted there at 12:05.
Impact location: British AA gun position approx. 4 kilometers south-west of Gambut. *Courtesy of Penn Templeman*

This report likely describes Marseille's downing of Australian Pilot Officer Wooley of 73 Squadron RAF. According to other sources, the other two Hurricane pilots he downed that day were able to bail out. This combat report shows Marseille's accuracy in placing his shots within the engine and cockpit. Thanks again to Frank Struppek for the translation.

Appendix 2: Different Theories for Air Combat

Dicta Bölcke[1]

1) Try to secure advantages before attacking. If possible, keep the sun behind you.
2) Always carry through an attack when you have started it.
3) Fire only at close range, and only when your opponent is properly in your sights.
4) Always keep your eye on your opponent, and never let yourself be deceived by ruses.
5) In any form of attack it is essential to assail your opponent from behind.
6) If your opponent dives on you, do not try to evade his onslaught, but fly to meet it.
7) When over the enemy's lines never forget your own line of retreat.
8) For the *Staffel*: attack on principle in groups of four or six. When the fight breaks up into a series of single combats, take care that several do not go for one opponent.

Marseille sporting his Knight's Cross and German Cross in Gold. Note his scarf tucked partially beneath his collar. *Courtesy of Penn Templeman*

Sailor Malan's Ten Rules for Air Fighting[2]

1) Wait until you see the whites of his eyes. Fire short bursts of one or two seconds, and only when your sights are definitely "ON."
2) Whilst shooting, think of nothing else, brace the whole of your body, have both hands on the stick, and concentrate on your ring sight.
3) Always keep a sharp lookout. "Keep your finger out!"
4) Height gives You the initiative.
5) Always turn and face the attack.
6) Make your decisions promptly. It is better to act quickly even though your tactics are not the best.
7) Never fly straight and level for more than thirty seconds in the combat area.
8) When diving to attack, always leave a proportion of your formation above to act as top guard.
9) INITIATIVE, AGGRESSION, AIR DISCIPLINE, and TEAMWORK are words that MEAN something in air fighting.
10) Go in quickly – Punch hard – Get out!

Erich Hartmann's Method[3]

1) See – You must first locate the enemy.
2) Decide – The pilot must look at the situation in its entirety (position, location, number of enemy aircraft) and then decide whether an attack is in his favor or not. Whether the enemy can be surprised is of utmost importance.
3) Attack – If the pilot decides the attack is in his favor, he must attack quickly and decisively. After the attack, the pilot must break away.
4) Reverse – If the pilot decides the situation is not in his favor, he should retreat and live to fight another day. Don't get into a turning battle with an opponent who knows you are there. Once the element of surprise is forfeited, move on.

Courtesy of author

The "Ace of Aces." Erich Hartmann led all pilots with 352 aerial victories. *Courtesy of author*

Another mission to go. *Courtesy of E & C Collection*

Boyd's OODA Loop[4]

1) Observe – Analyze the current situation
2) Orient – Favorably position oneself for an attack. Decide exactly what to do.
3) Decide – After analyzing all relevant information, make a decision and follow it through.
4) Act – Take decisive action based upon your decision.

Appendix 3:
Hans-Joachim Marseille's Major Awards and Decorations

Awards	**Date**
Flugzeugführerabzeichen	01 FEB 1940
Iron Cross Second Class	09 SEP 1940
Iron Cross First Class	17 SEP 1940
Ehrenpokal	03 NOV 1941
German Cross in Gold	11 NOV 1941 (07 DEC 1941 Pinned On)
Knight's Cross of the Iron Cross	22 FEB 1942
Knight's Cross with Oak Leaves*	06 JUN 1942
Knight's Cross with Oak Leaves and Swords	**18 JUN 1942
Medaglia d' Oro al Valor Militare	06 AUG 1942
Knight's Cross with Oak Leaves, Swords and Diamonds***	03 SEP 1942

Other Awards and Decorations
Silver Italian *Tapferkeitsmedaille*
Frontflugspange für Jäger in Bronze
Frontflugspange für Jäger in Silver
Frontflugspange für Jäger in Gold
Ärmelband Africa

* Marseille was the 43rd *Luftwaffe* member to receive this award.
** Marseille was the 10th *Luftwaffe* member to receive this award.
*** Marseille was the 4th *Luftwaffe* member to receive this award. (Marseille died before receiving the Diamonds)

Marseille proudly displays his new German Cross in Gold. *Courtesy of Paul Upton*

These two photographs taken on 7 December 1941 show Marseille being awarded the German Cross in Gold by Edu Neumann with Field Marshal Kesselring in the background. Half a world away, America was suddenly thrust into the war. *Courtesy of E & C Collection*

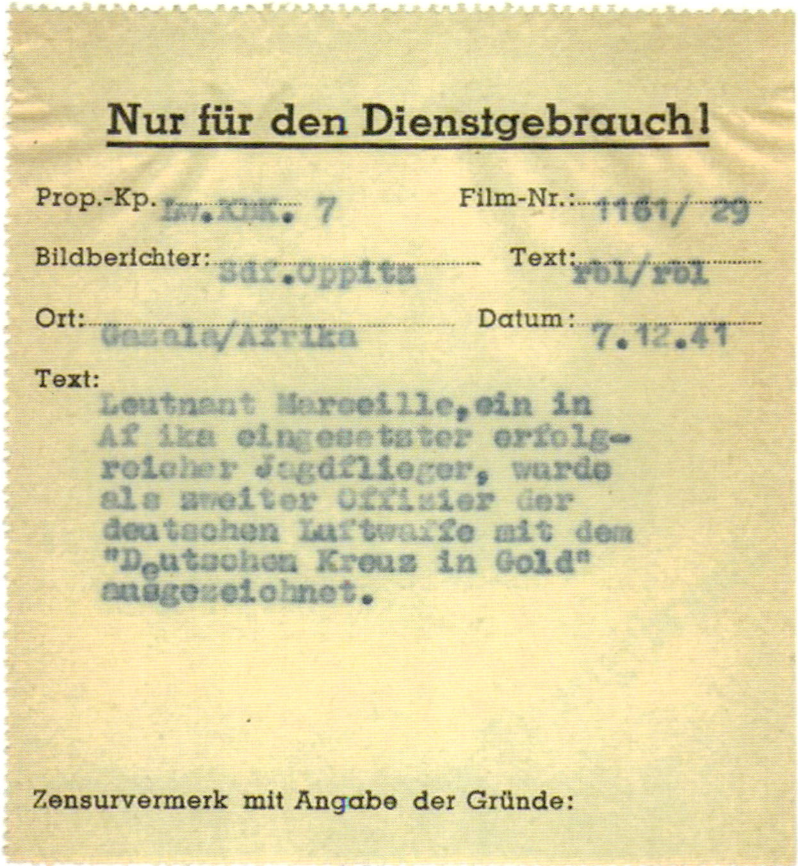

Nur für den Dienstgebrauch!

Prop.-Kp. Lw.KBK. 7 Film-Nr.: 1161/ 29

Bildberichter: Sdf.Oppitz Text: Fbl/Fbl

Ort: Gazala/Afrika Datum: 7.12.41

Text:
Leutnant Marseille, ein in Af ika eingesetzter erfolgreicher Jagdflieger, wurde als zweiter Offizier der deutschen Luftwaffe mit dem "Deutschen Kreuz in Gold" ausgezeichnet.

Zensurvermerk mit Angabe der Gründe:

The document states "Leutnant Marseille, ein in Afrika eingesetzter erfolgreicher *Jagdflieger*, wurde als zweiter Offizier der Deutschen *Luftwaffe* mit dem 'Deutschen Kreuz im Gold' ansgezeichnet." "Leutnant Marseille, a successful fighter pilot stationed in Africa was the second officer in the German *Luftwaffe* to be awarded the German Cross in Gold." At this time, Marseille had recently returned from Germany retraining on the new Bf-109F Trop. On this day Marseille claimed his 29th victory; a 274 Squadron Hurricane piloted by a Flight Lieutenant Hobbs, 20 km South of Sidi Omar. *Courtesy of Paul Upton*

Left and following: On 19 October 1942, Marseille was awarded the *Ehrenpokal*, or Fighter Pilot's Trophy (actually presented to him on 11 November 1941). At this time Marseille had gained 25 aerial victories. Although thought lost to history, it is shown here, for the first time since the end of the war, in a series of photographs. The owner wishes to remain anonymous. *All Courtesy of undisclosed source*

HANS-JOACHIM
LEISTUNG

1939
AM 19.10.41
KRIEG • FÜR

LEUTNANT HANS
BESONDERE

AM 19.10.41
KRIEG FÜR

HANS-JOACHIM
LEISTUNG

MARSEILLE
IM

PARISER

Postverlagsort Köln — Verlag und Schriftleitung: Paris, 100, rue Réaumur, Postanschrift: Köln I, Postfach 621. Tel.: Gutenberg 80-60, Postscheckkonto Paris 2.655.94, Bankkonto Crédit Lyonnais, Agence H, Paris (2e), Nr. 43 523. — In Deutschland: Postscheckkonto der Dresdner Bank, Berlin Nr. 800, mit Vermerk „für Pariser Zeitung".

Nr. 155/ Jahrg. 2/

PREIS fFr. 2. - IM REICH 20 Pfg. - IN BELGIEN bFr. 1.25.

ZEITUNG

Montag, 8. Juni 1942

Die „Pariser Zeitung" erscheint täglich morgens, auch Sonntags. Sie ist an jedem Zeitungsstand oder im Monatsbezug durch die Post erhältlich. Der Bezugspreis beträgt in Frankreich monatlich Frs. 45.— im Vierteljahr Frs. 120.— Bezugspreis im Reich RM 3.— zuzügl. Zustellgebühr. Bestellungen in Frankreich beim Verlag direkt, im Reich bei jeder Postanstalt.

Das Eichenlaub zum Ritterkreuz für Oberleutnant Marseille

Berlin, 7. Juni.

Dem Staffelkapitän in einem Jagdgeschwader, Oberleutnant Marseille, hat der Führer das Eichenlaub zum Ritterkreuz des Eisernen Kreuzes verliehen und ihm nachstehendes Schreiben übermittelt:

„In dankbarer Würdigung Ihres heldenhaften Einsatzes im Kampf für die Zukunft unseres Volkes verleihe ich Ihnen als 97. Soldaten der deutschen Wehrmacht das Eichenlaub zum Ritterkreuz des Eisernen Kreuzes.

Adolf Hitler"

From the newspaper *Pariser Zeitung*, dated 8 June 1942, it has been announced that Marseille will be receiving the Knight's Cross with Oak Leaves. It also says he is the 97th soldier to be awarded the Oak Leaves. *Courtesy of author*

Erfolgreichster Jagdflieger über Afrika

Oberleutnant Marseille, Staffelkapitän in einem Jagdgeschwader, der kürzlich vom Führer mit dem Eichenlaub ausgezeichnet wurde, ist der erfolgreichste Jagdflieger an der nordafrikanischen Front. Er errang jetzt seinen 87. Luftsieg. Der erst 22 Jahre alte Eichenlaubträger stammt aus Berlin. Nach kurzem Einsatz auf dem Balkan wurde er mit seiner Staffel im April vorigen Jahres nach Afrika verlegt. Oberleutnant Marseille hat mit kühnem Mut und einem geradezu wunderbaren Jagdglück stetig seine Abschußziffer erhöht. Am 24. Februar 1942 wurde ihm für seinen 40. Luftsieg das Ritterkreuz zum Eisernen Kreuz von Generalfeldmarschall Kesselring persönlich überreicht. Wenn ihm jetzt der Führer in Würdigung seines heldenhaften Einsatzes das Eichenlaub zum Ritterkreuz verlieh, so fanden Tat, Leistung und der Geist bleibender Einsatzbereitschaft trotz der harten körperlichen und seelischen Bedingungen seines Lebens und Kämpfens in der Wüste durch diese hohe Auszeichnung die Anerkennung, die der deutsche Afrikakämpfer seinem erfolgreichsten Jagdflieger aus ehrlichem Herzen zollt.

Aufn.: Presse-Hoffmann

Another newspaper clipping announcing the awarding of the Knight's Cross with Oak Leaves to Marseille. *Courtesy of Penn Templeman*

On 18 June 1942, one day after achieving his 101st aerial victory, Marseille stood before Adolf Hitler to receive the Knight's Cross with Oak Leaves and Swords. *Courtesy of author*

These two color photographs show Marseille wearing his newly awarded Knight's Cross with Oak Leaves and Swords. *Courtesy of E & C Collection*

Courtesy of Author

Formal shot of Marseille wearing the Oak Leaves and Swords. *Courtesy of author*

Cashing in on Marseille's popularity in the summer of 1942, the German propaganda machine went into overdrive, exploiting the *Star of Africa's* successes in the desert. These photographs capture Marseille in a photo-op as one of Germany's most popular personalities. *All Courtesy of author*

Die höchste Auszeichnung für Oberleutnant Marseille

Eichenlaub mit Schwertern und Brillanten nach dem 125. Luftsieg

Berlin, 5. September

Der Führer hat Oberleutnant Marseille, Staffelkapitän in einem Jagdgeschwader, das Eichenlaub mit Schwertern und Brillanten zum Ritterkreuz des Eisernen Kreuzes verliehen und ihm folgendes Schreiben übermittelt:

„In Würdigung Ihres immerwährenden heldenmütigen Einsatzes im Kampf für die Freiheit unseres Volkes verleihe ich Ihnen anläßlich Ihres 125. Luftsieges als viertem Soldaten der deutschen Wehrmacht die höchste deutsche Tapferkeitsauszeichnung, das Eichenlaub mit Schwertern und Brillanten zum Ritterkreuz des Eisernen Kreuzes. Adolf Hitler."

Der Glückwunsch des Reichsmarschalls lautet:

„Mein lieber Marseille!

Ich bin unendlich stolz auf Ihre überragenden Erfolge. In unbeugsamem Kampf- und Siegeswillen haben Sie den britischen Gegner in der Luft bezwungen, wo Sie ihn nur trafen. Dankbar und voll Bewunderung beglückwünsche ich Sie zu der Ihnen vom Führer verliehenen höchsten deutschen Tapferkeitsauszeichnung. Seien Sie versichert, lieber Marseille, daß mit mir das ganze deutsche Volk in Ihnen einen seiner größten Helden dieses Krieges erblickt. Kämpfen Sie, vom immerwährenden Soldatenglück begünstigt, in diesem Geiste weiter für den Endsieg unserer Waffen.

Ihr Göring,
Reichsmarschall des Großdeutschen Reiches
und Oberbefehlshaber der Luftwaffe.

*

Der als Sohn eines Generalmajors am 13. Dezember 1919 zu Berlin-Charlottenburg geborene Oberleutnant Hans Joachim Marseille gehört zu den deutschen Jagdfliegern, deren Name eines Tages nach sich rasch steigernden Erfolgen in aller Mund war. Mit sieben Luftsiegen kam der damalige Oberfähnrich im Frühjahr 1941 nach Afrika, wo er kurz darauf Offizier wurde.

Aufnahme: Weltbild OKW.

Mit unbeirrbarem Kampfeswillen ein ebenso draufgängerischer wie besonnener Jagdflieger, stellte er seine Gegner, schoß einen nach dem anderen ab und erhielt nach 46 Luftsiegen am 22. Februar 1942 das Ritterkreuz des Eisernen Kreuzes. Er wurde Oberleutnant und Staffelkapitän, entwickelte sich immer mehr zum gefürchtetsten deutschen Jagdflieger in Nordafrika und wurde nach seinem 75. Abschuß am 6. Juni 1942 vom Führer durch Verleihung des Eichenlaubes zum Ritterkreuz ausgezeichnet. Aber seine Siegeskurve stieg noch steiler in die Höhe. Nur elf Tage später war ein weiteres Viertelhundert britischer Flugzeuge abgeschossen: der 101. Luftsieg war errungen, und Oberleutnant Marseille erhielt das Eichenlaub mit Schwertern zum Ritterkreuz des Eisernen Kreuzes. Und nun, am 2. September 1942, erkämpfte er an der ägyptischen Front den 125. Luftsieg, nachdem er allein tags zuvor 16 britische Gegner abgeschossen hatte und damit eine einzigartige Leistung vollbrachte. Nach Mölders, Galland und Gollob wurden ihm nun die Brillanten zum Ritterkreuz des Eisernen Kreuzes mit Eichenlaub und Schwertern als höchste Tapferkeitsauszeichnung verliehen. Die von ihm bezwungenen Gegner sind ausschließlich Engländer, in der Hauptsache Jagdflieger.

Newspaper clipping anncunces the awarding of the diamonds to Marseill≥ after his 125th aer al victory. *Courtesy of Pern Templeman*

Appendix 4: Ranks of Hans-Joachim Marseille

Date	Rank	U.S. Equivalent
07 NOV 1938	*Flieger*	No Equivalent Rank*
13 MAR 1939	*Fahnenjunker*	No Equivalent Rank*
01 MAY 1939	*Fahnenjunker-Gefreiter*	No Equivalent Rank*
01 JUL 1939	*Fahnenjunker-Unteroffizier*	No Equivalent Rank*
01 NOV 1939	*Fähnrich*	No Equivalent Rank*
01 MAR 1941	*Oberfähnrich*	No Equivalent Rank*
01 APR 1941	*Leutnant*	2 Lieutenant
16 JUN 1941	*Leutnant* (Pinned On)	2 Lieutenant
01 APR 1942	*Oberleutnant*	1 Lieutenant
08 MAY 1942	*Oberleutnant* (Pinned On)	1 Lieutenant
08 JUN 1942	*Staffelkapitän* 3/ JG 27	Squadron Commander
01 SEP 1942	*Hauptmann* in the *Luftwaffe*)	Captain (Youngest
16 SEP 1942	*Hauptmann*	Captain (Pinned On)

Note: The *Luftwaffe* retained several junior pilot ranks for which there was no equivalent in any Allied air force. Likewise, the *Luftwaffe* maintained several "cadet officer ranks"(*). These positions were a sort of "holding pattern" for young pilots until they demonstrated the maturity to hold an officer's commission. Notice how long Marseille remained in this category; an indication of how little respect authorities had for the young, impetuous Berliner.

Also, the position of Squadron Commander (*Staffelkapitän*) did not necessarily carry with it the rank of "Captain" (*Hauptmann*). The two were not synonymous.

Two photographs showing Marseille's W.Nr. 8693 being refueled. Note how the sand has removed the paint from the prop, which is now one-half bare metal. The desert climate was certainly harsh on all mechanical equipment. Above: *Courtesy of E & C Collection* Below: *Courtesy of Paul Upton*

Appendix 5: Photo-Cards, Postcards, and Autographs

Like any well oiled machine, the German propaganda mill continually churned out information to help sell their cause and promote the men and machines that served the Reich. To accomplish this, many tools were used to include weekly news reels (The *Wochenschau*), postcards, photo opportunities with their military celebrities, and newspaper and magazine articles. There was never a shortage of attempts by the National Socialists to sway public opinion in their favor.

One interesting aspect of these propaganda attempts was the creation of postcards by companies like Hoffmann, Röhr, and Hansmann. Much like baseball cards traded by American kids today, these postcards showed the images of some of the more successful and popular *Wehrmacht* soldiers and airmen. German kids would trade these cards with one another, and often send them off to be signed by the member featured on the card. With Marseille's extreme good looks and success in the desert, he was the perfect poster child for the regime. To this end, the companies making these postcards eagerly included Marseille's image whenever possible. On the next several pages you will find several postcards featuring Marseille that I have been fortunate enough to gather over the years.

Another aspect of this phenomenon was that after soldiers had become famous, people would not only send these postcards to be signed, but they would also take photographs from magazines like *Der Adler*, *Die Berliner Illustrierte Zeitung*, and *Die Wehrmacht*, cut them out, affix them to paper or cardstock, and then send them to be signed by their hero. It has been mentioned that with Marseille's "Rock Star" like status and popularity, he would regularly get sacks of mail from adoring fans asking for autographs, photos, and whatever he might be willing to offer up. In this section, you will also see two examples of these photos signed by Marseille.

Today, the interest in Marseille has waned very little. Through many avenues, collectors can still find these historical Marseille items. For those with deep pockets and the willingness to own original Marseille artifacts, items such as autographs, letters, postcards, and photographs can still be found on the market. Some of these are also shown below.

Another signed card from "Der Adler" on cardstock. This photograph shows Marseille climbing from his Messerschmitt, and is dated 26 September 1942. It is interesting that this card was signed by Marseille on the day he achieved his final victory. *Courtesy of author*

Signed photo on cardstock. Marseille is pictured standing on the wing of a downed Kittyhawk H5-A. Marseille signed this card on 2 September 1942. The card reads: "Als Andenken u. Erinnerung Joachim Marseille, *Oberleutnant* u. *Staffelkap*. Afrika, 2.9.42." In discussions with Australian historian Russell Brown, it is possible this photograph shows the aircraft of Squadron Leader Pedro Hanbury (260 Squadron RAF) after Marseille claimed to have shot him down on 25 April 1942. *Courtesy of author*

A Hoffman Feldpost. The original shows considerable aging, while the other image has been saved in a grayscale tone to show its original appearance. Unlike other Hoffman style postcards, the Feldpost actually opens up to allow a letter to be written inside. *Both Courtesy of author*

A signed Hoffmann postcard showing Marseille in his desert "Bum Freezer" uniform. This photograph was likely taken immediately after being awarded the Knight's Cross with Oak Leaves and Swords. Once again, I have saved the original image and also made another image of the original in grayscale to remove the fading. Both the front and back of the postcard are displayed. *Courtesy of author*

A Hoffman postcard (366) front and back. *Courtesy of author*

Another Hoffman postcard (R-219) front and back. *Courtesy of author*

A Röhr postcard, front and back. *Courtesy of author*

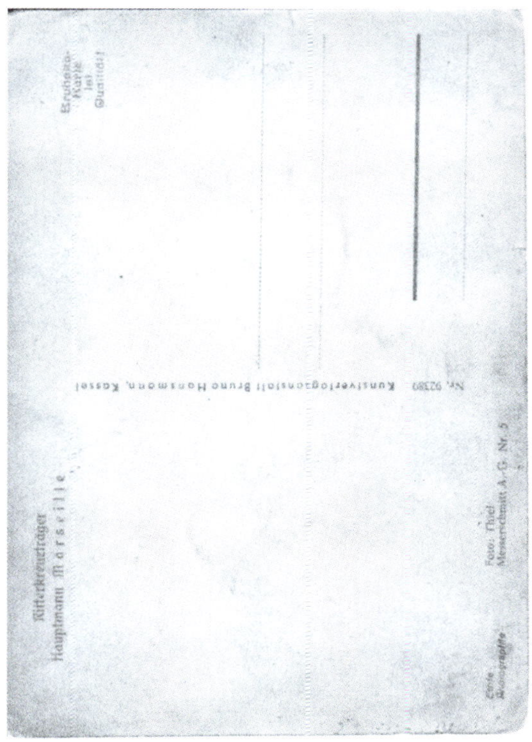

A Bruno Hansmann card, front and back. During Marseille's summer leave of 1942, he visited the Messerschmitt factory in Augsburg. There he met with Willy Messerschmitt and had the opportunity to fly a new Bf-109 G-2, the same type of aircraft that would kill him a little over a month later. This photograph was taken during Marseille's visit to the Messerschmitt factory. *Courtesy of author*

An interesting photograph I received in my collection over 15 years ago. This photograph at one time allegedly belonged to Werner Schrör and came from his personal collection. As translated by my good friend Frank Struppek, the other side of the photograph reads, "Du kannst mich mal an meiner 6. Hose riechen. Jochen." Directly translated, this salutation says, "You can sniff the 6 o'clock position of my pants, Jochen." In other words, the playful Marseille is telling Schrör to "Kiss his bottom." Another interesting thing about this photograph and the one of Marseille in front of the Hotel Regina is that when he signed a very personal card he called himself "Jochen," which of course was his nickname to his friends and comrades. For the more impersonal autographs, he normally signed his name as Hans-Joachim Marseille, Joachim Marseille, *Hauptmann*, *Staffelkäpitan*, or simply Marseille. His personal touch of "Jochen" makes this photograph a bit more interesting to me. *Courtesy of author*

Interesting photo dated 14 March 1942 while Marseille was on leave in Germany. The caption on the reverse states: "Where are we going today, Werner? To eat caviar with bread! You have to pay, Werner!! Jochen, Munich, 14.3.42." Werner refers to Marseille's good friend and comrade, Werner Schrör. In a letter sent to a Mr. Herbst, Schrör is unable to identify the second man, although he does state the photograph was taken in front of the Regina Hotel in Munich. *Courtesy of author*

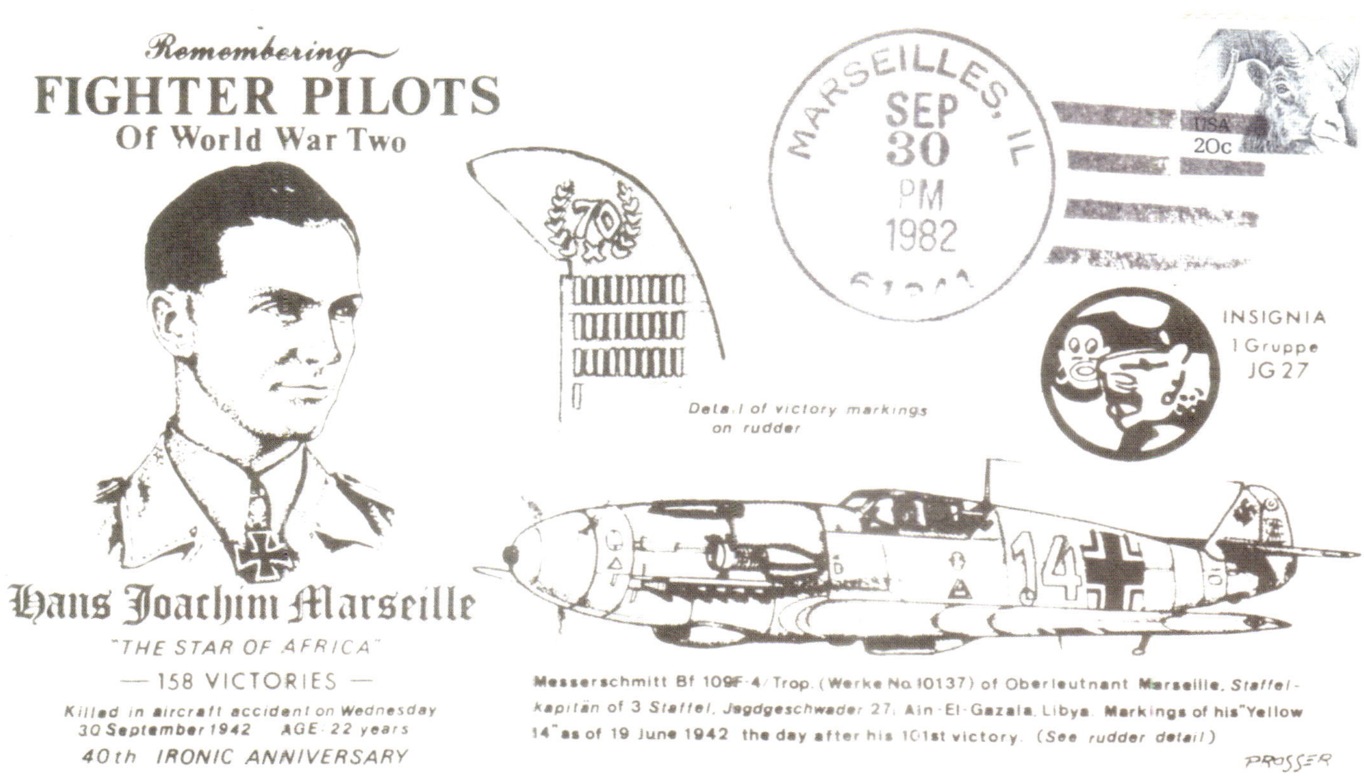

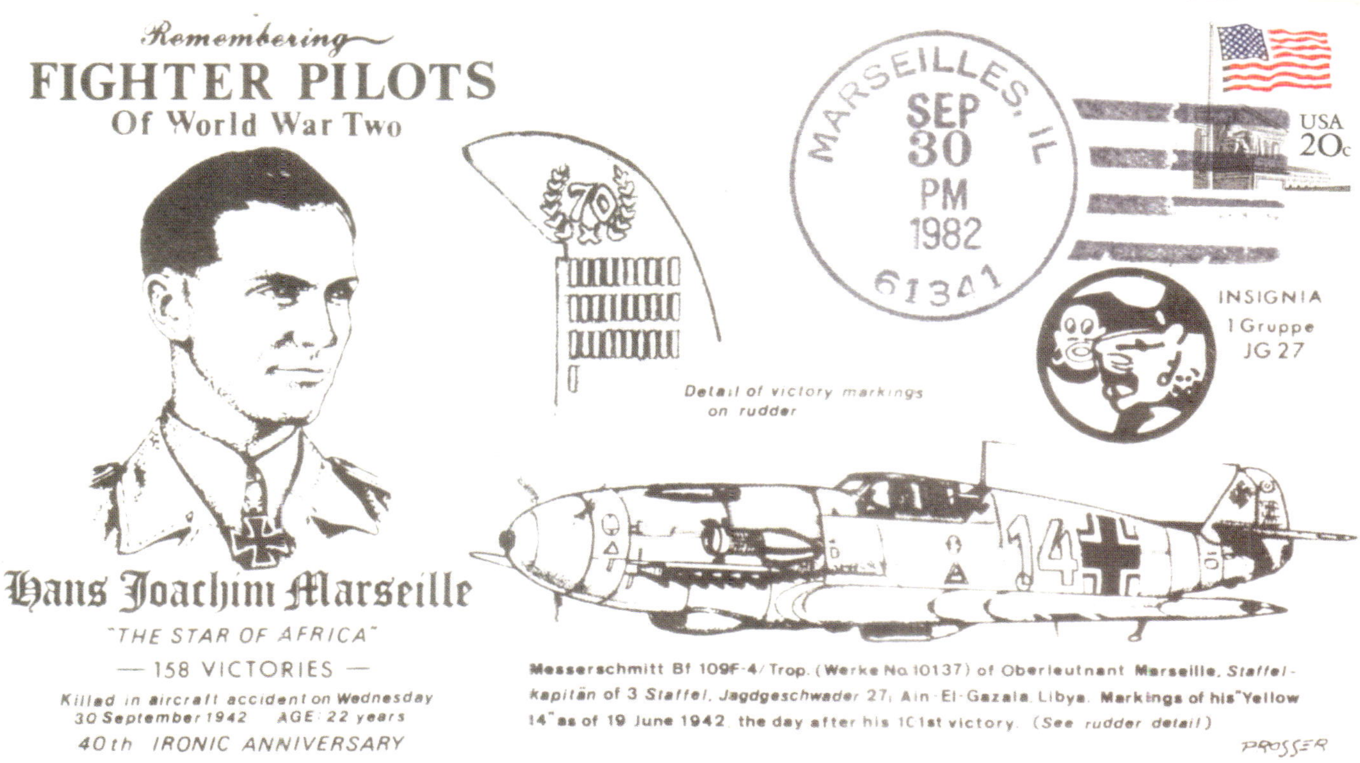

Two commemorative envelopes marking the 40th anniversary of Marseille's death. *Photo courtesy of author*

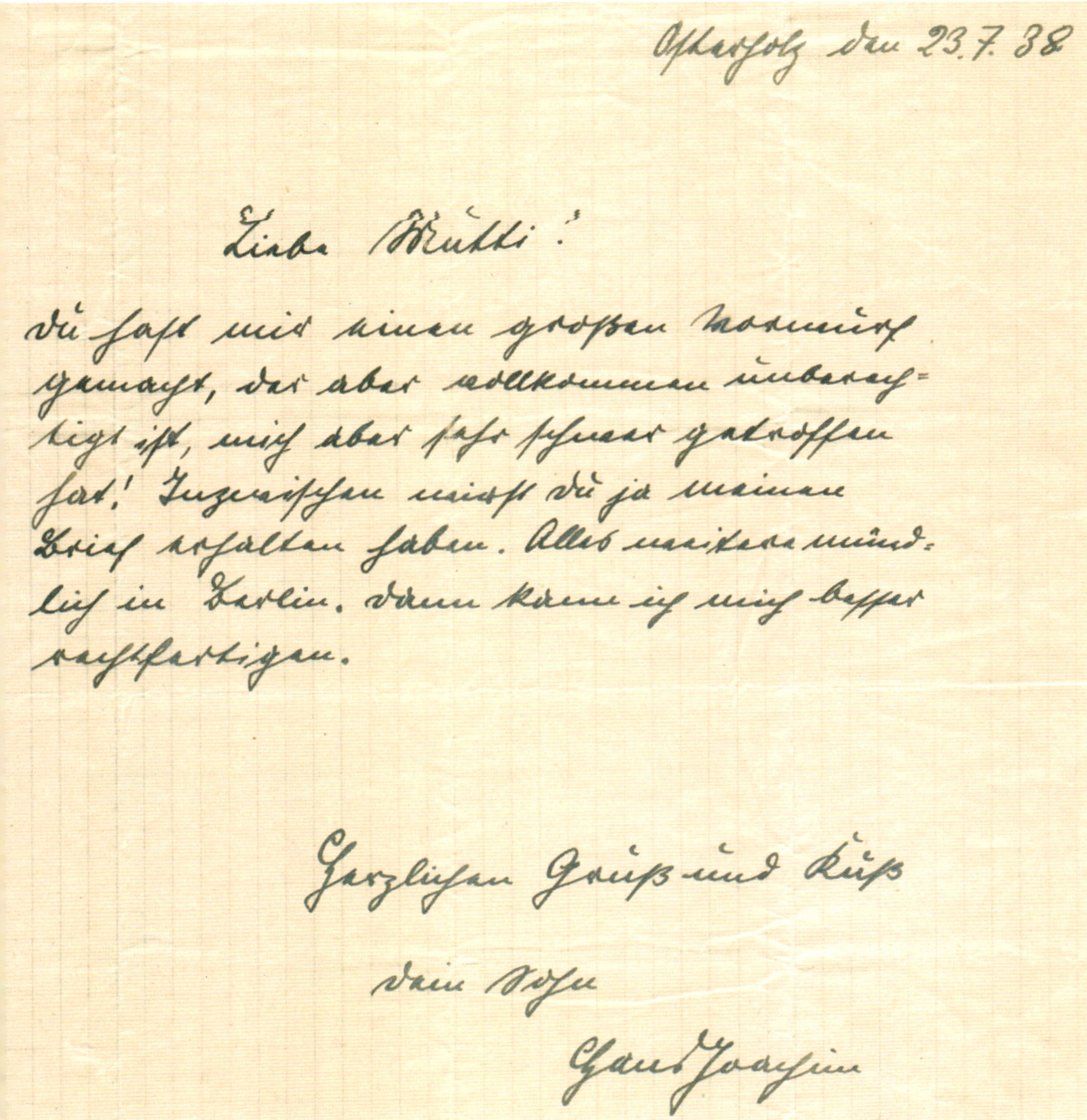

Osterholz den 23.7.38

Liebe Mutti!

Du hast mir einen grossen Vorwurf gemacht, der aber vollkommen unberechtigt ist, mich aber sehr schwer getroffen hat! Inzwischen wirst du ja meinen Brief erhalten haben. Alles weitere mündlich in Berlin. dann kann ich mich besser rechtfertigen.

Herzlichen Gruß und Kuß

dein Sohn

Hans Joachim

Courtesy of Author

Dear Mutti,

You have made a large accusation, which has no founda
but which hurt me deeply! In the meantime, you must
have received my letter. Anything further verbally in Be
there it will be better to exonerate myself. (or set things
straight,)

Dearest greetings and a kiss,

Your son,

Hans Joachim.

This is a handwritten letter Marseille wrote to his mother on 23 July 1938. The translation appears next to the letter. Although it is apparent that he and his mother had some sort of disagreement, the respect he has toward his mother remains evident.

Appendix 6: I/JG 27 North African Airfields

Location	Dates
	1941
Ain el Gazala, Libya	22 APR–7 DEC
Tmimi, Libya	07 DEC–12 DEC
Martuba, Libya	12 DEC–17 DEC
Magrum, Libya	17 DEC–23 DEC
Sirte, Libya	23 DEC–26 DEC
Arco Philaenorum, Libya	26 DEC–01 JAN
	1942
Agedabia, Libya	01 JAN–22 JAN
El Agheila, Libya	22 JAN–27 JAN
Agedabia, Libya	27 JAN–01 FEB
Benina, Libya	01 FEB–07 FEB
Martuba, Libya	07 FEB–22 MAY
Tmimi, Libya	22 MAY–14 JUN
Derna, Libya	14 JUN–16 JUN
Ain el Gazala, Libya	16 JUN–22 JUN
Gambut, Libya	22 JUN–25 JUN
Sidi Barrani, Egypt	25 JUN–27 JUN
Bir el Astas, Egypt	27 JUN–02 JUL
Mumin Busak, Egypt	02 JUL–07 JUL
Turbiya, Egypt	07 JUL–20 JUL
Quotaifiya, Egypt	20 JUL–02 OCT

*See North African Map in Appendix 1

A photograph of 2 *Staffel* JG 27 Bf 109Es in the desert. *Courtesy of Penn Templeman*

Although never used for its original purpose, Benito Mussolini's Triumphant Marble Arch stands on the Libyan coast as a testimony to failed Italian aspirations in North Africa. *Courtesy of Paul Upton*

An excellent close-up view of Mussolini's triumphant arch. *Courtesy of E & C Collection*

A rare photograph of 2 *Staffel* Bf 109Fs. In the distance you can clearly see the Arco Philaenorum, Mussolini's "Triumphant arch." This photograph dates between 26 December 1941 and 01 Jan 1942, when I/JG 27 was stationed in that part of Libya. *Courtesy of Penn Templeman*

Appendix 7: Primary DAF Squadrons and Aircraft Flown

RAF Squadrons	Aircraft Flown
6	Hurricane 2D
33	Hurricane 2C
46	Beaufighter
55	Baltimore
73	Hurricane 2C
80	Hurricane 2B
89	Beaufighter
92	Spitfire V
94	Hurricane 2B and Spitfire V
112	Kittyhawk
127	Hurricane 2B
145	Spitfire V
208	Hurricane 2B
213	Hurricane 2C
223	Baltimore
238	Hurricane 2C
250	Kittyhawk
260	Kittyhawk
274	Hurricane 2C
335	Hurricane 2B
417	Hurricane 2B and Spitfire V
601	Spitfire V

Royal Australian Air Force Sq.	Aircraft Flown
3 RAAF	Tomahawk
450 RAAF	Kittyhawk
451 RAAF (Recon)	Hurricane Mk. 1
South African Air Force Sq.	
1 SAAF	Hurricane 2C
2 SAAF	Kittyhawk
4 SAAF	Kittyhawk
5 SAAF	Tomahawk
7 SAAF	Hurricane 2D
12 SAAF	Boston
21 SAAF	Baltimore
24 SAAF	Boston
40 SAAF	Hurricane 2B
60 SAAF	Baltimore
USAAF Sq.	
64, 65, 66 Squadrons	P-40F Warhawk
81,82, 83, 434 Squadrons	B-25 Mitchell

Appendix 8:
Chronological Listing of RAAF Pilots Downed by Marseille

This is a list of Australian pilots downed by Marseille. Either these pilots flew with RAAF squadrons or were part of RAF Squadrons in the desert. Information for this section was graciously provided by author Mr. Russell Brown. Both photographs and photo captions were obtained, with his permission, from his book on Australian fighter pilots in North Africa titled *Desert Warriors: Australian P-40 pilots at war in the Middle East and North Africa 1941-1943*.

Name	Date	Squadron	Fate
FO Roberts	12/10/41	3 RAAF	Crash Landed
Sgt. Scott	12/10/41	3 RAAF	Landed with damage
FO Trimble	13/12/41	3 RAAF	Crash Landed
Sgt. Reid	15/02/42	3 RAAF	KIA
FO Briggs	15/02/42	3 RAAF	Baled Out
PO Hart	27/02/42	3 RAAF	Baled Out
Sgt. Jennings	27/02/42	3 RAAF	KIA
FO Pace	13/05/42	3 RAAF	KIA
Sgt. McDiarmid	13/05/42	3 RAAF	Baled Out
Sgt. Teede	16/05/42	3 RAAF	Crash Landed on Fire
PO Parker	16/05/42	450 RAAF	Baled Out
Sgt. Metherall	16/05/42	450 RAAF	KIA
Sgt. Young	19/05/42	450 RAAF	Crash Landed
Unk.	19/05/42	450 RAAF	Cat II Damaged
Sgt. Buckland	30/05/42	250 RAF	KIA
Sgt. Halliday	13/06/42	450 RAAF	KIA
Sgt. Stone	13/06/42	450 RAAF	KIA
PO Osborne	13/06/42	450 RAAF	Crash Landed
Sgt. Drew	17/06/42	112 RAF	KIA
PO Donald	15/09/42	3 RAAF	Baled Out (POW)
Sgt. Scribner	15/09/42	3 RAAF	KIA
Sgt. Ewing	15/09/42	450 RAAF	POW

* Parker's airplane collided with Metherall's. Marseille did not claim this.

This Tomahawk was originally CO Alan Rawlinson's, hence the "R." It was flown by Dudley Parker on this date (12/10/41) when he was shot down, probably by Rudolf Sinner, but its significance is that it was in the first fight Marseille had with 3 RAAF. Most of their aircraft had been re-camouflaged by this date, but AN335 was still wearing dark green and dark earth. *Courtesy of Russell Brown*

This photograph shows three of Marseille's RAAF victims. FO Roberts is on top of the fuselage, Sgt. Reid is standing in front of the lower propeller blade, and FO Trimble is standing on the far right. Of the 15 pilots shown in this photograph, only two came through the war without being injured, captured, or killed. *Courtesy of Russell Brown*

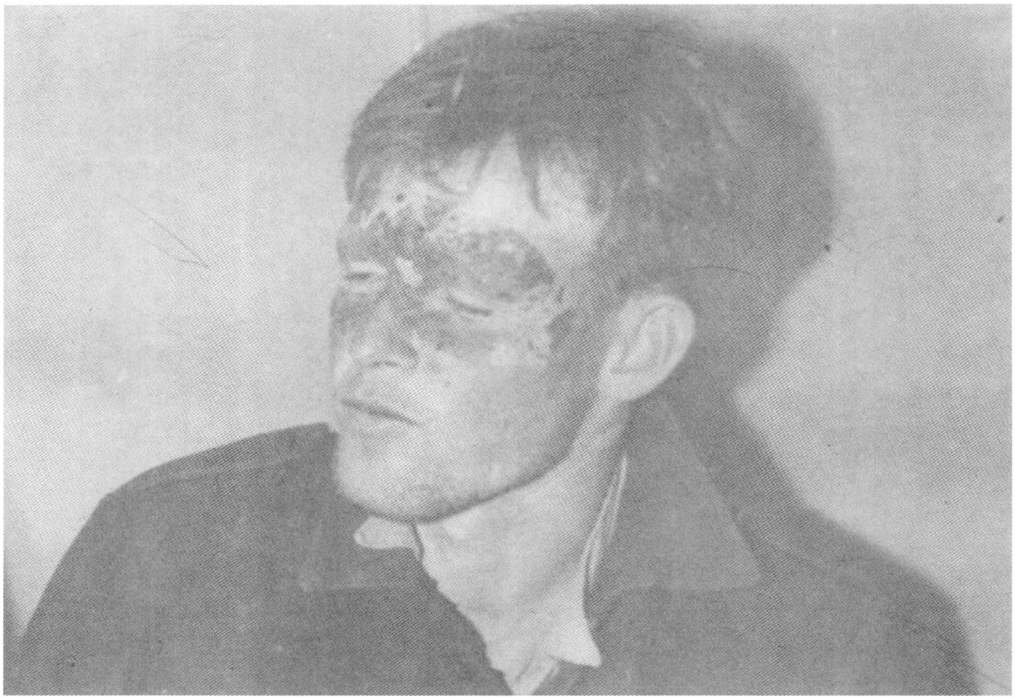

Photograph shows the burns FO Tom Trimble received after his encounter with Marseille on 13 December 1941. *Courtesy of Russell Brown*

3 RAAF pilots at LG (Landing Ground) 102, Sidi Heneish, September 1941. In this picture, five of Marseille's victims can be seen: 1: FO "Robbie" Roberts, 2: Sgt. Frank Reid, 3: Sgt. Dudley Parker, 4: Sgt. Derek Scott, and 5: FO Tom Trimble. *Courtesy of Russell Brown*

Five men at Msus, January 1942. FO Graham Pace, Marseille's 57th victory, stands in the middle. *Courtesy of Russell Brown*

The following is a scan from a contemporary newspaper. Although the quality is not too good, Tommy Briggs (15/02/42), Dick Hart (27/02/42), and Graham Pace (13/05/42) are found in this interesting photograph. *Courtesy of Russell Brown*

Above: A group of 450 Squadron pilots at LG91, mid-1942. Left to right rear: Rod Hughes, (Canadian) George O'Neill, Max Jenkins, and F.E. Parker. Front, left to right: Don McBurnie, Frank Schaaf, and Gordon Lindsay. F.E. Parker was Marseille's 60th victory. After parachuting to safety, it was Parker's aircraft that collided with Sgt. W.J. Metherall. *Courtesy of Russell Brown* Below: A group of 450 RAAF pilots with their "battle buggy." Sgt. Ivan Young, Marseille's 62nd victory, sits in the back seat wearing the cap. The marking on the mudguard identifies this vehicle as belonging to 8 Panzer Regiment, 15 Panzer Division. *Courtesy of Russell Brown*

Sergeant William "Bubba" Halliday. At nineteen, he was the youngest pilot in 450 Squadron. Marseille's 84th victory poses on the wing of his slightly damaged Kittyhawk. *Courtesy of Russell Brown*

Sgt. Drew of 112 Squadron. He was shot down and killed by Marseille on 17 June 1942. He was likely Marseille's 100th victory. *Courtesy of Russell Brown*

Left to Right: Danny Boardman, Garth Neill, Gordon Scribner, and Jack Donald of 3 RAAF at Aboukir beach camp, August 1942. Both Donald and Scribner were shot down on 15 September, but as already discussed in detail, with the much over claiming done that day, there is no way to be certain that Marseille did in fact shoot these two men down. *Courtesy of Russell Brown*

3 RAAF Kittyhawks taking off in September 1942. The second aircraft, CV-1, is a late model Mark IA, in spite of its extended fin. This aircraft (EV322) was the plane Gordon Scribner was flying when he was shot down and killed on 15 September 1942. Scribner was flying the Kittyhawk in the foreground on 8 September when he claimed a 109 destroyed. *Courtesy of Russell Brown*

PO Dick Hart's airplane. *Courtesy of Russell Brown*

Australian author and good friend, Russell Brown. *Courtesy of Russell Brown*

Appendix 9: *Der Stern von Afrika* (1957)

Principle Actors

Hans-Joachim Marseille	Joachim Hansen
Brigette (Hanne-Lies)	Marianne Koch
Robert Franke	Hansjörg Felmy
Albin Droste	Horst Frank
Answald Sommer	Peer Schmidt
Hauptmann Krusenberg	Carl Lange
Werner Haydenreich	Werner Bruhns
Frau Marseille (mother)	Gisela von Collande
Herr Marseille (father)	Arno Paulson
Matthias	Roberto Blanco

Directed by Alfred Weidenmann
Written by Herbert Reinecker and Udo Wolter

In 1957, Neu Münchener Lichtspielkunst G.m.b.H produced this film portraying the exploits of Hans Marseille. Although it was never a well received movie or "blockbuster" film, I still applaud the producers for having the courage to make this movie so close to the end of World War II in an atmosphere that was not receptive to showing German soldiers as heroes.

The film begins with Marseille during peacetime gunnery training and points to some of his difficulties with authority, such as unauthorized aerobatic flying and the infamous story of his landing on the Autobahn. The movie then moves into the Battle of Britain, but then focuses mostly on his contributions in North Africa. The movie is not incredibly accurate in its portrayal of Marseille or the *Luftwaffe* in North Africa, and I believe misses the point on many of Marseille's most important attributes and characteristics. It does, however, do a fairly decent job of showing Marseille's change from the gung-ho fighter pilot eager for combat to the tortured young man, fed up with the war, the killing, and wanting to live his life and have a family.

Made in 1957, you can imagine how sophomoric the flying sequences are with model airplanes slowly moving around the screen, or even the very "cheesy" scene of Matthias dancing without his shirt or shoes on before cheering *Luftwaffe* pilots (see photograph 15). But looking past this and several other detractors, I believe this movie is an interesting "tribute" to Marseille. If you do watch this movie, I recommend viewing it in German with English subtitles. In the English version, for example, the actors keep calling Marseille "Johann" instead of the correct "Jochen."

Over the years I have collected many movie stills and posters from this movie. They are recreated here for you to see. This film can be purchased from International Historic Films or, of course, on eBay.

Note: All photographs, posters, and lobby cards seen in this chapter are part of the author's private collection.

The "Star of Africa." Joachim Hansen as Hans Marseille. *Courtesy of author*

Hansen with co-star Marianna Koch. Koch played Marseille's girlfriend. *Courtesy of author*

Above: Hans Jörg Felmy played Marseille's good friend and fellow pilot, Robert. *Courtesy of author* Below: Hansen and Peer Schmidt in a scene during Marseille's training. *Courtesy of author*

Above: A concerned Marseille sweats the downing of his friend Robert over the Channel. *Courtesy of author* Below: Hansen climbs out of his Messerschmitt. Don't ask why there are two "Yellow 14s." *Courtesy of author*

Ground crew paint "Yellow 14" on yet another Marseille aircraft. *Courtesy of author*

Both Courtesy of Author

Although this movie was made in 1957, the flying sequences and the director's attempts to show the camaraderie in the desert are worthy representations of life for the *Luftwaffe* pilots and ground crew in North Africa. *Courtesy of author*

"Marseille and Hanne-Lies" in Rome discussing their future together. *Courtesy of author*

Above: "Marseille and Hanne-Lies" during their vacation in Italy *Courtesy of author* Below: After "Marseille" and his girlfriend, Brigette, discuss the future of their lives together, Robert arrives in Italy to take Marseille back to Egypt. *Courtesy of author*

Marseille back in the desert, now fighting with a vengeance. *Courtesy of author*

In reality, it was upon his return to North Africa that Marseille met up with his future batman, Matthias, played by the still popular singer Roberto Blanco. Without a doubt, this was the worst scene in the entire movie. All I can ask is, "Why?' *Courtesy of author*

As *Der Stern von Afrika* was released to the German audiences in 1957, true to Hollywood style releases of the day, the studio offered various different film programs hyping their newest movie. These were four-page sheets with written comments and photographs from the movie. Here are three such movie releases. They have been copied and placed together as one image to show the entire program. *All programs Courtesy of Author*

NEUES Film-PROGRAMM
Der Stern von Afrika
„NEUES FILMPROGRAMM"
1957
Der Stern von Afrika

DER
STERN
VON
AFRIKA
HERZOG
DER STERN VON AFRIKA

Der Stern von Afrika

In addition to the film programs, the studios, just like today, offered full size posters of their newest releases. These two images are full color posters of *Der Stern von Afrika*. *Courtesy of Author*

Joachim Hansen
Hansjörg Felmy
Horst Frank
Peer Schmidt
Karl Lange
Werner Bruhns
Alexander Kerst
Marianne Koch
Der Stern von Afrika
Ein Alfred Weidenmann-Film
Drehbuch:
von Udo Wolter Bild: Helmut Ashley
Luftaufnahmen: Jost Graf Hardenberg Musik:
: Rüdiger Freiherr von Hirschberg
Produktion: Neue Münchener Lichtspielkunst GmbH.
Madrid Verleih: Mercator-Film

To coincide with the Spanish release, Juan Kopecky Films created several movie Lobby Cards for "La Estrella de Africa." Here are five examples, each depicting a movie image set on a standard background. These Lobby Cards are similar to the Lobby Cards released for new Hollywood movies of the same period. *All Lobby Cards Courtesy of Author*

J.K.
JOACHIM HANSEN · MARIANNE KOCH en
La ESTRELLA de AFRICA
¡ESPECTACULARES COMBATES AEREOS!
VERIDICA HISTORIA DEL AS DE LA AVIACION ALEMANA QUE DERRIBO MAS DE 100 AVIONES INGLESES!
·DISTRIBUIDA POR: Distribuidora CINEMATOGRAFICA AMERICA S.A. · MONTERREY 150 ·

J.K.
JOACHIM HANSEN · MARIANNE KOCH en
La ESTRELLA de AFRICA
¡ESPECTACULARES COMBATES AEREOS!
VERIDICA HISTORIA DEL AS DE LA AVIACION ALEMANA QUE DERRIBO MAS DE 100 AVIONES INGLESES!
·DISTRIBUIDA POR: Distribuidora CINEMATOGRAFICA AMERICA S.A. · MONTERREY 150 ·

J.K.
JOACHIM HANSEN · MARIANNE KOCH en
La ESTRELLA de AFRICA
¡ESPECTACULARES COMBATES AEREOS!
VERIDICA HISTORIA DEL AS DE LA
·DISTRIBUIDA POR: Distribuidora CINEMATOGRAFICA AMERICA S.A. · MONTERREY 150 ·

In addition to the Lobby Cards, movie posters, and stills, the partial soundtrack for the "Star of Africa" was also released to the public. The song "Bolero," by Hans-Martin Majewski, was released on 45 by Polydor Records, while the same song, additionally titled "Du bist der Stern in dunkler Nacht" (You are the star in the dark of night), was released by Columbia records in Germany. This song was the theme music heard throughout the movie. *Courtesy of author*

Appendix 10: Magazine Covers

Much like the photo cards displayed earlier, Marseille's likeness graced dozens of newspapers and magazines during 1942. It is obvious that he was incredibly popular with the German people. Following the war, Marseille's image continued to adorn magazine covers as well as professional journals. Below are several wartime as well as post war examples. With the exception of the DMZ cover, all of the images in this section come from the author's private collection.

"Berlin is Proud of Him." Cover of the *Berliner Illustrierte Zeitung* dated 4 July 1942. *Courtesy of author*

Der Adler, French edition dated 14 July 1942. *Courtesy of author*

Der Adler

HEFT 14 / BERLIN, 7. JULI 1942

PREIS 20 Pf.

HERAUSGEGEBEN UNTER MITWIRKUNG DES REICHSLUFTFAHRTMINISTERIUMS

Unser Aß in Afrika

Der Adler, German edition dated 7 July 1942. Marseille was home on leave when this edition came out. *Courtesy of author*

Rear cover of *Signal* magazine, dated September 1942. *Courtesy of author*

Koralle: Magazine for Entertainment, Knowledge and Lifestyle. This issue highlights both Marseille and Gordon Gollob being awarded the Knight's Cross with Oak Leaves, Swords, and Diamonds. Ironically, this edition was released on Wednesday, 30 September 1942, the day Marseille died. *Courtesy of author*

Die Wehrmacht, color edition dated 28 October 1942. *Courtesy of author*

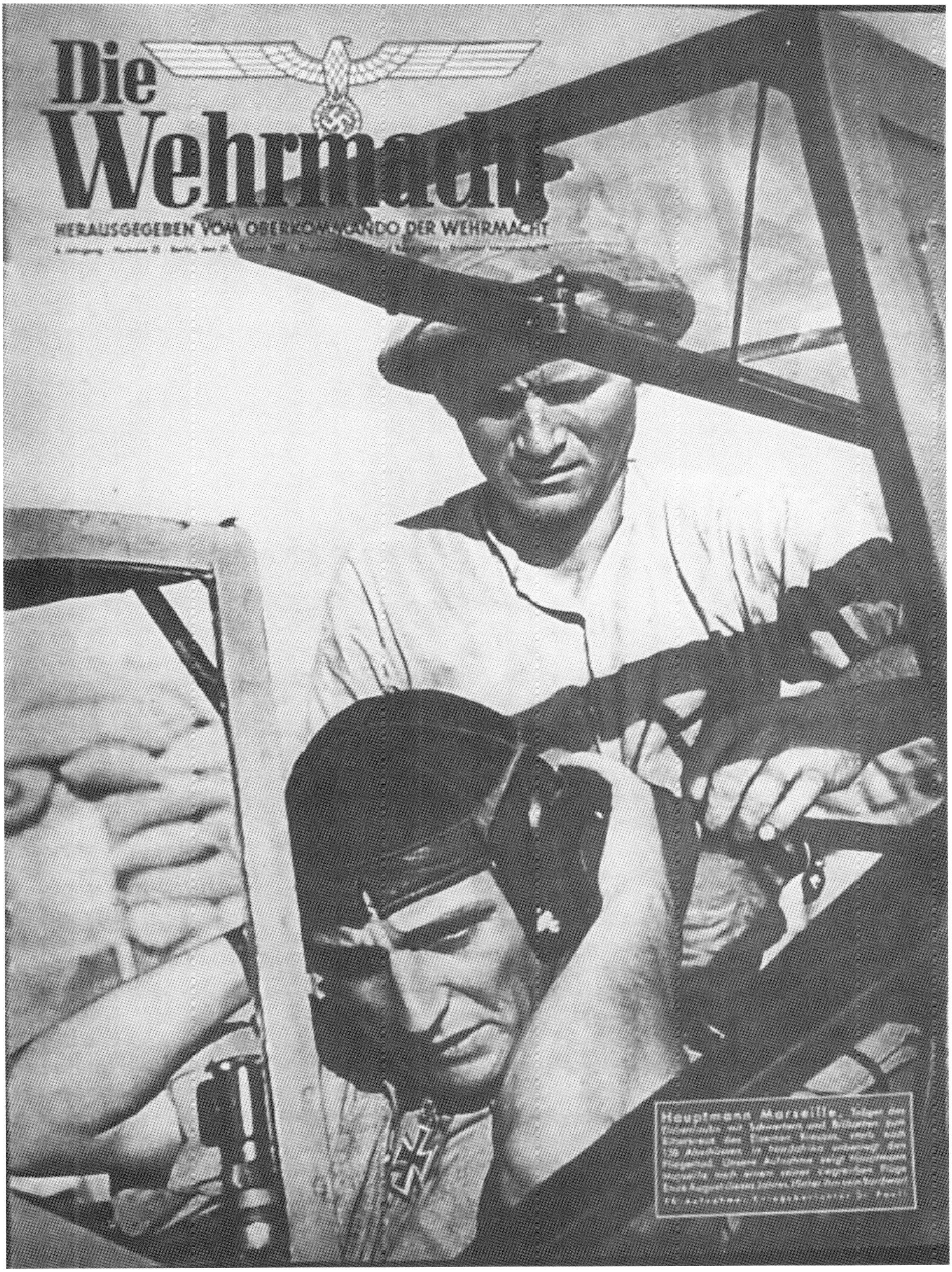

Die Wehrmacht, dated 21 October 1942. Note how the photographs on the two *Die Wehrmacht* covers have been reversed. *Courtesy of author*

Der Front Soldat, Nr. 10. Undated. *Courtesy of author*

Der Landser Grossband, "Hans-Joachim Marseille" by Hans Holl. Undated. *Courtesy of author*

Review, dated 3 April 1954. *Courtesy of author*

Fliegergeschichten. "Fighter pilot stories": Hans-Joachim Marseille – The Eagle of Africa by Hans Peter Holl. *Courtesy of author*

Der Landser Ritterkreuzträger: "Hans-Joachim Marseille, the Star of the South," by Bertold Jochim. *Courtesy of author*

Deutsche Militärzeitschrift (DMZ) quarterly journal. April thru June 1997. *Courtesy of Paul Upton*

DER LANDSER

Die authentischen Erlebnisberichte zur Geschichte des Zweiten Weltkrieges

Österreich S 6,50 Schweiz sfr 1,20 Frankr. NF 1,50
Italien L 200 Lux.,Belg.frs 14,- Holland hfl 1,-
1,- DM

H. Peter

Nr. 574

Hans-Joachim Marseille

1942. In 388 Feindflügen besiegte der „Adler von Afrika" 158 britische Gegner im Luftkampf. Neun Monate nach der Auszeichnung mit dem Ritterkreuz folgte die Verleihung der Brillanten.

Der Landser: "Hans-Joachim Marseille" by H. Peter. Undated. *Courtesy of author*

Appendix 11:
List of People Quoted

Bick, Dr. Oberarzt. Regimental doctor for *Panzergrenadierregiment* 115 in North Africa.

Clade, Emil. Oberleutnant. Pilot with JG 27, survived the war with 8 desert and 26 total victories.

Cundy, Ron. Flt/Lt (DFC, DFM, MID). RAAF pilot who flew with 260 Squadron RAF in North Africa and 452 Squadron RAAF in the pacific. He scored 5 aerial victories.

Denis, James. Sous-Lt DFC. 274 Squadron pilot. Likely shot down Marseille on two occasions.

Deere, Alan. Air Commodore (DSO, OBE, DFC and bar, DFC (US), Croix de Guerre (FR). Deere was a fighter pilot from New Zealand that rose to fame during the Battle of Britain. He scored a total of 22 confirmed kills during the war with 10 probable victories and 18 damaged. He was shot down 7 times during the war.

Dettmann, Fritz. German war reporter and correspondent. Author of the wartime novel, *My Friend Marseille*.

Duke, Neville Frederick. Sqdn. Leader (DFC, DSO, OBE). 28 confirmed victories, with 3 probables and 6 damaged. Flew with 112 and 92 squadrons in the Middle East, survived the conflict and became a test pilot at Hawker Aircraft after the war.

Düllberg, Ernst. Oberleutnant. II/ JG 27, 10 desert victories and 50 total.

Franzisket, Ludwig. Major. Survived the war and scored 24 desert victories with I/ JG 27 in the desert and another 19 later in the war. He is the pilot that recovered Marseille's body.

Filson, Floyd V. Biblical scholar, researcher and author.

Galland, Adolf. General of the Fighters. 104 kills, survived the war. Called Marseille the "unrivalled virtuoso" among WWII fighter pilots.

Gibbes, Bobby. Squadron Leader (DSO, DFC with Bar). Gibbes scored 10 1/2 desert victories flying with 3 RAAF. He survived the war and died in April 2007.

Gilpin-Barnes, Derek. DAF intelligence officer.

Hart, Basil Liddell. Served as a Captain in the British Army during the First World War and became arguably the most prolific and thought provoking military strategist of the 20th century.

Ihlefeld, Herbert. Oberst. Scored 132 victories in over 1000 combat missions, including 15 four-engine bombers. He was Marseille's first commander in LG 2.

Jabs, Hans-Joachim. Oberstleutnant. Jabs was both a day and night fighter pilot ace scoring a total of 50 aerial victories, 28 of those at night.

Johnson, James Edgar "Johnnie." Air Vice-Marshal (CB, CBE, DSO and two Bars, DFC and Bar). Johnson was the top scoring RAF pilot in WWII with 38 confirmed victories. Johnson survived the war.

Keefer, George Clinton. Wing Commander (DSO, DFC and bar, *Croix de Guerre*). RCAF pilot who ended the war with 12 aerial victories.

Keller, Friedrich. Hauptmann. Flew with I and II/ JG 27 and survived the war with 13 victories.

Kesselring, Albrecht von. Generalfeldmarschall. Smiling Albert. In December 1941, Kesselring was appointed Commander-in-Chief South with command of all *Luftwaffe* units in the Mediterranean and North African theaters.

Körner, Friedrich (Fritz). Oberleutnant. 2/ JG 27, 36 kills, POW (04-07-42). Retired from the New German Air Force in June 1979 as a Major General.

Krupinski, Walter. "The Count." Major. Survived the war with 197 victories, mostly on the Russian Front. He flew with JG 52, JG 5 and the Me-262 unit JV 44.

Lavigne, Michel. Canadian aviation historian who has written several outstanding books on Canadian fighter pilots and their significant contributions to WW II aviation. He has also authored several articles on Hans Marseille.

Marseille, Hans-Joachim. Hauptmann. 3/ JG 27, 158 total kills, KIA (30-09-42).

Matthew P. Letuku "Mathias." Corporal. The black South African prisoner of war that became Marseille's personal batman and friend.

Morley-Mower, Geoffrey. Wing Commander (DFC, AFC). Before his death in December 2005, he served as an associate professor in the English department of James Madison University. Morley-Mower flew Hurricanes in North Africa as part of 451 Tactical Reconnaissance Squadron RAAF and wrote the book *Messerschmitt Roulette*.

Neumann, Eduard "Edu." Major. Commander JG 27, 5 desert kills with 13 total victories.

Paetzold, Professor. One of Marseille's grade school teachers.

Pöttgen, Rainer. Oberfeldwebel. Marseille's Wingman, 7 total victories, survived.

Rall, Günther. Generalleutnant. Rall was the third highest scoring ace of the war with 275 victories in 621 sorties. Shot down 5 times during the war, Rall flew primarily with JG 52, JG 11 and JG 300 on both the Western and Eastern Fronts.

Ring, Hans. Historian and author of several books on *Luftwaffe* aviation. Served as the Historian for the German Association of former Fighter Pilots. He has written extensively for *Der Jäger Blatt* and has co-authored the definitive study of the air war in North Africa, *Fighters Over the Desert*.

Roba, Jean-Louis. World War II historian and author.

Schrör, Werner. Perhaps the most underrated of the *Luftwaffe* "Experten." Credited with 61 desert victories, Schrör scored a total of 114 kills in only 197 missions. In the desert he flew with I and III/ JG 27.

Shores, Christopher. Historian and author of several books including the definitive *Fighters Over the Desert*.

Sims, Edward Howell. Historian and author of several books dealing with WWII fighter combat including *The Greatest Aces* and *Aces Talk*.

Sinner, Rudolf. Major. Survived the war with 39 aerial victories. While assigned to JG 27, he flew with I and II *Gruppen*.

Smith, W.G.G. Duncan. Group Captain (DSO with bar, DFC with 2 bars). Author of Spitfire into Battle, Smith was credited with 19 total victories.

Stahlschmidt, Hans-Arnold "Fifi." Oberleutnant. 2 JG 27 with 59 confirmed victories. Close personal friend of Marseille, shot down and presumed KIA, (07-09-42).

Steinhoff, Johannes "Macky" Oberstleutnant. Although horribly burned in a Me-262 accident on 18 April 1945, he survived the war with 176 victories in over 990 operational sorties to become one of the senior *Luftwaffe* officers in the new West German Air Force. Steinhoff flew with JG 7, JG 26, JG 52, JG 77, *Kommando* Nowotny and JV 44.

Tozer, Aiden Wilson. A well known American pastor, author of over forty books, magazine editor and spiritual mentor.

Trimble, Tom. Pilot Officer. Kittyhawk pilot with 3 RAAF shot down by Marseille on 13 December 1941.

Waddy, John Lloyd. Group Captain. From Sydney, Australia, Waddy served with Nos 250, 260, 4 SAAF and 92 Squadrons in the Western Desert flying Tomahawks, Kittyhawks and Spitfires. Waddy became the third highest scoring Allied pilot in the African Campaign with 15.5 victories.

Weiler, Anton. Author and historian.

Yindrich, Jan. Polish war correspondent and author of the book *Fortress Tobruk*.

Endnotes

For over 35 years, I have collected magazine articles, excerpts from books, interviews, and any other relevant information surrounding Hans Marseille. I must admit that when I was younger, my skills at logging and verifying information left much to be desired. I would often copy information and paste it in a large book to read over and over again. That leads me to this case in point. As you read through the endnotes, you will find the following note several times: *Unknown Source**. This is then followed by a page number. Over twenty years ago, I found a book in the library that had several interesting pages on Marseille. When I copied those pages, either I forgot to copy the title page or, after several moves around the U.S., Germany, or Saudi Arabia, that page has long since disappeared. What I am left with is ten pages copied from a book with no identifying information. These "Unknown Sources" come from this section of the book that identifies an interview with Werner Schrör, in Ottobrunn, West Germany, 1982. Likewise, two Edu Neumann quotes came from the same book under a section subtitled, "He was the Best." The book mentions that Neumann was quoted by Von Günther Stiller in his series *Der Playboy mit dem Retterkreuz*: Bild am Sonntag, Hamburg, September 1979.

I am using these quotes because they are relevant to the Marseille story, and Edu Neumann's and Werner Schrör's first hand accounts of Marseille, his flying genius, and his character are irreplaceable. With this being said, I first want to apologize for not having the full reference and hope that a reader out there can forward that information to me at some time. Should this tribute be released for a second edition, this updated information will be included. Likewise, I want the readers to realize that in no way am I claiming this information as my own. I thank you in advance for your understanding.

Introduction

[1] After Allied resurgence in early 1942 and the stunning defeats in September, morale of German and Italian airmen began to wane. A.I.K. Report No. 266/1942 titled Losses, Morale, etc. For September, 1942 discusses general Luftwaffe morale in the Middle East for the month of Marseille's death. During interrogation of German prisoners of war, several general attitudes were uncovered. The report stated, "Most P/W are now becoming resigned to a lengthy struggle, and in the general view the war will last at least another two years." It goes on to state, "Underlying this veneer of confidence [of German and Italian prisoners of war], however, there were indications of definite misgivings both as to the duration and outcome of the war" and "morale of P/W shows a slight downward tendency." Further, the report states that 9 out of 26 prisoners interrogated, those from KG 77, "gave an impression of tiredness and disillusion; the comparative failure of their operations over Malta had destroyed their faith in the invincibility of the Luftwaffe." While some Luftwaffe crews reported being "operationally tired and not over-anxious to face the British air defenses" on the Western Front, two of the remaining P/Ws interrogated anticipated a "compromise peace" after defeating Russia. As for the Luftwaffe's Italian allies, "Italian morale remained as before: general apathy, with hopes for a compromise peace." September was indeed a turning point for the Luftwaffe in the Middle East.

[2] Transvaal: A province of northern South Africa from 1910-1994. Although the province no longer exists, it is still a commonly used geographical term that retains much of its historical identity.

Chapter 1: Marseille and the Historical Great Man

[1]Note: In the historical context, the Great Man can indeed be a woman. The discussion that follows uses the term "he" throughout, but is not meant to discount historical contributions of women. Certainly history is replete with historically Great women like Elizabeth 1 of England and Catharine of Russia.

[2]Greg Boyington. *Baa Baa Black Sheep* (New York: Bantam Books, 1979) 374

[3]Note: *Experten* – Term used to describe the *Luftwaffe* "Super aces."

[4]Franz Kurowski. *German Fighter Ace HJM: The Life Story of the Star of Africa* (PA: Schiffer Military History, 1994) 70-71

[5]Carl G. Gustavson. *A Preface to History* (NY: McGraw-Hill, 1955) 129

[6]Gustavson 130.

[7]Gustavson 123.

[8]Gustavson 124.

[9]Gustavson 124.

[10]Note: Desert Air Forces (DAF) – Allied pilots from Great Britain, Canada, New Zealand, Australia, and South Africa that flew against the *Luftwaffe* and Italians in North Africa.

[11]Friedrich Körner (2/ JG 27 pilot), interview by author, 7-94.

[12]Gustavson 130.

[13]Gustavson 130.

[14]Gustavson 130.

[15]Hans Ring and Christopher Shores, *Fighters Over the Desert: The Air Battles in the Western Desert June 1940 to December 1942* (NY: Arco Publishing, 1969) 239-40, 241.

[16]Gustavson 130.

Chapter 2: Fighter Pilot Qualities

[1]Mike Spick. *The Ace Factor: Air Combat and the Roles of Situational Awareness* (England: Airlife Publishing, 1988) v.

[2]Fritz Dettmann. *My Friend Marseille* (Berlin: Heimbücherei, 1944) 139.

[3]Raymond Toliver and Trevor Constable. *Horrido!: Fighter Aces of the Luftwaffe* (NY: Bantam Books, 1968) 104.

[4]Geoffrey Morley-Mower, telephone interview conducted by author summer 2003.

[5]James R. Whelan. *Hunters in the Sky: Fighter Pilots of WW II* (Washington, DC: Regnery Publishing Inc., 1991) 147.

[6]Whelan 147.

[7]Richard Smith and Martin Pegg. *Jagdwaffe: War Over the Desert June 1940-June 1942* (Surrey, UK: Ian Allan Publishing, 2003) 272.

[8]"Hans-Joachim Marseille" Video (Chicago: International Historic Films, 1990)

[9]Marseille Video.

[10]Robert Jackson. *Fighter Pilots of World War II* (NY: Barnes and Nobel, 1995) 139.

[11]Unknown Source 152.*

[12]Kurowski 73.

[13]Edward H. Sims. *The Greatest Aces* (NY: Ballantine Books, 1967) 137.

[14]Heinz Nowarra. *Marseille: Star of Africa* (CA: Caler Illustrated Series, 1968) 8.

[15]Toliver and Constable, *Horrido*! 103.

[16]Ron Cundy DFC, DFM, MID. *A Gremlin on my Shoulder* (Australia: Australian Military History Publications, 2001) 22.

[17]Leadership Now. Quotes on confidence. http://www.leadershipnow.com/confidencequotes.html.

[18]Dettmann 63.

[19]Dettmann 63.

[20]Dettmann 63.

[21]Toliver and Constable, *Horrido!* 86.

[22]Richard Exley. *Man of Valor: Every Man's Quest for a Life of Honor, Conviction and Character* (Lakeland, FL: White Stone Books, 2005) 188.

[23]Sims 143.

[24]Ring and Shores 220.

[25]Ring and Shores 222.

[26]Ring and Shores 224.

[27]Marseille Video.

[28]Ring and Shores 166.

[29]Nowarra 9.

[30]Ring and Shores 222.

[31]Ring and Shores 231-232.

[32]Friedrich Körner (2/ JG 27 pilot), interview conducted by author, 7-94.

[33]Dettmann 141.

[34]Whelan 147.

[35]Whelan 147.

[36]Unknown Source 150.

[37]Unknown Source 152.*

[38]Unknown Source 151-151*

[39]Sims 139.

[40]Unknown Source 152.*

[41]Sims 144.

[42]Marseille Video.

[43]Marseille Video.

[44]Paul Carell. *The Foxes of the Desert* (NY: Bantam Books, 1962) 279.

[45]Unknown Source 151.*

[46]Günther Fraschka. *Knights of the Reich: The 27 Most Highly Decorated Soldiers of the Wehrmacht in World War II* (PA: Schiffer Military History, 1994) 62.

[47]Kurowski 181-182.

[48]Sims 144.

[49]Smith and Pegg 211.

[50]Toliver and Constable, *Horrido!* 103.

[51]Note: John Boyd was called "40 Second Boyd" because as an instructor pilot at the Air Force Weapons School, he had a standing $40 bet that with any pilot on his tail, within 40 seconds, he could position himself into a firing position against his adversary. In numerous combats with pilots from around the world, there is no evidence that he ever lost his bet and was never defeated in mock aerial combat.

[52] Unknown Source 152.*

[53]Dettmann 16.

[54]Sims 145.

[55]Walter J. Boyne. *Aces in Command: Fighter Pilots as Combat Leaders* (Dulles, VA: Brassey's Inc., 2001) 16.

[56]Johannes "Macky" Steinhoff. *Messerschmitts Over Sicily* (Baltimore, MD: The Nautical and Aviation Publishing Company, 1987) 119-120.

[57]Kurowski 73.

[58]Sims 144.

[59]Smith and Pegg 211.

[60]Unknown Source 151

[61]Marseille Video.

[62]Michel Lavigne, "Hans-Joachim Marseille" (Military Journal, Pt.3) 33.

[63]Michel Lavigne 34.

[64]Marseille Video.

[65]Mike Spick. *The Ace Factor* (Shrewsbury, UK: Airlife Publishing, 1988) 171.

[66]Cundy 88.

Chapter 3: Tactics

[1]Marseille Video.

[2]Dave Schueler, "The Vic Down in Flames," GMT Games Down in Flames, www.relativerange.com/dif/variants.htm#TheVicInDownInFlames. (last accessed 24 June 2007) 1.

[3]Schueler 1.

[4]Ring and Shores 224.

[5]Ring and Shores 225.

[6]Ring and Shores 231.

[7]Ring and Shores 235.

[8]Kurowski 91-92.

[9]Russell Brown. *Desert Warriors: Australian P-40 Pilots at War in the Middle East and North Africa 1941-1943* (Australia: Banner Books, 2000) 258.

[10]Liddell Hart. *Strategy* (NY: Signet Books, 1974) 323.

[11]Sun Tzu. *The Art of War*, translated by Thomas Cleary (Boston: Shambhala, 1991) 93.

[12]Hart xii.

[13]Hart 5.

[14]Hart 4.

[15]Hart 327.

[16]Hart 6.

[17]Dettmann 15.

[18]Lavigne, Hans-Joachim Marseille, Pt.1

[19]Carell 279.

[20]Ring and Shores 166.

[21]Kurowski 72-73.

[22]Toliver and Constable 109. (As quoted from Fritz Dettmann)

[23]Toliver and Constable 110. (As quoted from Fritz Dettmann)

[24]Brown 109.

[25]Brown 109.

[26]Brown 110.

[27]Kurowski 76-77.
[28]Unknown Source 152.*
[29]Ring and Shores 232.
[30]Friedrich Körner (2/ JG 27 pilot), interview by author, 4-93.
[31]Friedrich Körner (2/ JG 27 pilot), interview by author, 7-94.
[32]Friedrich Körner (2/ JG 27 pilot), interview by author, 7-94.

Chapter 4: Victories
[1]HJM, Military Journal, Michel Lavigne, Pt.1.
[2]HJM, Military Journal, Michel Lavigne, Pt.1.
[3]Boyne 1.
[4]David M. Glantz and Jonathan House. *When Titans Clashed: How the Red Army Stopped Hitler*, (KS: University Press of Kansas, 1995) 306.
[5]Ring and Shores 218.
[6]Ring and Shores 228.
[7]Adolf Galland. *The First and the Last* (NY: Bantam Books, 1991) 125.
[8]Jan Yindrich. *Fortress Tobruk* (London: Ernest Benn Limited, 1951) 178.
[9]Brian Cull. *Hurricanes over Tobruk: The Pivotal Role of the Hurricane in the Defense of Tobruk, January – June 1941* (London: Grub Steet, 1999) 140.
[10]Yindrich 178-180.
[11]Michel Lavigne. *Kittyhawks Over the Sands: The Canadians and the RCAF Americans* (Canada: Lavigne Aviation Publications, 2002) 248.
[12]Ring and Shores 79.
[13]Don Darbyshire, "Desert Flamer," *Flypast*, August 2001, 58-59.
[14]Toliver and Constable, *Horrido!* 112.
[15]Ring and Shores 170.
[16]Lavigne, *Kittyhawks* 82-83.
[17]Cundy 89.
[18]Bruce D. Callander, "The Aces That History Forgot," *Air Force Magazine Online*. http://www.afa.org/magazine/1991/0491aces.asp (Last accessed 24 June 2007).
[19]Douglas Tidy, "Myths of the Battle of Britain," http://www.battle-of-britain.com/BoB2/General/Myths-of-battle.htm (Last accessed 24 June 2007).
[20]Brown x.
[21]Brown 281-282.
[22]Nowarra 9.
[23]Carell 281.
[24]Toliver and Constable, *Horrido!* 15-16.

Chapter 5: Personality
[1]Whelan 147.
[2]Whelan 146.
[3]Colin D. Heaton. "Interview with WWII *Luftwaffe* Eagle Johannes Steinhoff." *World War II Magazine* (May 1998) 31.
[4]Jackson 135.
[5]Jackson 137.
[6]Heaton 31.
[7]Sims 143.
[8]Nowarra 3.
[9]Lavigne, "Hans-Joachim Marseille Pt.3" 33.
[10]Smith and Pegg 211.
[11]Smith and Pegg 224.
[12]Marseille Video.
[13]Unknown Source 151.*
[14]Unknown Source 151.*
[15]Toliver and Constable, *Horrido!* 101.
[16]Marseille Video.
[17]Günther Kaufmann. *Botschaft Gefallenen: Briefe aus dem II. Weltkrieg* (Germany: VGB – Verlagsgesellschaft 82335).
[18]Dettmann 17.
[19]Dettmann 111-112.
[20]Lavigne, "Hans-Joachim Marseille Pt.1" 27.
[21]Kurowski 12-13.
[22]Lavigne, "Hans-Joachim Marseille Pt.1" 27.
[23]Marseille Video.
[24]Marseille Video.
[25]Unknown Source 152.*
[26]Unknown Source 152.*
[27]Nowarra 7.
[28]Jean-Lous Roba and Martin Pegg. *Luftwaffe Colors - Jagdwaffe: The Mediterranean 1942-43* (Surrey, UK: Ian Allan Publishing, 2003) 124.
[29]Lavigne, "Hans-Joachim Marseille Pt.1" 27.
[30]Kurowski 204.
[31]Dettmann 139.
[32]Dettmann 139.
[33]Marseille Video.
[34]Toliver and Constable 116.
[35]Kurowski 70-71.
[36]Unknown Source 152.*
[37]Ring and Shores 35.
[38]Toliver and Constable 106.
[39]Toliver and Constable 106.
[40]Unknown source 152.*
[41]Dettmann 167.
[42]Raffael Scheck. *Hitler's African Victims: The German Army Massacres of Black French Soldiers in 1940* (NY: Cambridge University Press, 2006) 98.
[43]Scheck 100.
[44]Scheck 106.
[45]"Jazz in Germany 1939-1945." Translated by Jill Benz http://www.return2style.de/swingaring/amijazz3.htm (Last accessed 24 June 2007).
[46]Benz, "Jazz in Germany."
[47]"German Swing Youth." No author cited. http://www.return2style.de/amiswhei.htm#mode (Last accessed 24 June 2007)
[48]"German Swing Youths."
[49]"German Swing Youths."
[50]Richard Bessel. *Life in the Third Reich* (Oxford: Oxford University Press, 1987) 37.
[51]Bessel 38.
[52]"German Swing Youths."
[53]"German Swing Youths."
[54]Bessel 39.
[55]Bessel 39.
[56]Ring and Shores 35.
[57]Sims 142.
[58]Toliver and Constable 86.
[59]Friedrich Körner (2/ JG 27 pilot) interview conducted by author 4-93.

Chapter 6: Enemy Perspectives
[1]W.G.G Duncan Smith. *Spitfire Into Battle* (London: John Murray Publishers, 1981) 226-227.
[2]Ring and Shores 233.
[3]Johnnie Johnson. *Wing Leader* (NY: Ballantine Books, 1957) 287.
[4]Ring and Shores 170.
[5]Cull 134.

[6]Cull 152.
[7]Cundy 89-90.
[8]Fraschka 59.
[9]Ring and Shores 225.
[10]Ring and Shores 226.
[11]Fraschka 59.

Chapter 7: Stories
[1]Friedrich Körner (2/ JG 27 pilot), interview conducted by author 4-93.
[2]Geoffrey Morley-Mower. *Messerschmitt Roulette* (MN: Phalanx Publishing, 1993) 61-66.
[3]Ring and Shores 223.
[4]Nelson Gilboe, "An Airman's Adventure," http://www.geocities.com/vienna/5373/gilboe-war-diaries.htm (Last accessed 24 June 2007).

Chapter 8: Death of Marseille
[1]Kurowski 170.
[2]Dettmann 130.
[3]Unknown Source 152.*
[4]Kurowski 209.
[5]Kurowski 209.
[6]Carell 282.
[7]Marseille Video.
[8]Kurowski 211-212.
[9]Ring and Shores 220.
[10]Friedrich Körner (2/ JG 27 pilot), interview conducted by author 4-93.
[11]Carell 282.
[12]Kurowski 213.
[13]Marseille Video.
[14]Marseille Video.
[15]Cundy 35.
[16]Kurowski 215.
[17]Marseille Video.
[18]Kurowski 213.
[19]Marseille Video.
[20]Lavigne, *Kittyhawks* 368.
[21]Lavigne, *Kittyhawks* 368.
[22]Lavigne, *Kittyhawks* 369.
[23]Fraschka 66.

Chapter 9: Marseille's Aircraft
[1]J.R. Smith and J.D. Galaspy. *Luftwaffe Camouflage and Markings Vol. 2* (Melbourne: Kookabura Books, 1976) 53.
[2]Jerry Scutts. *Bf 109 Aces of North Africa and the Mediterranean* (London: Osprey Publishing, 1994) 73.
[3]Smith and Pegg 248.

Appendix 2: Theories of Air Fighting
[1]Spick 50.
[2]Spick 94.
[3]Raymond Toliver and Trevor Constable. *The Blonde Knight of Germany: A Biography of Erich Hartmann* (PA: Aero Books, 1970) 54.
[4]"What OODA 'loop' speed really means," Kettle Creek Corporation, 2006. http://www.d-n-i.net/richards/boyds_ooda_loop.ppt#323, (Last accessed 24 June 2007).

Bibliography

Beaman, John R. and Jerry L. Campbell. *Messerschmitt Bf-109 in Action: Part 1*. Carrollton, TX: Squadron/Signal Publications, 1980.
Beaman, John R. *Messerschmitt Bf-109 in Action: Part 2*. Carrollton, TX: Squadron/Signal Publications, 1983.
Becker, Cajus. *The Luftwaffe War Diaries*. New York, NY: Ballantine Books, 1972.
Boyington, Greg "Pappy." *Baa Baa Black Sheep*. New York, NY: Bantam Books, 1977.
Boyne, Walter J. *Aces in Command: Fighter Pilots as Combat Leaders*. Dulles, Virginia: Brassey's Inc., 2001.
Brown, Russell. *Desert Warriors: Australian P-40 Pilots at War in the Middle East and North Africa 1941-1943*. Queensland, Australia: Banner Books, 2000.
Caiden, Martin. *Me-109*. New York, NY: Ballantine Books, 1972.
Carell, Paul. *The Foxes of the Desert*. New York, NY: Bantam Books, 1962.
Cull, Brian. *Hurricanes Over Tobruk: The Pivotal Role of the Hurricane in the Defense of Tobruk, January – June 1941*. London, UK: Grub Street, 1999.
Cundy, Ron DFC, DFM, MID. *A Gremlin on My Shoulder*. Loftus, Australia: Australian Military History Publications, 2001.
Dettmann, Fritz. *Mein Freund Marseille*. Berlin, Germany: Heimbücherei, 1944.
Exley, Richard. *Man of Valor: Every Man's Quest for a Life of Honor, Conviction and Character*. Lakeland, FL: White Stone Books, 2005.
Fraschka, Guenther. *Knights of the Reich: The 27 Most Highly Decorated Soldiers of the Wehrmacht in World War II*. Atglen, PA: Schiffer Military Aviation, 1994.
Galland, Adolf. *The First and the Last*. New York, NY: Bantam Books, 1991.
Glantz, David M. and Jonathan House. *When Titans Clashed: How the Red Army Stopped Hitler*. Lawrence, Kansas: University Press of Kansas, 1995.
Gustavson, Carl G. *A Preface to History*. New York, NY: McGraw-Hill Paperbacks, 1955.
Hart, Liddell. *Strategy*. New York, NY: Signet Books, 1974.
Hitchcock, Thomas H. *Bf 109 F: Monogram Close-Up 9*. Sturbridge, MA: Monogram Aviation Publications, 1990.
Jackson, Robert. *Fighter Pilots of World War II*. New York, NY: St. Martins, 1976.
Johnnie Johnson. *Wing Leader*. New York, NY: Ballantine Books, 1957.
Kaufmann, Gunter. *Botschaft Gefallenen: Briefe aus dem II. Weltkrieg*. Berg am Starnberger See, Germany: VGB-Verlagsgesellschaft 82335, 1996.
Kurowski, Franz. *German Fighter Ace Hans-Joachim Marseille: The Life Story of the Star of Africa*. Atglen, PA: Schiffer Military History, 1994.
Lavigne, Michel. *Kittyhawks Over the Sands: The Canadians and The RCAF Americans*. Victoriaville, Canada: Lavigne Aviation Publications, 2002.
Morley-Mower, Wing Commander Geoffrey. *Messerschmitt Roulette: The Western Desert 1941-1942*. St. Paul, MN: Phalanx Publishing, 1993.
Musciano, Walter A. *Messerschmitt Aces*. Blue Ridge Summit, PA: Tab/Aero Books, 1989.
Nowarra, Heinz. *Marseille: Star of Africa*. Sun Valley, CA : Caler Illustrated Series, 1968.
Ring, Hans and Werner Girbig. *Jagdgeschwader 27: Die documentation ueber den Einsatz an allen Fronten 1939-1945*. Stuttgart, Germany: Motorbuch Verlag, 1991.
Roba, Jean-Louis and Martin Pegg. *Luftwaffe Colors Vol.4 Section 2: The Mediterranean 1942-43*. Surrey, UK: Ian Allan Publishing, 2003.
Scheck, Raffael. *Hitler's African Victims: The German Army Massacres of Black French Soldiers in 1940*. New York, NY: Cambridge University Press, 2006.
Scutts, Jerry. *Bf 109 Aces of North Africa and the Mediterranean*. London, UK: Osprey Publishing, 1994.
Shores, Christopher and Hans Ring. *Fighters Over the Desert: The Air Battles in the Western Desert June 1940 to December 1942*. New York, NY: Arco Publishing, 1969.
Sims, Edward H. *The Aces Talk*. New York, NY: Ballantine Books, 1972.
Sims, Edward H. *The Greatest Aces*. New York, NY: Ballantine Books, 1967.
Smith, J.R. and J.D. Galaspy. *Luftwaffe Camouflage and Markings Vol. 2*. Melbourne, Australia: Kookabura Books, 1976.

Smith, Richard J. and Martin Pegg. *Luftwaffe Colours Vol. 3, Section 3. Jagdwaffe: War Over the Desert North Africa June 1940 – June 1942*. Surrey, UK: Ian Allan Publishing, 2003.
Smith, W.G.G. Duncan. *Spitfire Into Battle*. London, UK: John Murray Publishing, 1981.
Spick, Mike. *The Ace Factor: Air Combat and the Roles of Situational Awareness*. Shrewsbury, UK: Airlife Publishing, 1988.
Spick, Mike. *Luftwaffe Fighter Aces*. London, UK: Greenhill Books, 1996.
Steinheiff, Johannes. *Messerschmitts Over Sicily*. Baltimore, MD: The Nautical and Aviation Publishing Company, 1987.
Sun Tzu. Translated by Thomas Cleary. *The Art of War*. Boston, MA: Shambhala, 1991.
Toliver, Raymond and Trevor Constable. *Horrido! Fighter Aces of the Luftwaffe*. New York, NY: Bantam Books, 1968.
Toliver, Raymond and Trevor Constable. *The Blond Knight of Germany: A Biography of Erich Hartmann*. Blue Ridge Summit, PA: Aero Books, 1970.
Weal, John. *Jagdgeschwader 27 "Afrika"*. Osceola, WI: Osprey Publishing, 2003.
Woods, Tony (compiled by). *O.K.L. Fighter Claims: Chef für Ausz. Und Dizsiplin Luftwaffen-Personalamt L.P. (A) V Films and Supplementary Claims from Lists: Mediterranean and Southern Front 1941-1942*.
James R. Whelan. *Hunters in the Sky: Fighter Aces of WW II*. Washington, DC: Regnery Publishers, 1991.
Wübbe, Walter. *Marseille: Ein Jagdfliegerschicksal in Daten, Bildern und Dokumenten*. Schnellbach, Germany: Verlag Siegfried Bublies, 2001.
Yenne, William. *Aces: True Stories of Victory and Valor in the Skies of World War II*. New York, NY: Berkley Books, 2000.
Yindrich, Jan. *Fortress Tobruk*. London, UK: Ernest Benn Limited, 1951.

Interviews

Friedrich Körner, conducted by the author in his home in Bailly, France.
April 1993
October 1993
July 1994

Periodicals

Beaman, John and Jim Kitchens. "Marseille's Bf-109F Aircraft," *The IPMS/USA Quarterly*, Vol. 16, No.2 – (winter 1980).
Darbyshire, Don. "Desert Flamer," FlyPast, (August 2001).
Lavigne, Michel. "Hans-Joachim Marseille – Pt. 1." *Military Journal*, (undated).
Lavigne, Michel. "Hans-Joachim Marseille – Pt. 2." *Military Journal*, (undated).
Lavigne, Michel. "Hans-Joachim Marseille – Pt. 3." *Military Journal*, (undated).

Internet

Benz, Jill. Translator. "Jazz in Germany 1939-1945." 17 June 2007.
http://www.return2style.de/swingaring/amijazz3.htm
Callander, Bruce D. "The Aces That History Forgot." 17 June 2007. http://www.afa.org/magazine/1991/0491aces.asp
Gilboe, N.E. F/Lt, "Combat Diary of 1940 to 1946: An Airman's Adventure." 17 June 2007 http://www.geocities.com/vienna/5373/gilboe-war-diaries.htm
Leadership Now. "Quotes on Confidence." 24 June 2007. http://www.leadershipnow.com/confidencequotes.html
Schueler, Dave. "The Vic Down in Flames." 17 June 2007.
http://www.relativerange.com/dif/variants.htm#TheVicInDownInFlames
Tidy, Douglas. "Myths of the Battle of Britain." 17 June 2007. http://www.battle-of-britain.com/BoB2/General/Myths-of-battle.htm.
German Swing Youth. Translated by a Friend of the Swingstyle Syndicate. 17 June 2007. http://www.return2style.de/amiswhei.htm#mode

Videos

Hans-Joachim Marseille. Chicago, IL: International Historic Films, Item Number: 22744, 1990.

Maps

North African Coast. 802409(546325) Courtesy of the Air University Library, Maxwell Air Force Base, Montgomery, AL.